I0795696

IMAGES
of America

AROUND NEWFOUND LAKE

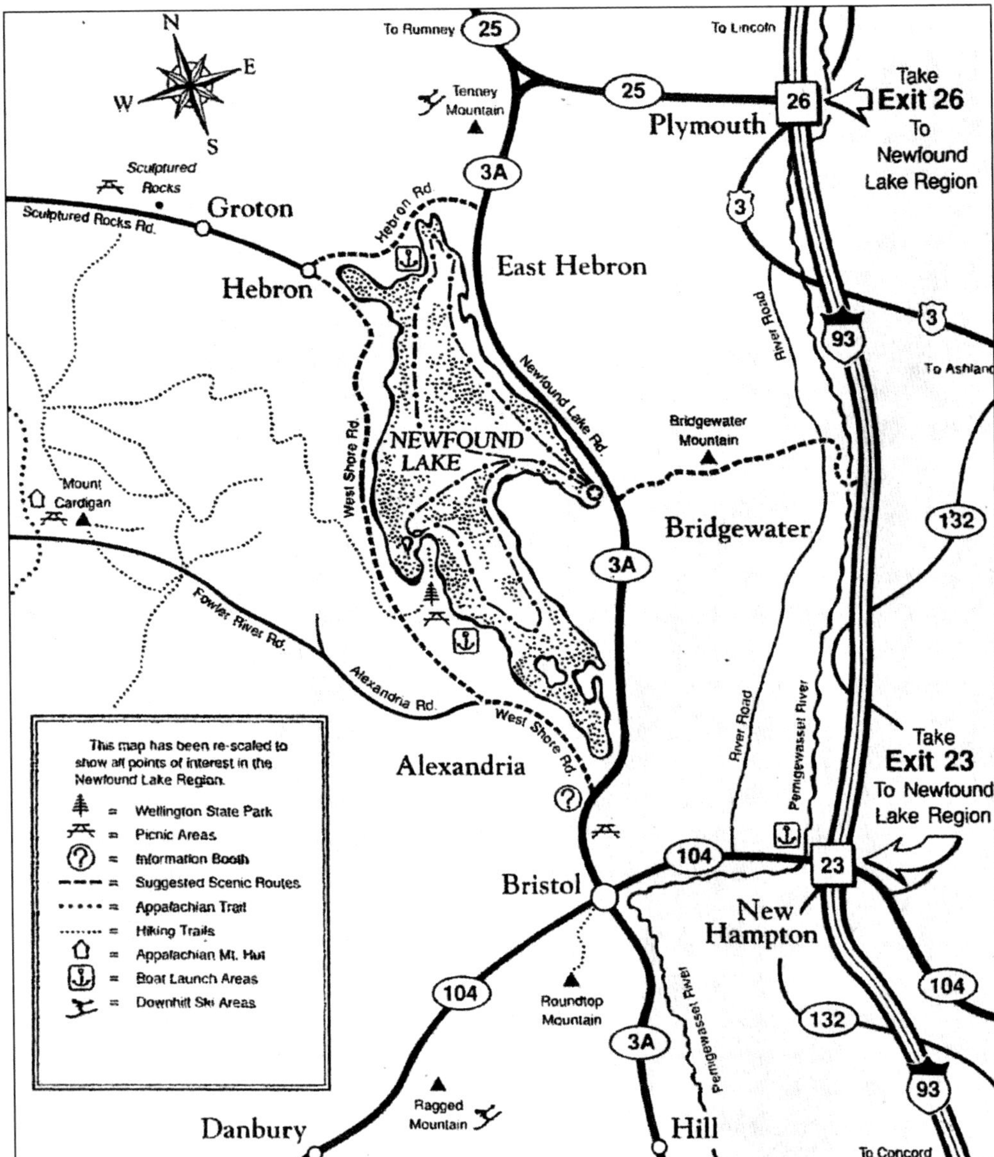

This is the Newfound Lake Region of New Hampshire.

IMAGES
of America

AROUND NEWFOUND LAKE

Janice Hugron Harvey

ARCADIA
PUBLISHING

ISBN 978-0-7385-0960-0

Published by Arcadia Publishing
Charleston, South Carolina

Printed in the United States of America

Library of Congress Catalog Card Number: 2001093045

For all general information contact Arcadia Publishing at:
Telephone 843-853-2070
Fax 843-853-0044
E-mail sales@arcadiapublishing.com
For customer service and orders:
Toll-Free 1-888-313-2665

Visit us on the Internet at www.arcadiapublishing.com

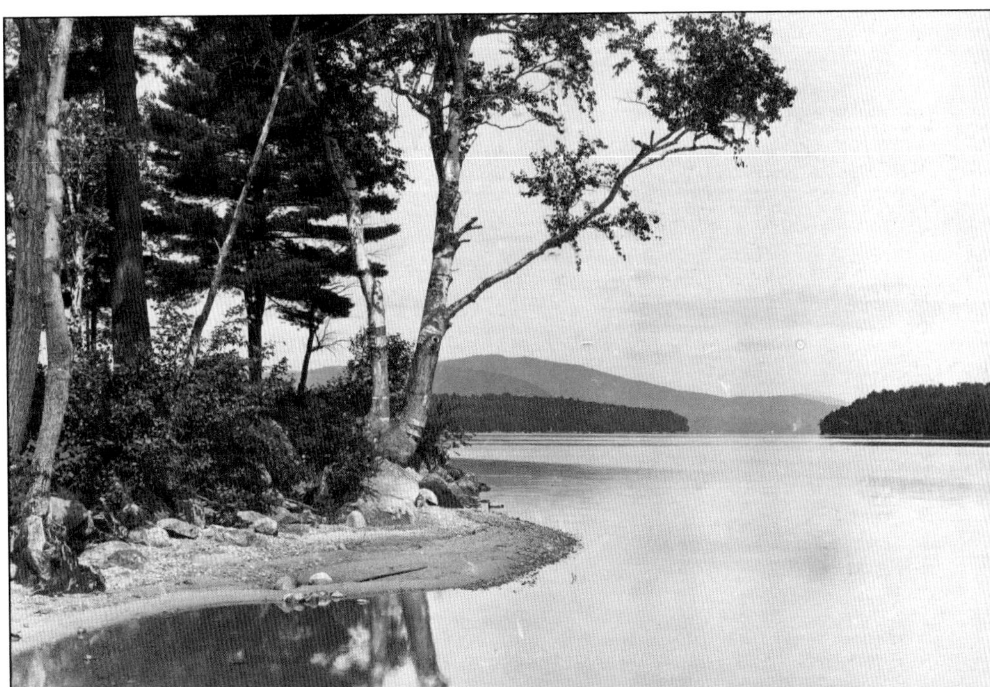

This book is dedicated to the memory of my parents, who loved the lakes of New Hampshire.

Contents

ACKNOWLEDGMENTS

The idea of creating a series of books consisting exclusively of vintage photographs is an idea par excellence. It is an idea that this author is delighted to have been involved in. Although innumerable hours of sometimes exhausting work have been required in the preparation of this work, it has been inspiring, educational, and fun. The project could not have been entered into or completed, however, without the generous assistance of the members and directors of local historical societies, librarians, historians, and other interested individuals. To each and every one who facilitated the selection of photographs and provided historical information, support, and encouragement, the author wishes to express her heartfelt thanks and appreciation.

The captions accompanying the photographs herein are credited with parenthesized initials to provide identity as follows:

Alexandria Historical Society (AHS.): Marilyn Ramsey
Bridgewater Historical Society (BWHS.): Judy Ferrin
Bristol Historical Society (BHS.): Beverly McKenna
Groton Historical Society (GHS.): Deb Johnson, Judy Demers, David Demers, Louise Traunstein, Ellen Anderson, and Jane Gilman
Hebron Historical Society (HBHS.): Howard Oedel and Ronald Collins
Hill Historical Society (HHS.): John Chandler, John Thierry, and Phyllis Kerkawich
New Hampton Historical Society (NHHS.): Jean Thompson
Newfound Lake Region Chamber of Commerce: Phyllis Berton
Camp Mowglis (CM.): Phillip Hart
Camp Pasquaney (CP.): Nelson Adams and Vincent Broadrick
Mason Westfall (MW.)
Webster Farms (WF.): Judy Ferrin
Doreen Powden (DP.)
June Phelps (JP.)
Beverly McKenna (BM.)
Barbara Maluchnik (BML.)
Cynthia Robie (CR.)

INTRODUCTION

I like small towns. I have yet to encounter one that is not endlessly fascinating. My favorite small towns do not have an architectural theme newly imposed upon all the buildings, complete with dishonest airs. Rather, in my favorite towns the buildings are grand through simplicity, built long ago and nicely preserved, giving an honest mix of style and function.

I like to walk through a small town and embrace its uniqueness. A manicured town common with maples, benches, memorial monuments, and perhaps a dove-white bandstand are mute reminders of the celebrations and dedications that have taken place there. I like to visit the library, the town hall, the historical society archives, and the churches. I like to talk with the merchants, farmers, historians, and town officials about their memories of the past in their small town.

The towns that make up the Newfound Lake Region are small towns to be sure and share certain physical, cultural, and historical attributes with one another, but each holds its own fascinating individual flavor and distinctive identity. For example, the town of Hill was first called New Chester in its original charter in 1753.

That year, a group of "Masonian" proprietors living in Chester bought 30,000 acres on the northern side of the John Tufton Mason land grant. They named this land New Chester. This acreage, along the Pemigewasset River, included what is now Bristol, Bridgewater, and part of Alexandria. New Chester changed its name to Hill in 1837 in honor of one of the state's most influential governors, Isaac Hill, the owner of the *New Hampshire Patriot* newspaper. In 1941, a new planned community was created for Hill on higher ground and the original land on the floodplain was used for a flood control project.

New Hampton, in its original charter of 1761, was known as Moultonbourough Addition and was granted by Gov. Benning Wentworth. In 1777, it was renamed after Col. Jonathan Moulton's native town of Hampton. In 1798, New Hampton's first meetinghouse and the New Hampton Literary Institution was founded.

Groton was incorporated in 1761 as Cockermouth, named after Charles Wyndham, the baron of Cockermouth and earl of Egremont. Once thought to be too remote, in 1776 the town was regranted as a viable and practical area for settlement and cultivation. A later grantee, Samuel Blood of Groton, Massachusetts, renamed the town Old Groton.

Hebron, nestled at the northern end of Newfound Lake, was formed in 1792 from parts of Cockermouth (Groton) and Plymouth and was incorporated as a township in 1792. It was largely a town of self-sufficient farmers and has been associated with the founding of several youth summer camps. Pasquaney Camp for boys was founded in 1895 by Aaron Wellington and Capt. John Wall Wilson. Mowglis was founded in 1903 by Mrs. Henry Hollister on the site of Redcroft, an earlier camp for girls.

Danbury was originally part of Alexandria. It was incorporated as a separate town in 1795 by its first moderator, Maj. Joshua Tolford, one of the proprietors of the New Chester land grant. Danbury later annexed additional land from the neighboring towns of Wilmot and New Chester (Hill). It also includes the villages of Elmwood and South Danbury. Ragged Mountain Golf Course and Ski Area brings hundreds of visitors annually to this town of nearly 1,000 residents.

The town of Alexandria obtained its grant in 1753 and was probably named after the city of Alexandria, Virginia. It was the birthplace of Luther E. Ladd, the first enlisted soldier to lose his life in the Civil War. One of the town's scenic attractions is Mount Mowglis, commemorating the hero of *The Jungle Book*, by Rudyard Kipling.

Bridgewater received its charter in 1783 after being annexed from New Chester. It includes a considerable portion of Newfound Lake. A family named Mitchell from Bridgewater, Massachusetts, was one of the first to settle in Bridgewater and appears to have chosen the town's name.

The prosperous, industrial town of Bristol was incorporated in 1819 and is situated on terrain that produced a type of alluvial deposit of fine sand used in Bristol, England, for the production of china, earthenware, and pottery. This deposit, in demand in the early 1800s, became known as Bristol sand and was also used to make a superior quality of brick, which was marketed as a Bristol brick. Early Bristol factories manufactured paper, leather, woolen goods, furniture, and other wooden items.

Newfound Lake is central to these eight towns of the region. This pristine lake is spring fed and is rated as one of the cleanest bodies of fresh water in the world. It covers an area of 4,106 acres, has 22.24 miles of shoreline, and is 183 feet deep.

This book begins with the lake and extends outward in eight directions. Its yield has required many hours of sifting through hundreds of photographs and is supplemented with other printed material, as well as the information obtained through personal interviews. It has been a complex, but inspiring task. It has summoned my presence at coffee shops, private homes, town halls, and basement archives. I have walked through the towns and dawdled on commons. I have wanted to adopt each town as my own.

—Janice Hugron Harvey
Hill, New Hampshire

One

The Lake

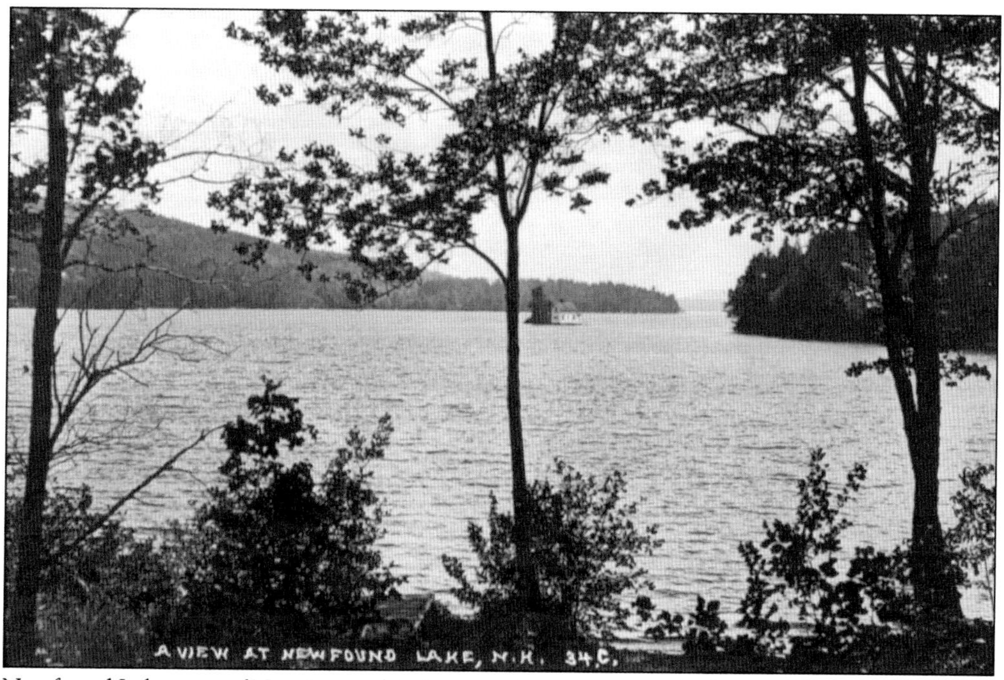

Newfound Lake, one of New Hampshire's natural treasures, has for decades drawn thousands to its shores. With the lake's enchanting islands and coves, dotted with cottages and year-round homes, elegant 19th-century inns and youth camps, it is little wonder that it has enticed these masses. Seen here, a cozy cottage consumes tiny Loon Island. This photograph was taken from Sleepy Hollow Cove in East Hebron. (MW.)

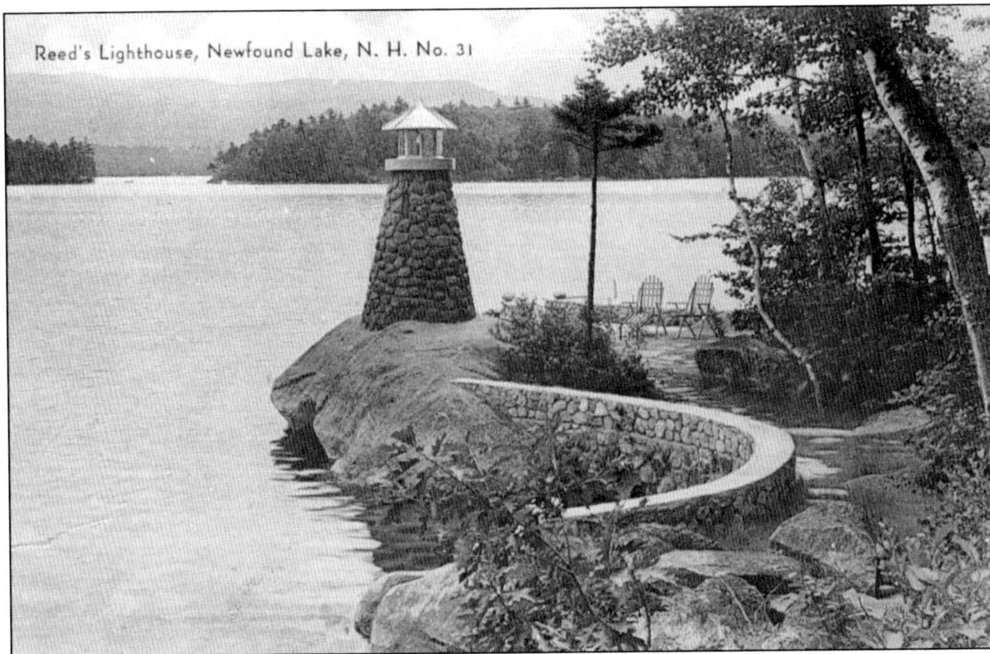

The light on the west shore was built by Mrs. A.B. Reed in 1932. It is 14 feet tall and 9 feet in diameter. Its blinking light is a cheerful guide and is a joy to see for boaters and lake residents alike. (MW.)

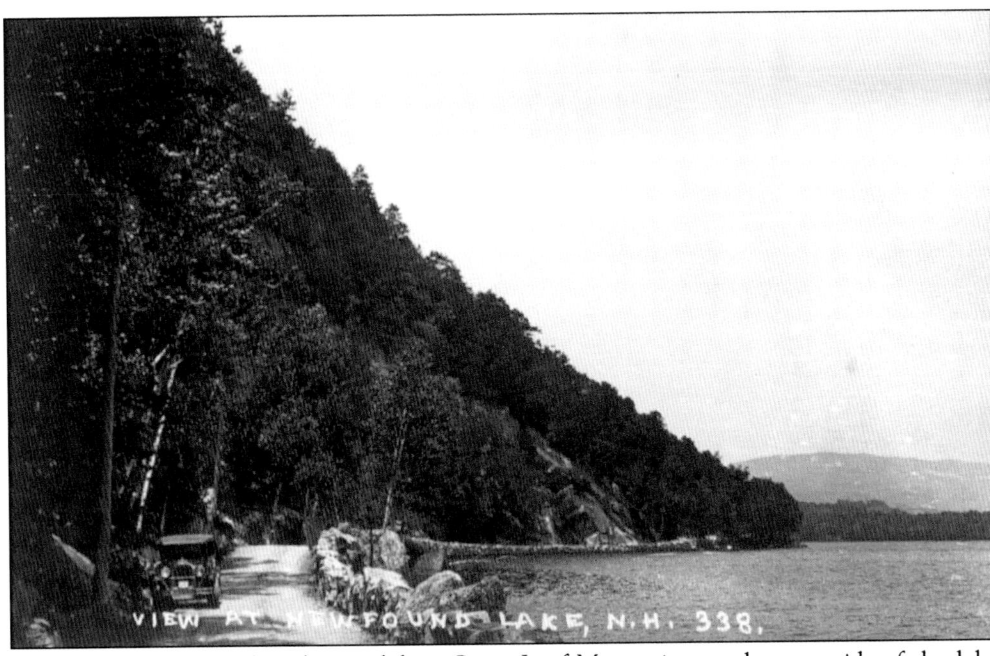

In 1861, the section of road carved from Sugar Loaf Mountain, on the west side of the lake in Alexandria, must have been a complex endeavor. Before that time the only highway from Bristol to Hebron was around the eastern side of the lake, a much greater distance. The project completed, this scenic area is known as the Ledges. (MW.)

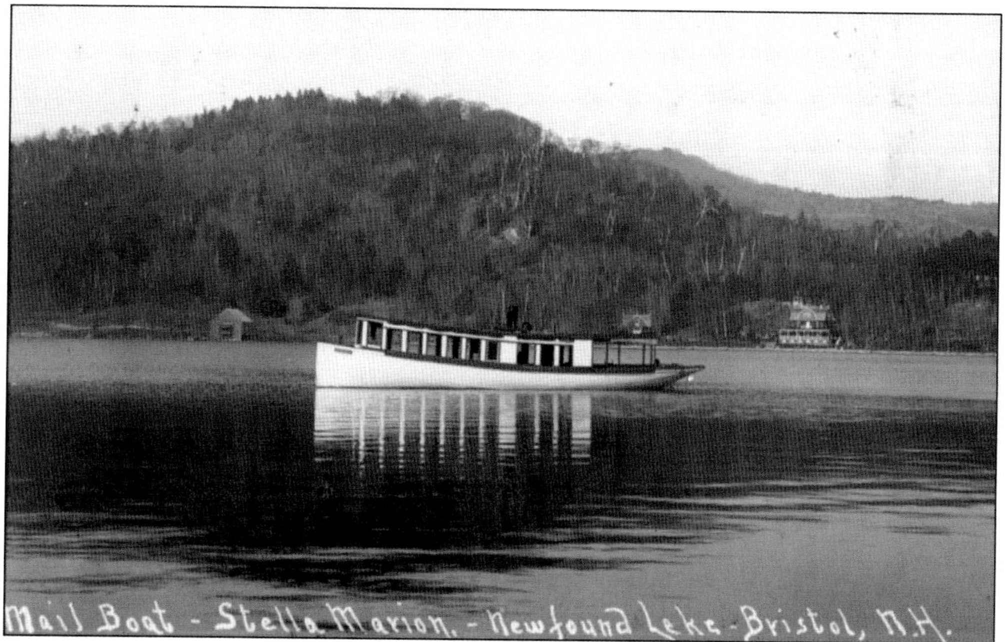

The *Stella-Marion*, built in 1901 by Ambrose Adams of Hebron, was named for his two daughters. The boat was utilized as a mail boat for many years and as a barge for towing logs down the lake to Merrill's sawmill in Bristol. But the boat was probably most remembered by Newfound guests for its joyous excursions around the lake. Sadly, the *Stella-Marion* was destroyed by fire in 1915. (MW.)

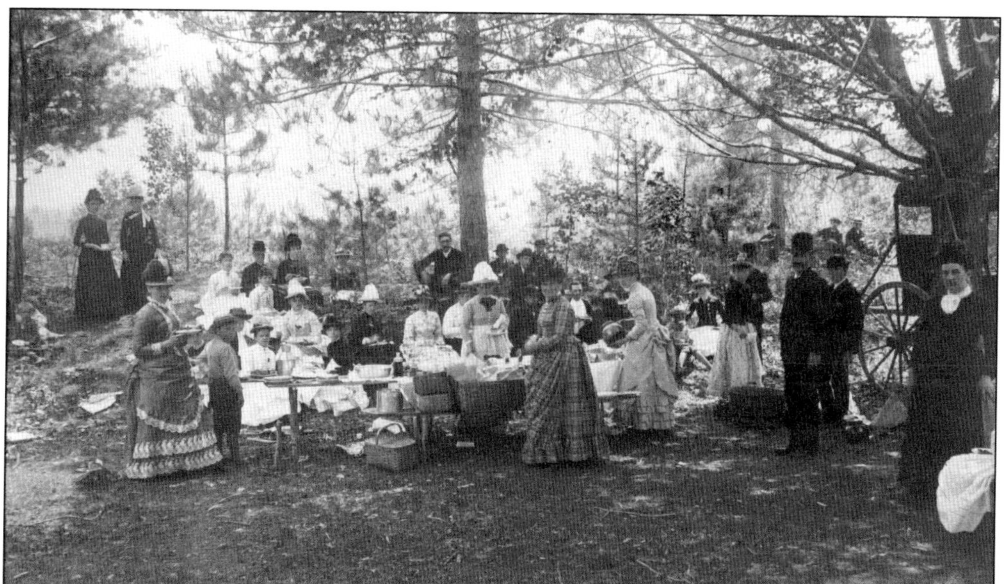
One of life's simple pleasures: an Independence Day picnic at Sanborn's Beach in Bristol, c. 1886. (HBHS.)

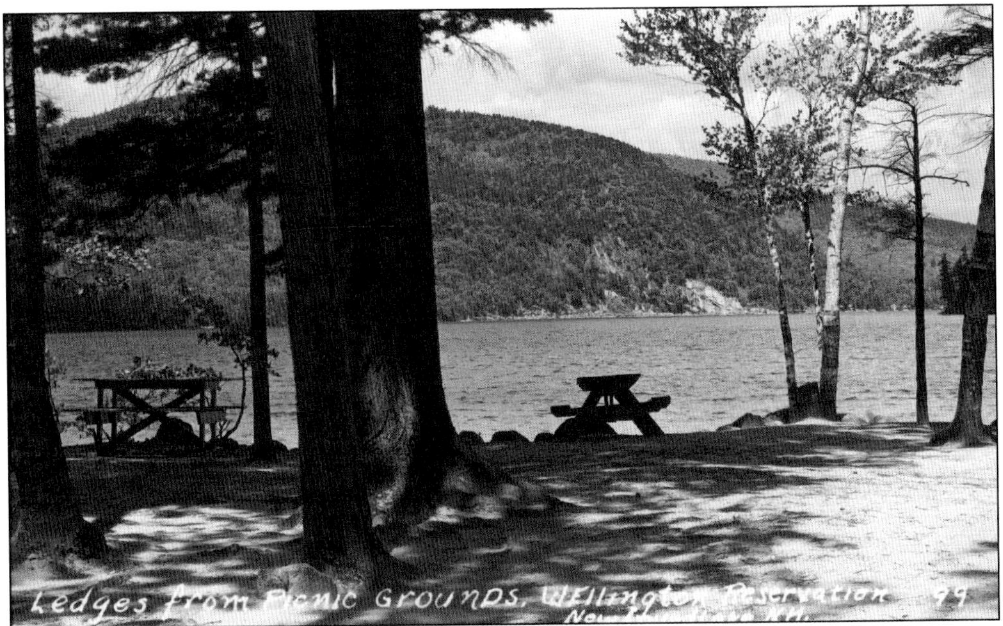

Wellington Park, located on the west shore of Newfound lake, covers 200 acres with numerous picnic areas, hiking trails, a half-mile-long beach for swimming, and a public boat ramp. Early summer boarders enjoyed excursions to the park, which was then known as Crescent Beach. (MW.)

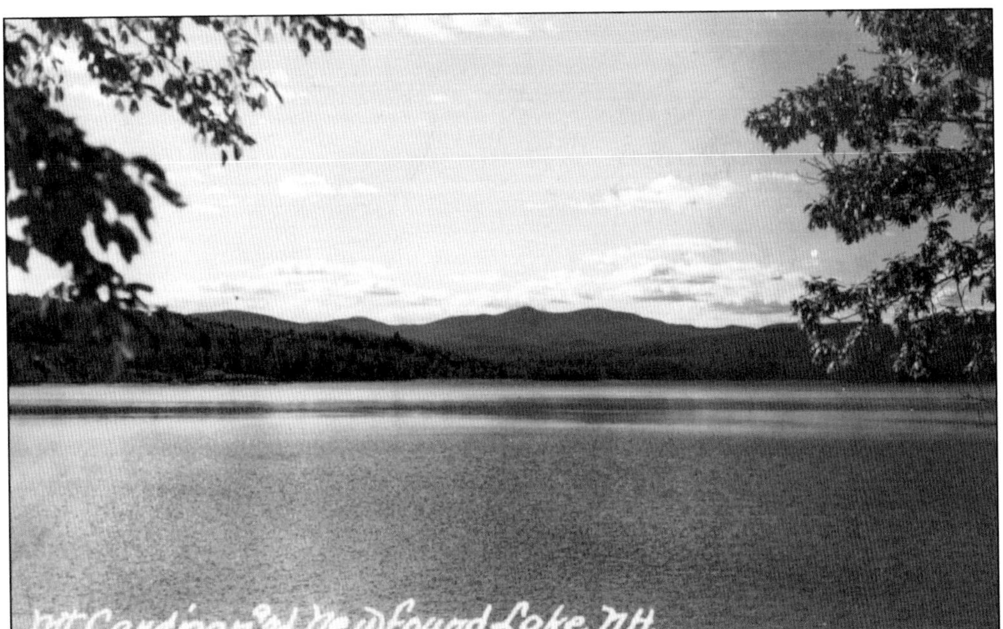

Mount Cardigan's summit is at 3,100 feet and offers sweeping views for the visiting hiker. At the base of the mountain, in Alexandria, is the Appalachian Mountain Club Lodge, from which more than 50 miles of trails extend to several area peaks. (DP.)

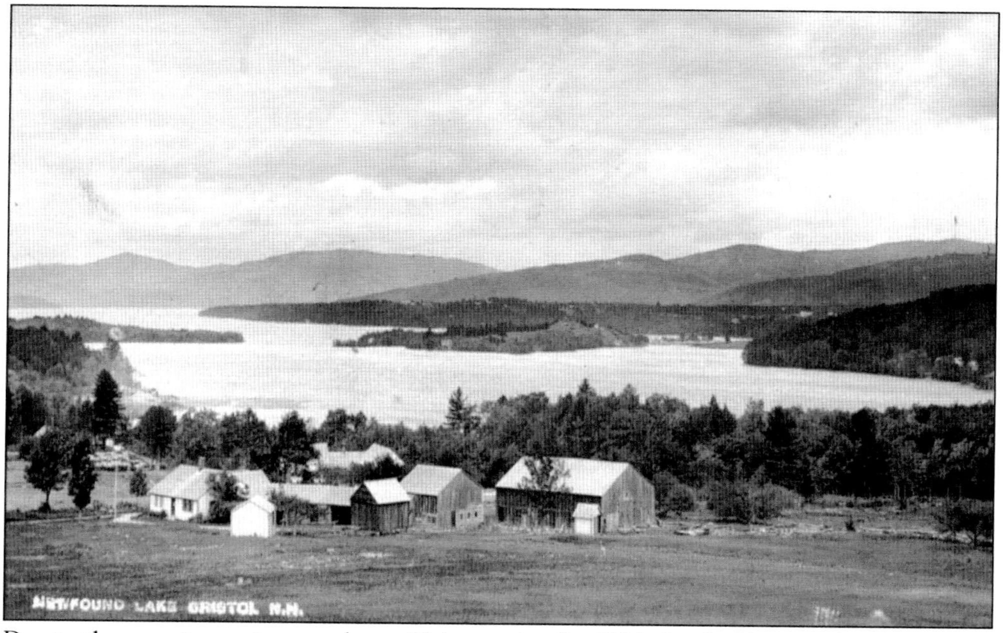

Due to the ever-increasing numbers of lake tourists by 1891, Jacob Akerman bought the old Sleeper Farm, shown here, on the west side of the lake and opened a tourist home. In 1910, his son Frank built the Akerman House, a three-story guesthouse with an enchanting view of the lake from a wraparound piazza. (CP.)

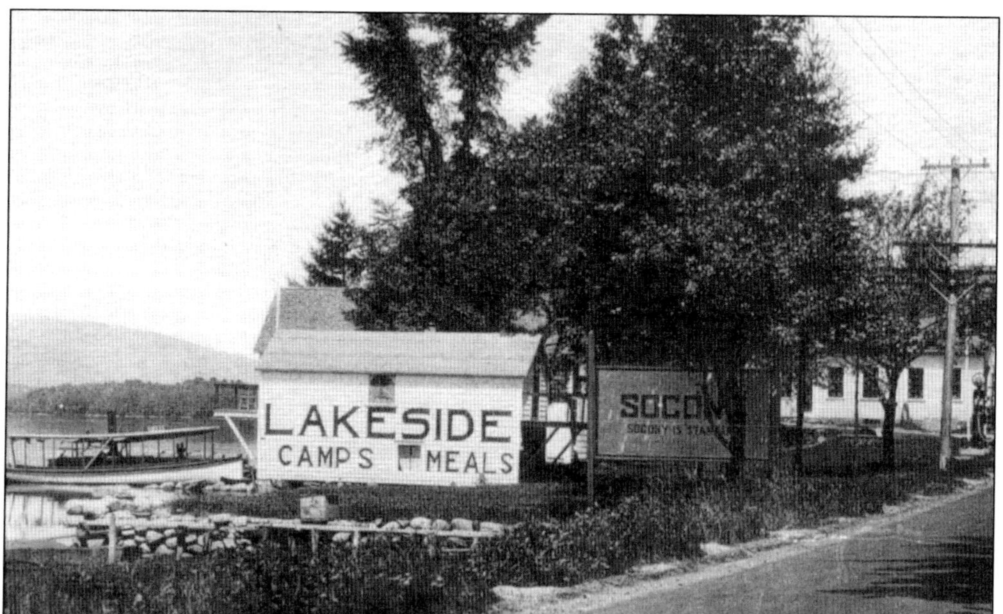

Adebahr's Lakeside Camps was one of several multifunction tourist sites along Route 3A in the 1930s. At Adebahr's, visitors were offered cottages, rooms, baths, cabins, boats, meals, bathing, fishing, and automobile fill-ups with Socony fuel. (MW.)

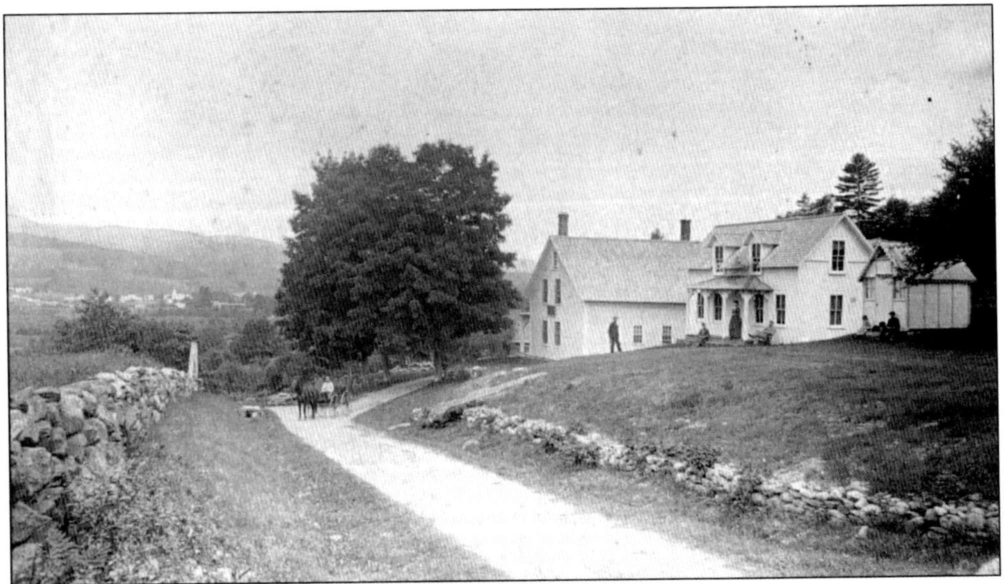

In 1875, Grove Hill Farm in Hebron, with proprietors Mr. and Mrs. John W. Sanborn, was the first to go into the boardinghouse business. Situated on a hill, the farm offered an unparalleled view of the lake. Guests enjoyed boating, fishing, bathing, and riding, as well as excursions to area attractions. (HBHS.)

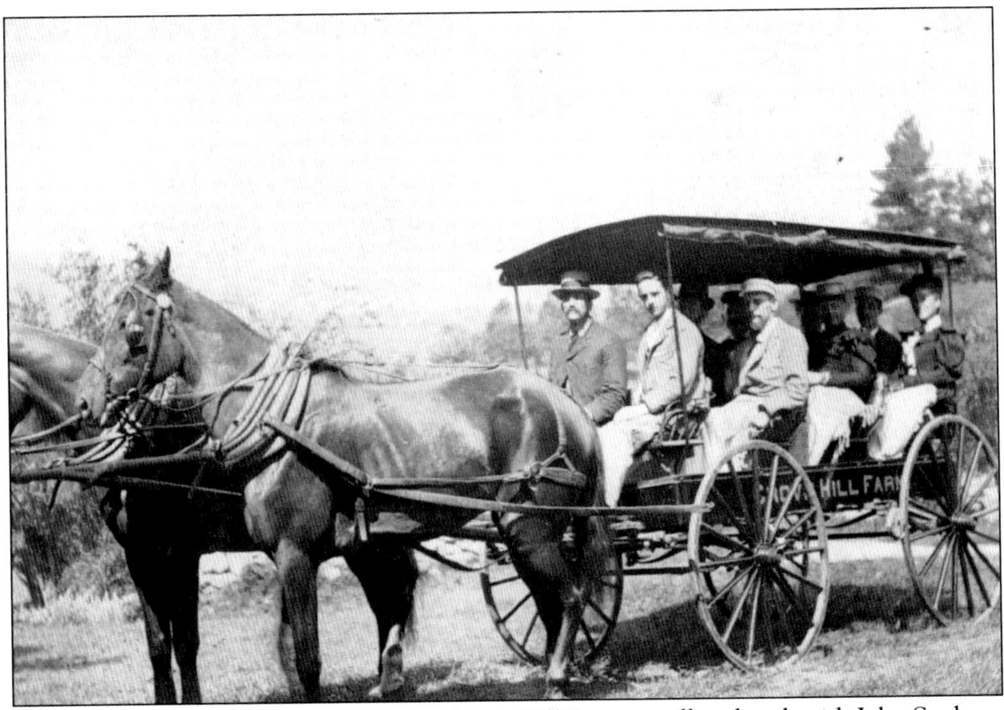

Seen in this c. 1894 photograph, guests at Grove Hill Farm are off to church with John Sanborn driving the team. (HBHS.)

A hand-written bill of fare lists a variety of delectable choices for Grove Hill guests.

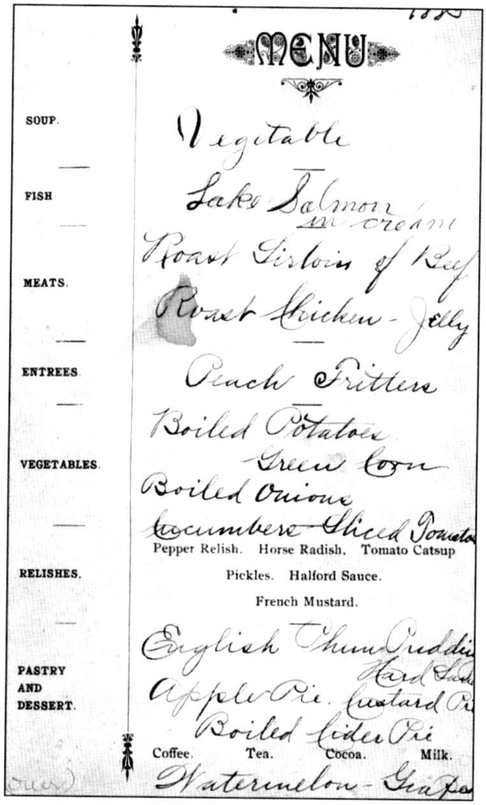

MENU

SOUP. Vegetable

FISH Lake Salmon in cream

MEATS. Roast Sirloin of Beef
Roast Chicken - Jelly

ENTREES. Peach Fritters

VEGETABLES. Boiled Potatoes
Green Corn
Boiled Onions
~~Cucumbers~~ Sliced Tomatoes

RELISHES. Pepper Relish. Horse Radish. Tomato Catsup
Pickles. Halford Sauce.
French Mustard.

PASTRY AND DESSERT. English Plum Pudding
Hard Sauce
Apple Pie. Custard Pie
Boiled Cider Pie

Coffee. Tea. Cocoa. Milk.

Watermelon - Grapes

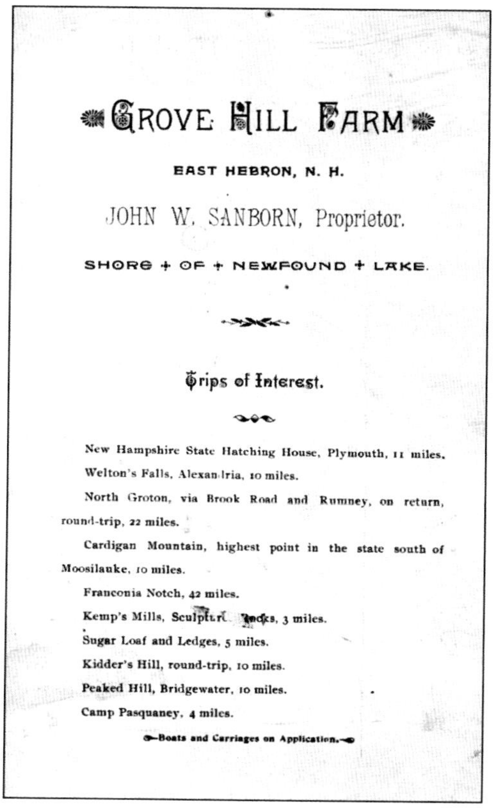

GROVE HILL FARM

EAST HEBRON, N. H.

JOHN W. SANBORN, Proprietor.

SHORE + OF + NEWFOUND + LAKE.

Trips of Interest.

New Hampshire State Hatching House, Plymouth, 11 miles.

Welton's Falls, Alexandria, 10 miles.

North Groton, via Brook Road and Rumney, on return, round-trip, 22 miles.

Cardigan Mountain, highest point in the state south of Moosilauke, 10 miles.

Franconia Notch, 42 miles.

Kemp's Mills, Sculptured Rocks, 3 miles.

Sugar Loaf and Ledges, 5 miles.

Kidder's Hill, round-trip, 10 miles.

Peaked Hill, Bridgewater, 10 miles.

Camp Pasquaney, 4 miles.

Boats and Carriages on Application.

An 1885 trip itinerary seems quite impressive considering the distances given for travel with horse and carriage. (HBHS.)

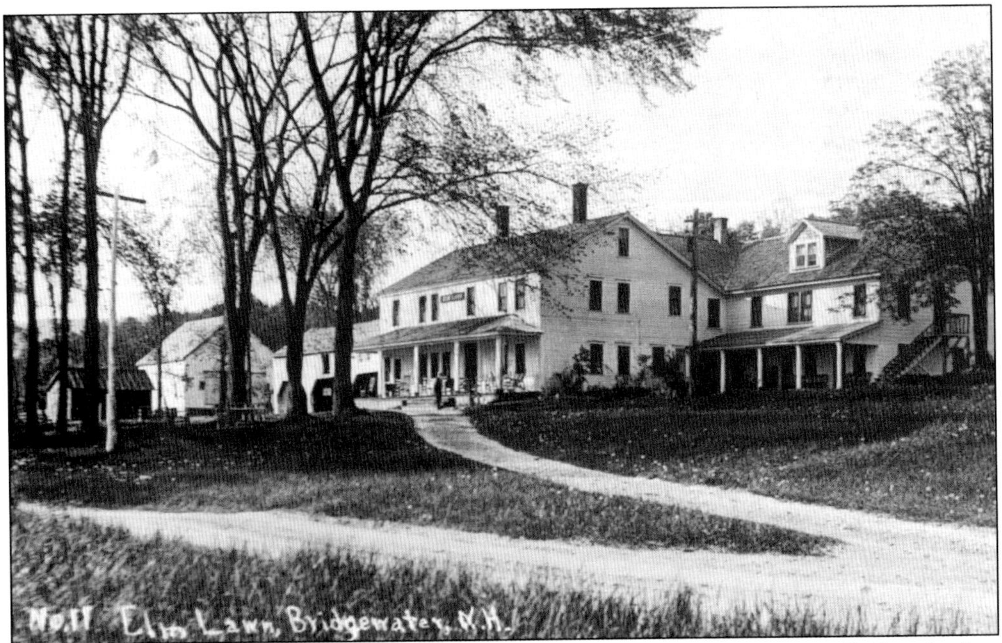

The old Hoyt Tavern in Bridgewater, having been refurbished by Mrs. Orin Dolloff in the late 1890s, became a summer boardinghouse known as Elm Lawn. (BWHS.)

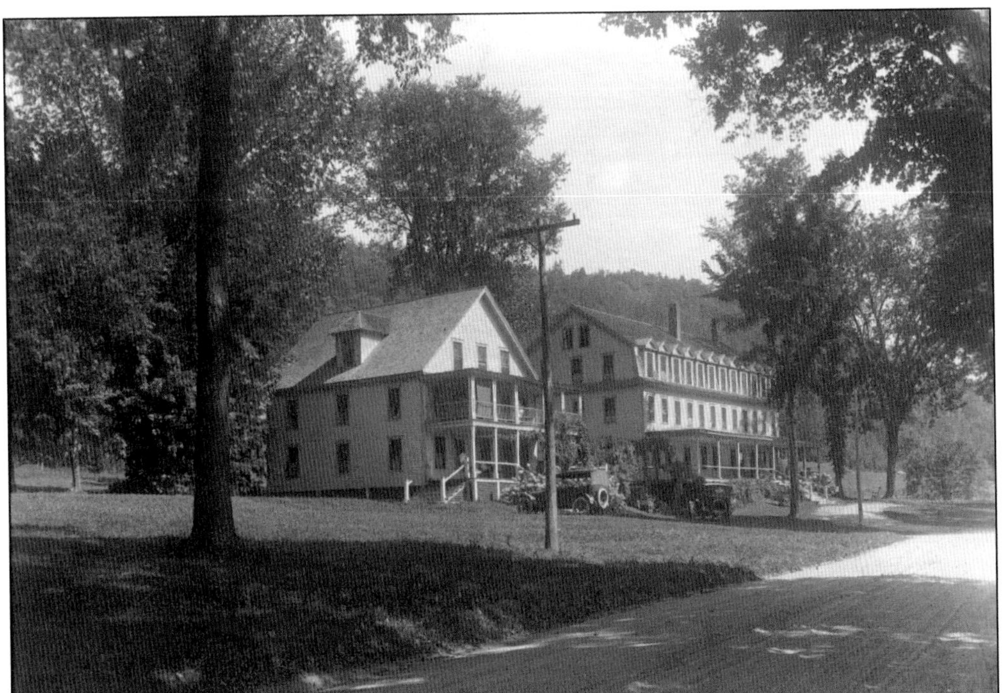
To meet the increasing demand for summer tourist accommodations, the elegant Pasquaney Inn was built in 1910, the same year the famous Masquebec Inn was demolished. (BWHS.)

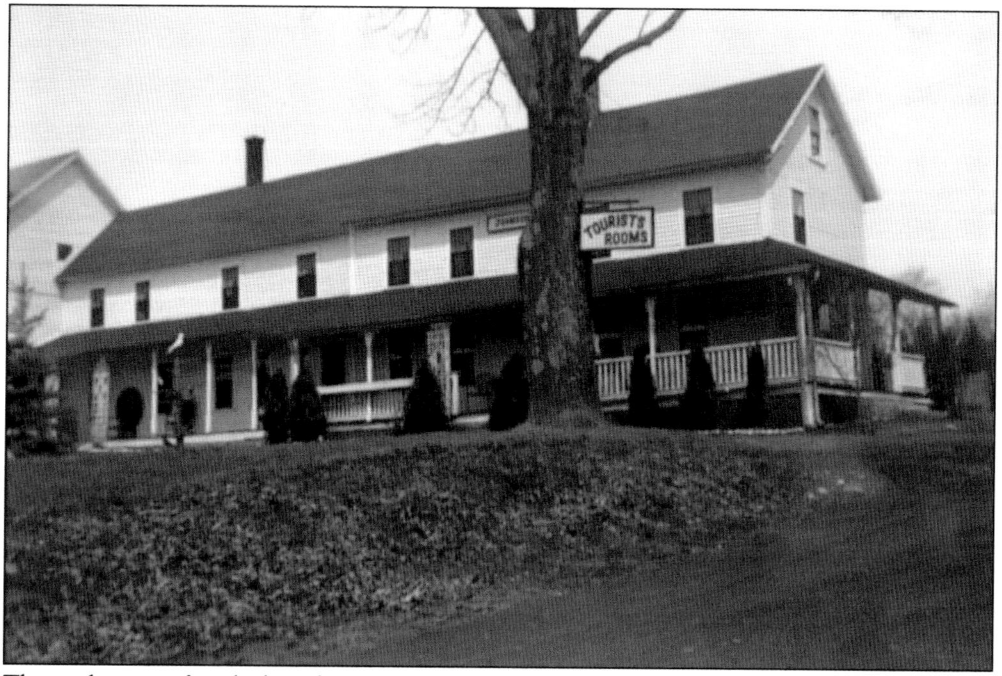

The ambiance of early boardinghouses was homey and unpretentious. Rooms were simply decorated, and bathrooms were shared. Guests were served healthy home-style meals and were entertained generously. The Bridgewater Inn, shown here, has provided decades of hospitality to Newfound Lake's summer visitors. (BWHS.)

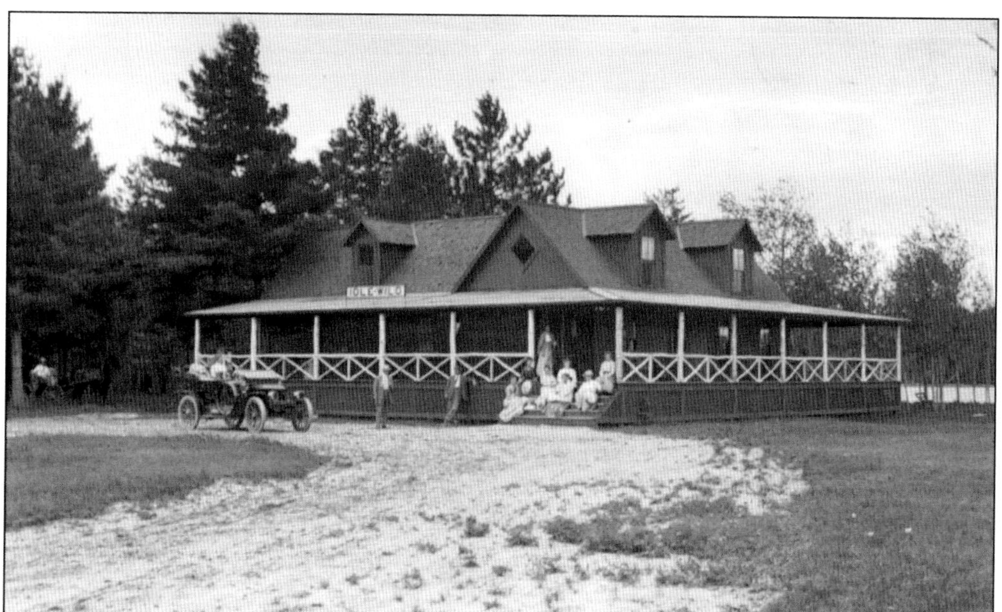

Another favorite tourist destination on the lake was the Idle Wild. Arriving in their sporty automobile, these guests were perhaps detained with sight-seeing but are warmly greeted by those already enjoying the inn's lavish porches. (BWHS.)

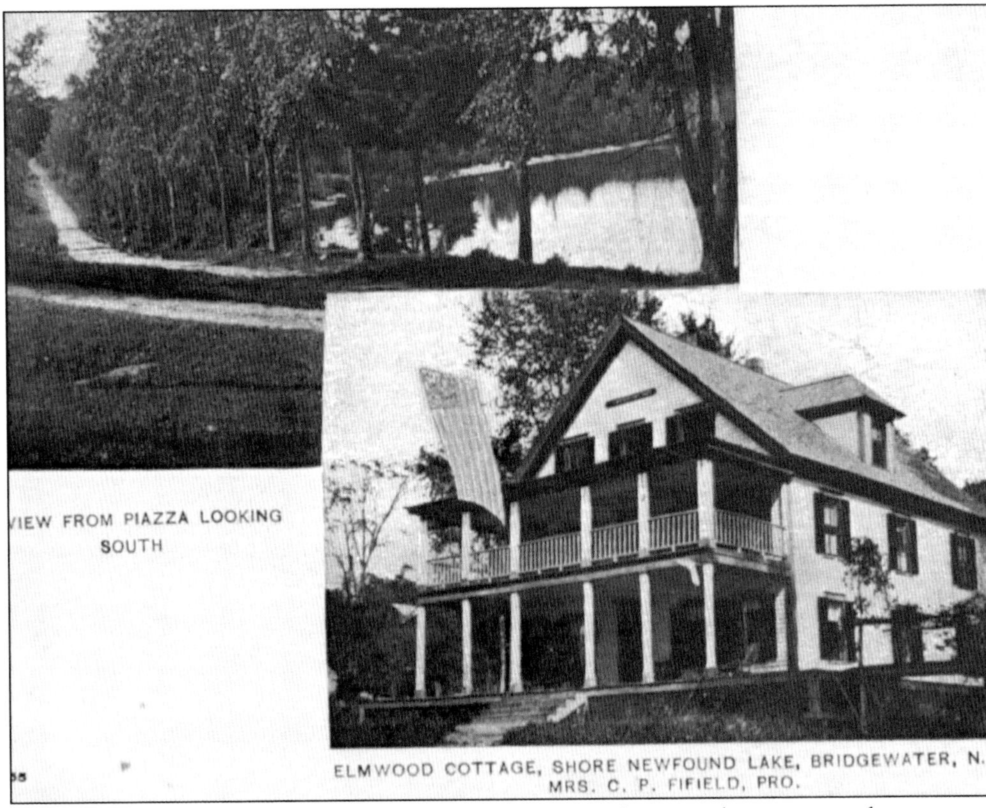

Elmwood Cottage, on the shore of Newfound Lake in Bridgewater, boasts its southern view of the lake from the piazza. Mrs. C.P. Fifield was the proprietor. (BWHS.)

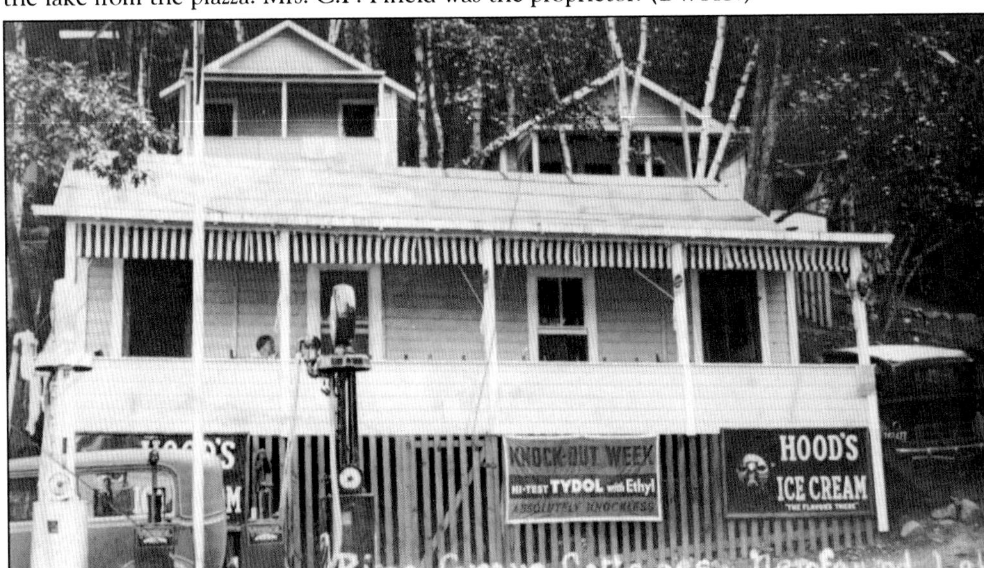

If guests took preference to a more private boarding arrangement, Pine Grove Cottages would accommodate their wishes, along with Tydol for their automobile and an ice-cream treat to boot. (MW.)

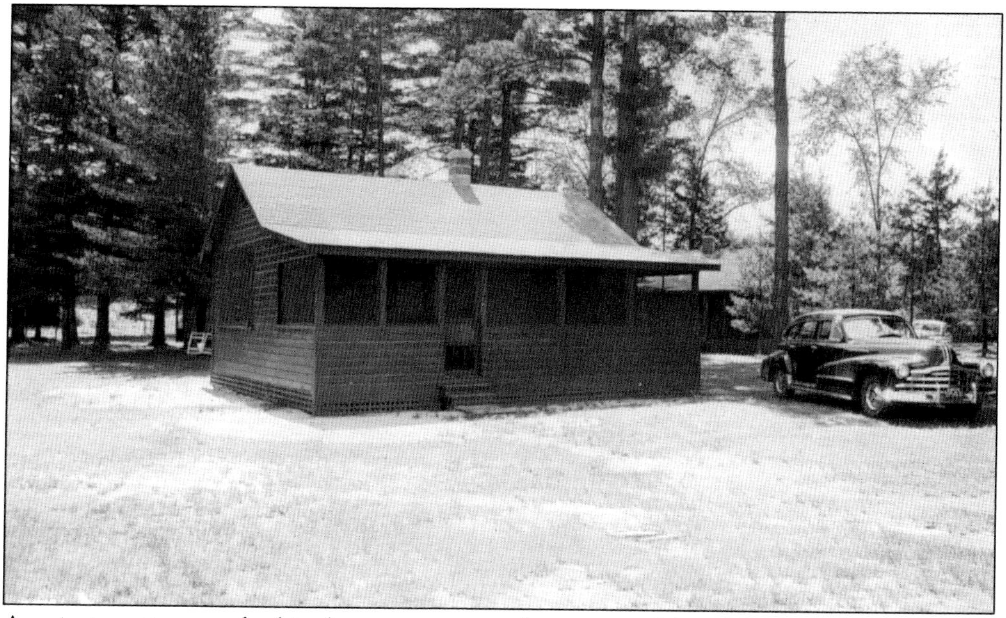

As private cottages and cabins became more popular, groups of them began to spring up around the lake. This one, located at Timberlock Lodge, would probably accommodate six people and has its own screened-in porch for bug-less summer evenings. (BWHS.)

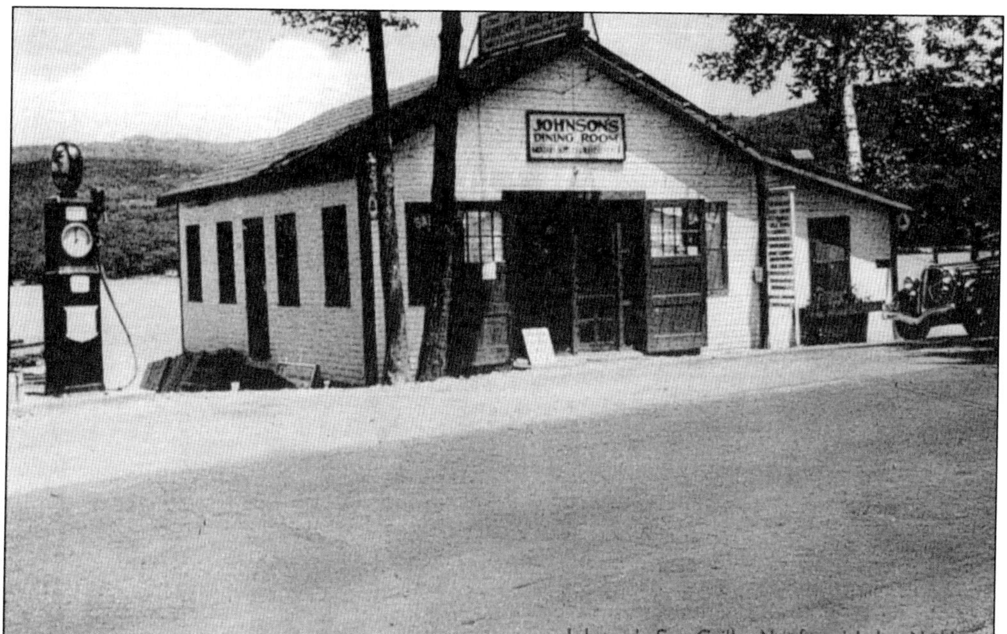

Vacationers enjoyed dinner at Johnson's Sea Grille Dining Room, which they traveled to by boat or automobile. This photograph was taken c. 1938. (MW.)

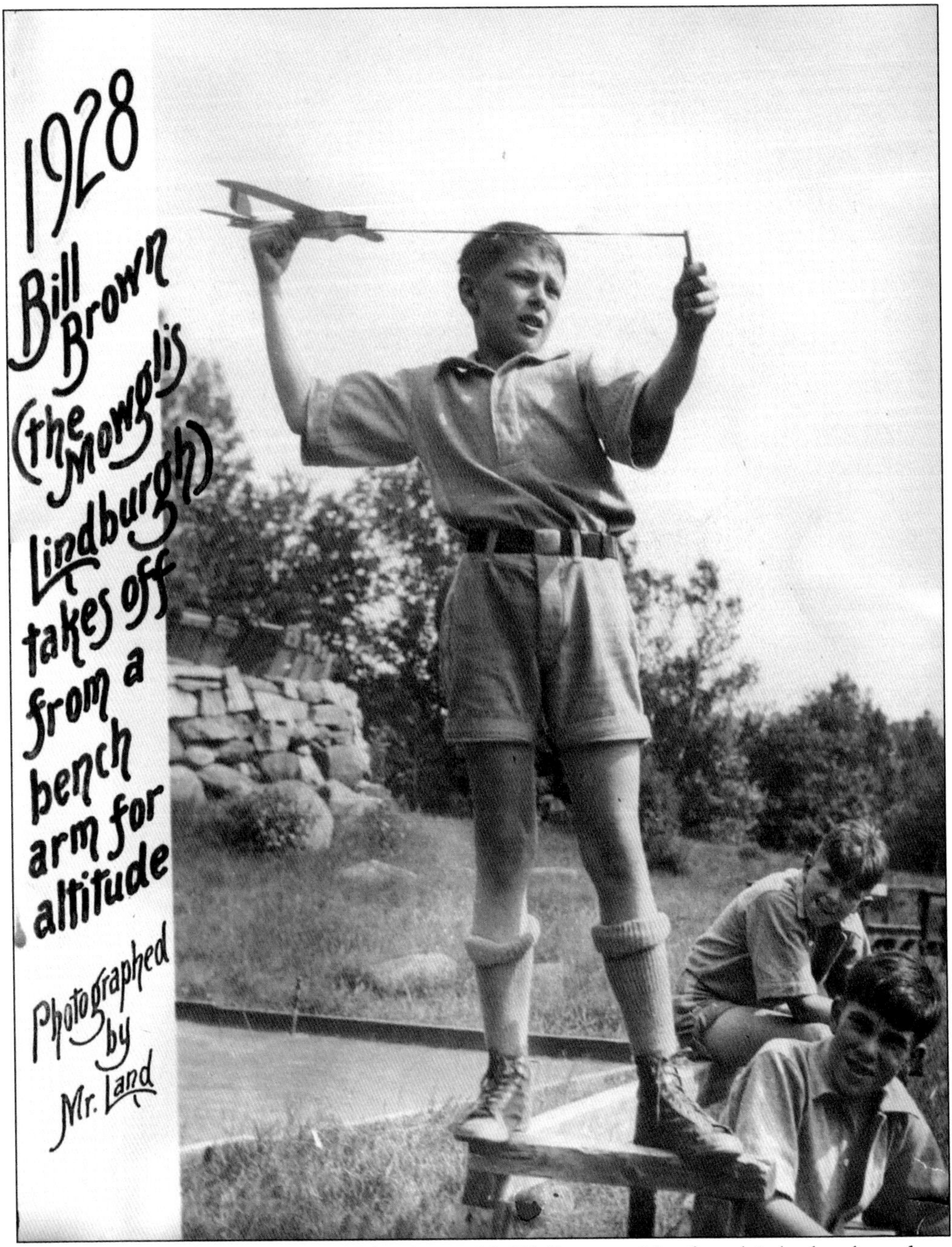

Almost since its discovery in 1888 by Aaron H. Wellington, Newfound Lake has been host to summer camps for boys and girls. Camp Pasquaney for boys was founded in 1895, Camp Mowglis for boys was founded in 1903, and Camp Onaway for girls was founded in 1911. Later camps were Camp Wah-Kee-Nah, Camp Berea, Darling Camp, Camp Wi-Co-Su-Ta, and Camp Wikiva. These youth camps, founded on a philosophy of good citizenship and ideals of integrity for future productivity, offered a wide variety of activities. Some of these activities were archery, riflery, rowing, sailing, photography, theater, water-skiing, and windsurfing. (CM.)

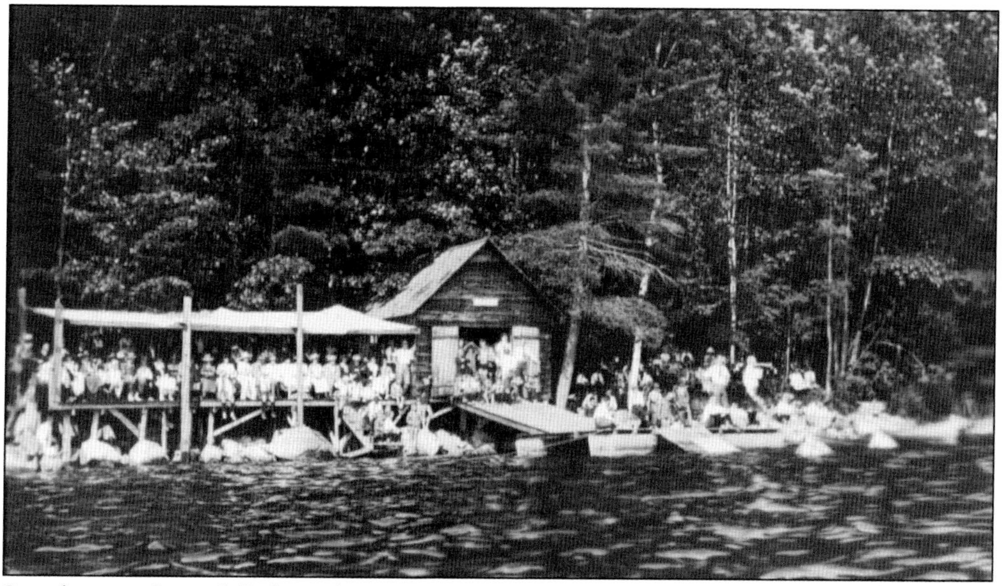

Seen here are beautifully-hatted parents at a water-sports day at Camp Pasquaney. (CP.)

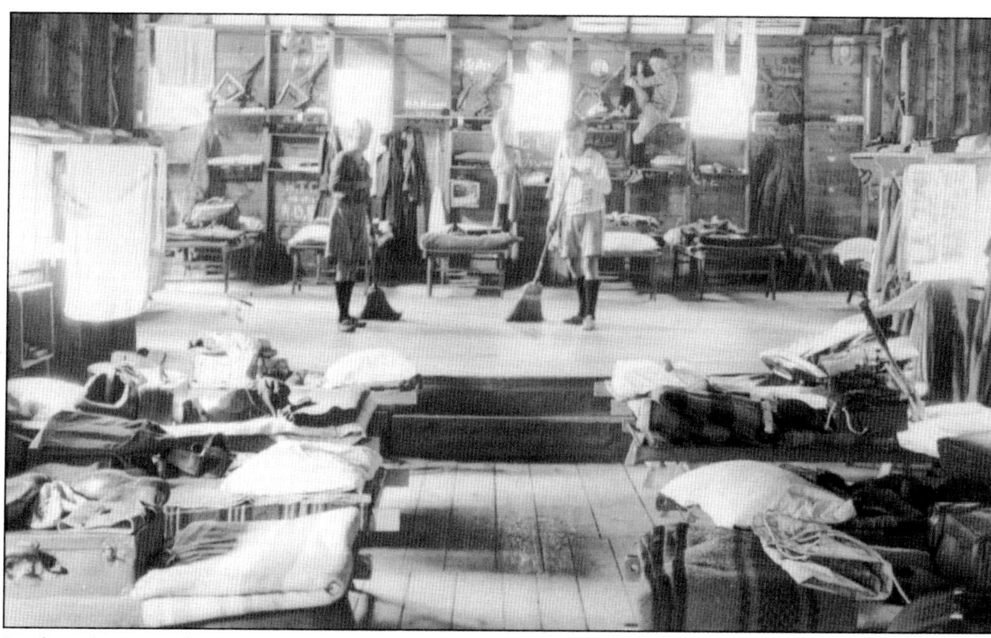

In this photograph, the Camp Pasquaney cleaning crew performs the daily tradition. (MW.)

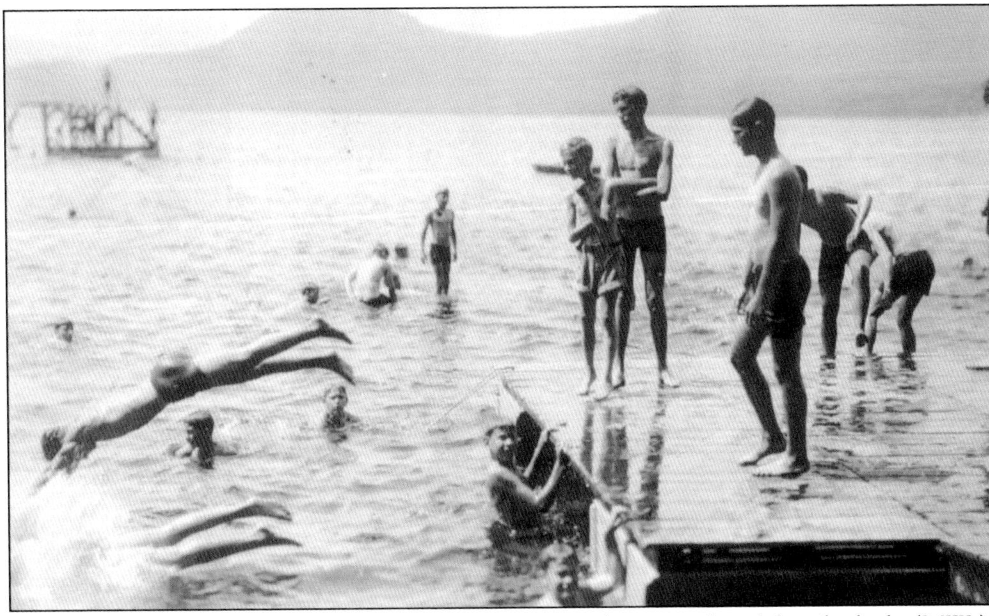

These Camp Pasquaney boys appear to be having a grand time at their lakeside dock. (MW.)

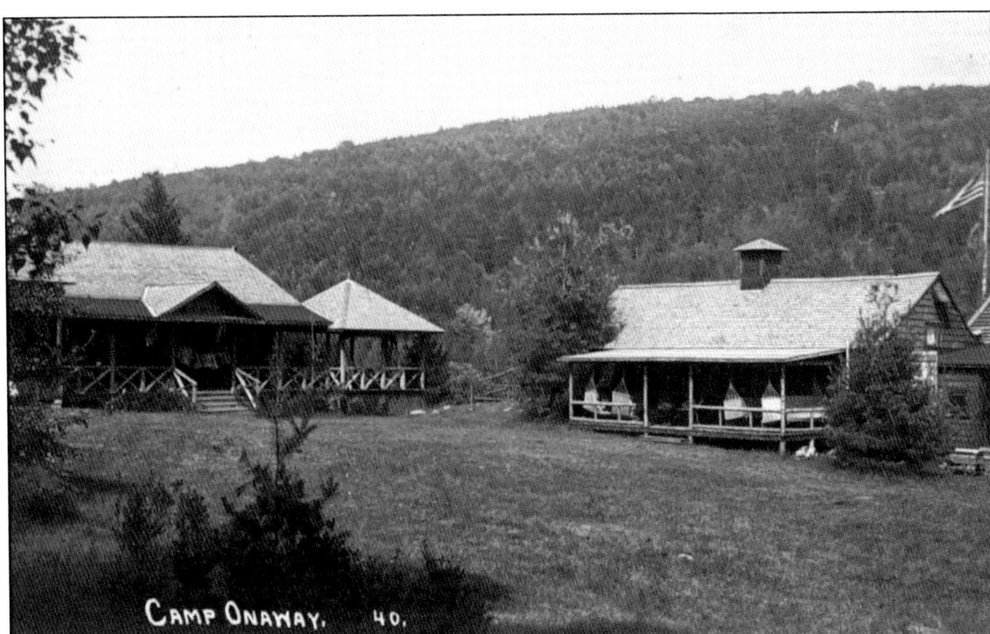

Camp Onaway for girls continues to promote leadership potential, recreational opportunities, and lasting friendships for its campers. (MW.)

Two

About Town

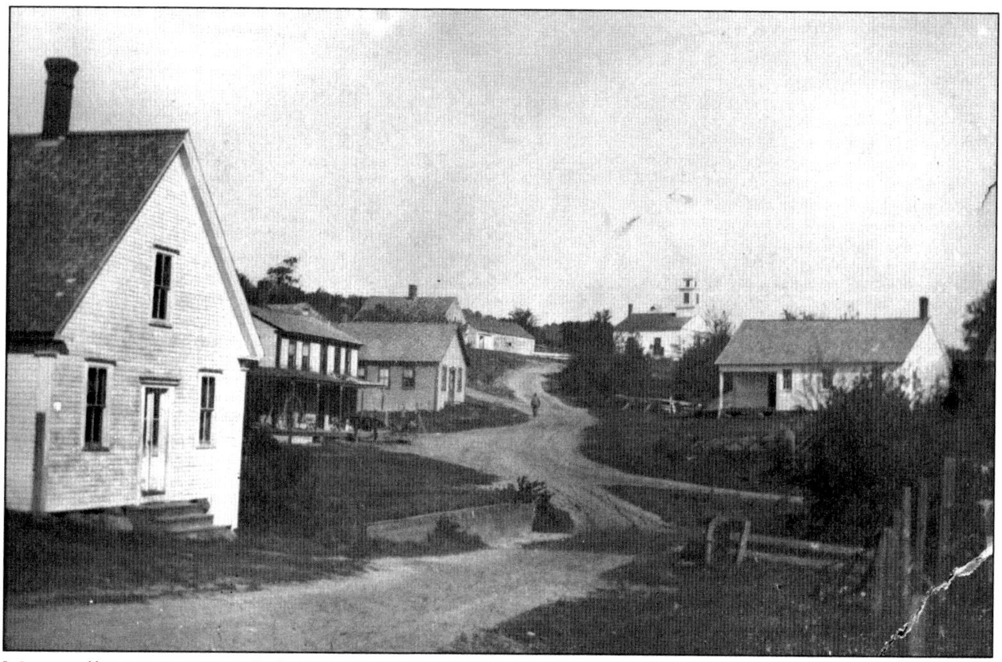

Most villages were settled according to the availability of resources from which to build a viable livelihood. Bridgewater, Bristol, Hill, and New Hampton were heavily reliant upon the Pemigewasset, Newfound, and Smith's Rivers to power the early sawmills and gristmills. Other communities were best suited to farming, fishing, or mining. The church, or meetinghouse, served as the center of religious, political, and social life in early New England villages. Taverns provided stopovers for stagecoach travelers and a post office. Some villages developed outwardly from a center green, or common, others were linear in pattern. Groton, the latter pattern, shown from the south in this c. 1885 view, was settled and became prosperous when mica and other minerals were discovered in the surrounding mountains. Seen here, from left to right, are the Grange Hall, Burley's General Store, the mica-processing shop, the Union Congregational Church, and the schoolhouse. (GHS.)

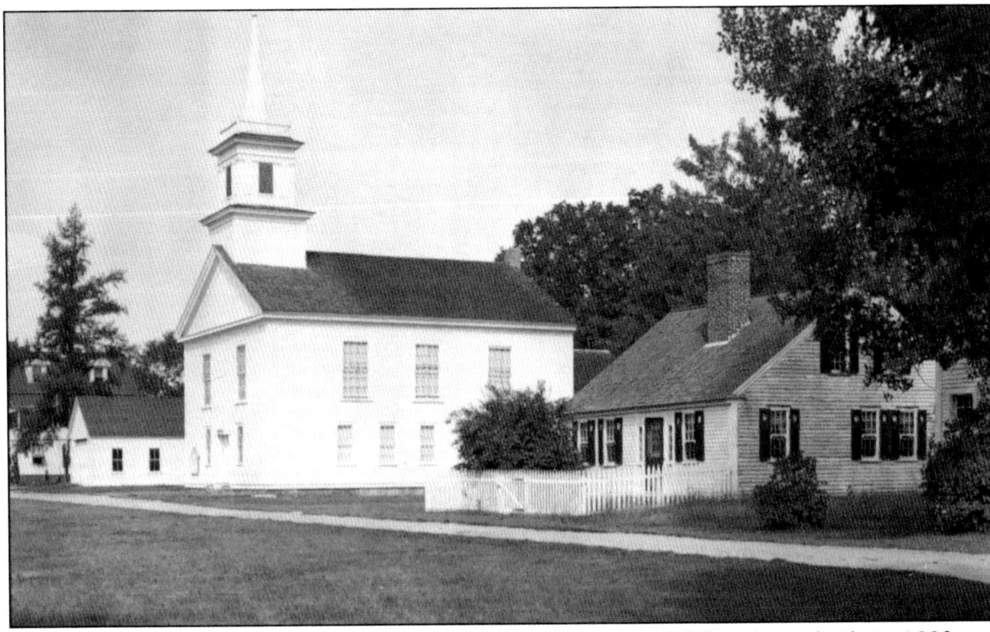

The original Union Congregational Church of Cockermouth (Hebron) was built in 1803 and was tragically destroyed by fire in 1945. Shown here is the new meetinghouse that replaced the original in 1953. (HBHS.)

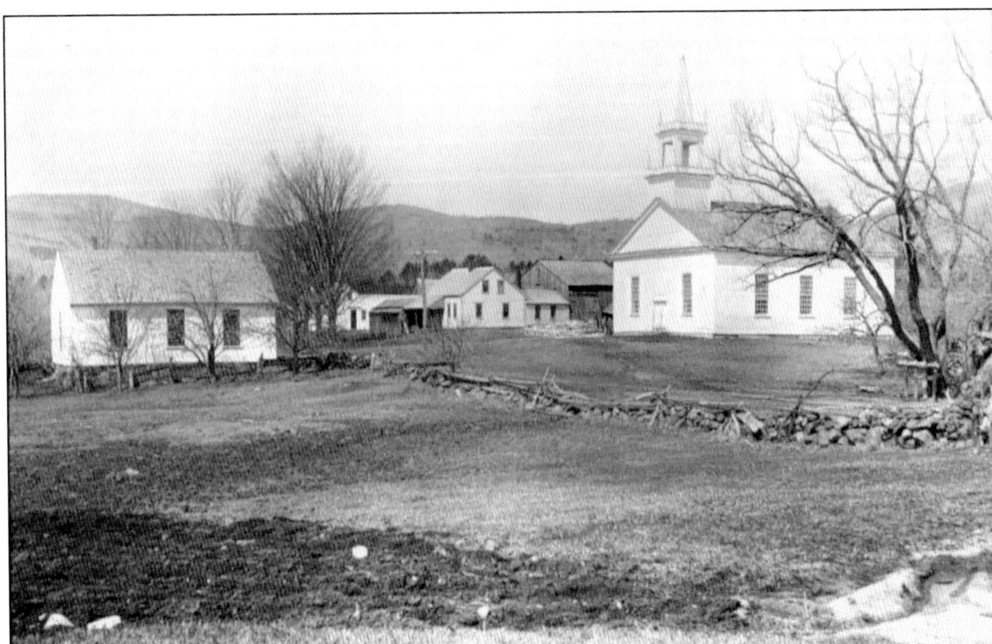

In New Chester (Hill), the first church, known as the West Meetinghouse, was built in 1800 on the hill at the "centre," a mile west of the old village. (HHS.)

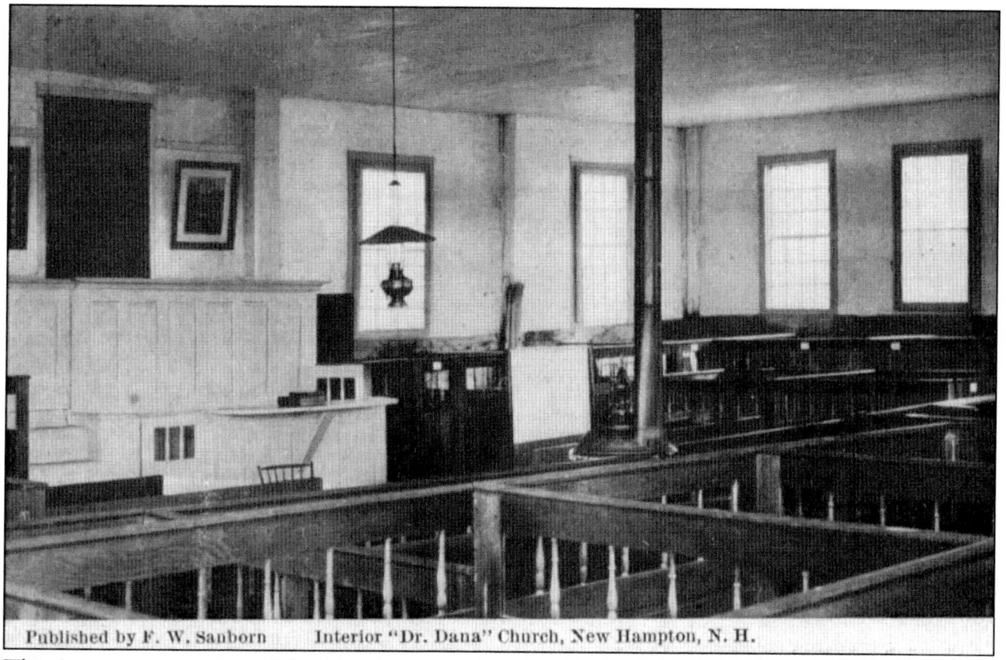

This is an interior view of the Free Baptist Church, also known as the Dana Meetinghouse or the "Dr. Dana" church, in New Hampton. This beautiful church was built in 1800 and features sheep-pen style pews. (NHHS.)

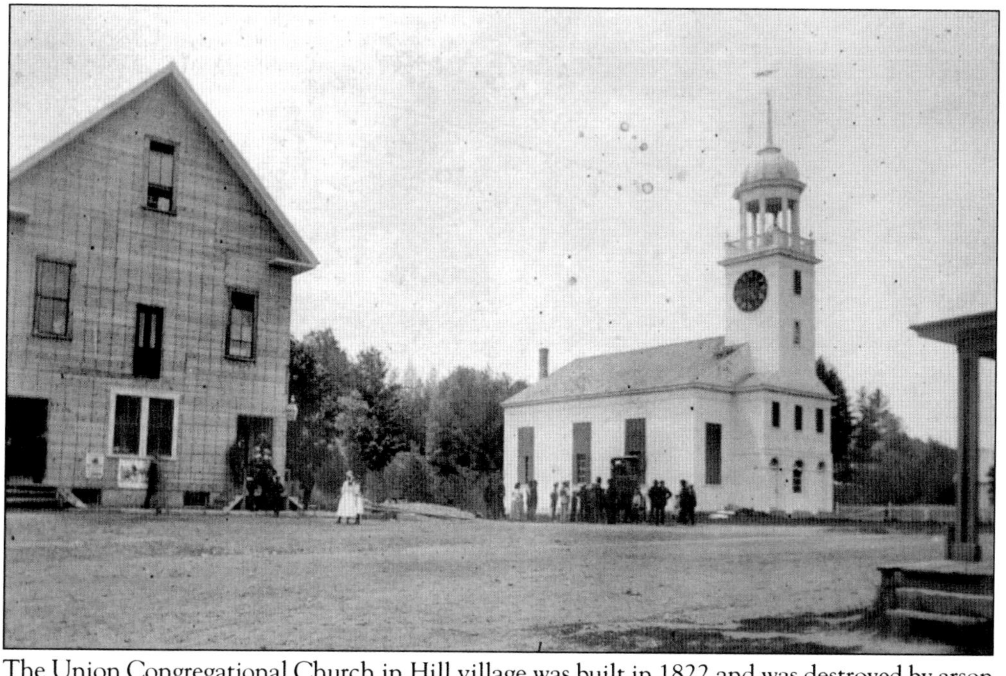

The Union Congregational Church in Hill village was built in 1822 and was destroyed by arson in 1887. On the left in this *c.* 1886 view is Woodward's Hall, which was built in 1886. On the right, in the foreground, is the E. Little Store. (HHS.)

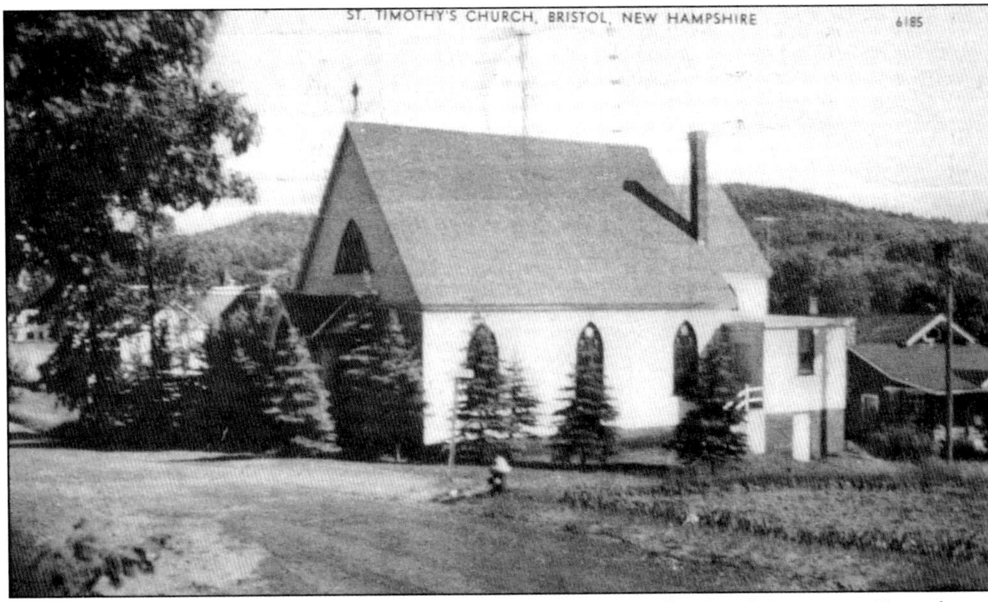

St. Timothy's Catholic Church, at the corner of Mayhew and School Streets in Bristol, was built in 1900 under the auspices of the Rev. Father Timothy W. Coakley. It was provided with "all modern conveniences." The church had finely frescoed ceiling and walls, nine memorial windows, and a marble altar. (BHS.)

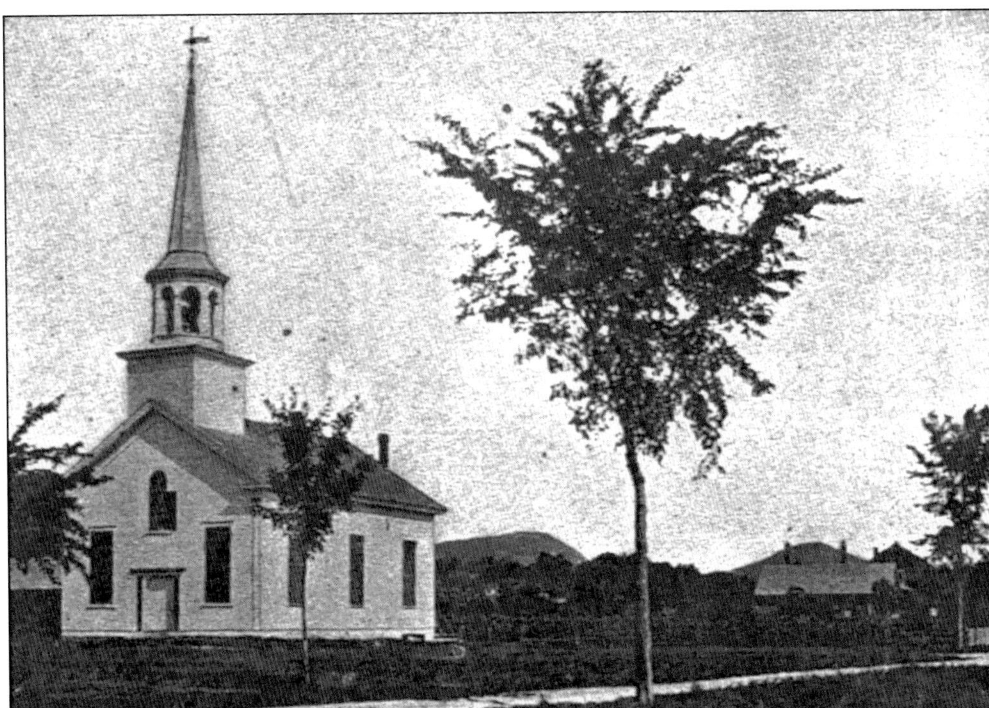

Seen here is the Methodist Church in Alexandria. (AHS.)

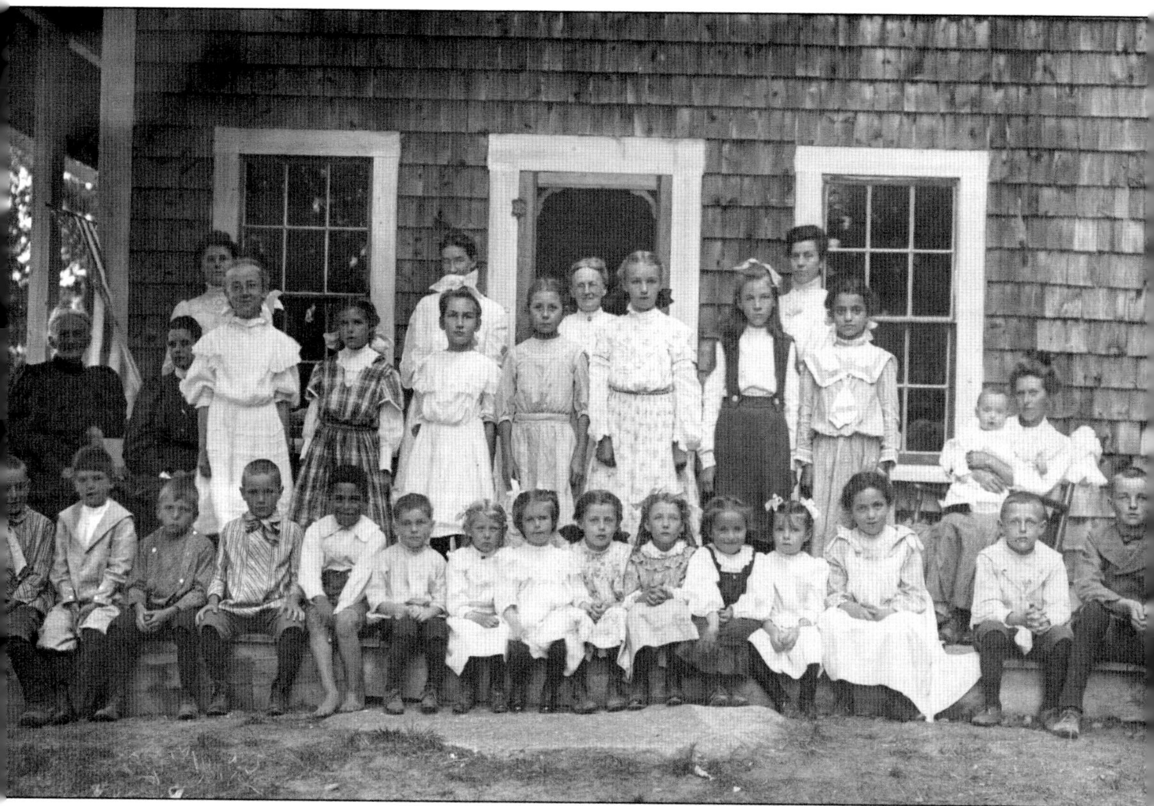

The concept of a Sunday school for area churches was first established in 1824 by N.S. Berry, William Lewis, and Jonathan Emmons. Early on, these schools were nondenominational, and classes were held in neighborhood schools. Later, each church had a Sunday school. The usual course of Sunday church services at that time was preaching in the morning, Sunday school at noon, preaching again at one o'clock, and a prayer meeting at five o'clock. This c. 1907 photograph of a Sunday school group was taken at Flint cottage in Groton. The church affiliation is unknown. (HBHS.)

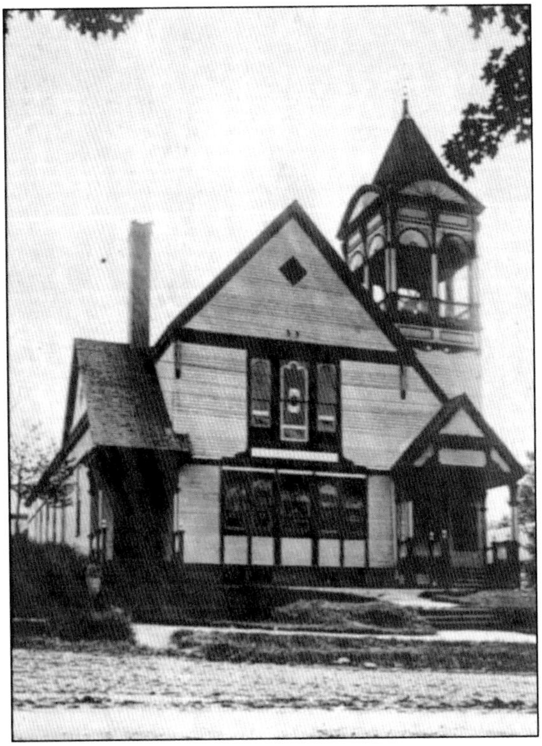

The original Methodist church in Bristol was a beautiful structure. It was built in 1872 at a cost of over $20,000, which included the lot and furnishings. In February 1889, the church was destroyed by fire. Shown here is the new Methodist church, which was built and dedicated in 1890. The entire cost of the rebuilding was $11,000. (MW.)

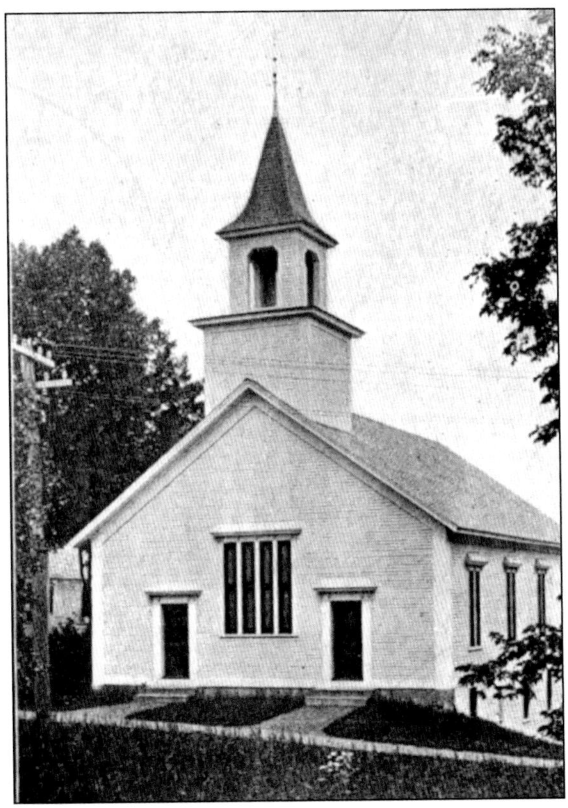

The Freewill Baptist denomination began in 1780 in New Durham. In 1845, the Bristol society was formed and was known as the Bristol and Alexandria Freewill Baptist Society. In 1850, the present church was constructed, with Rev. Samuel P. Fernald as pastor. (MW.)

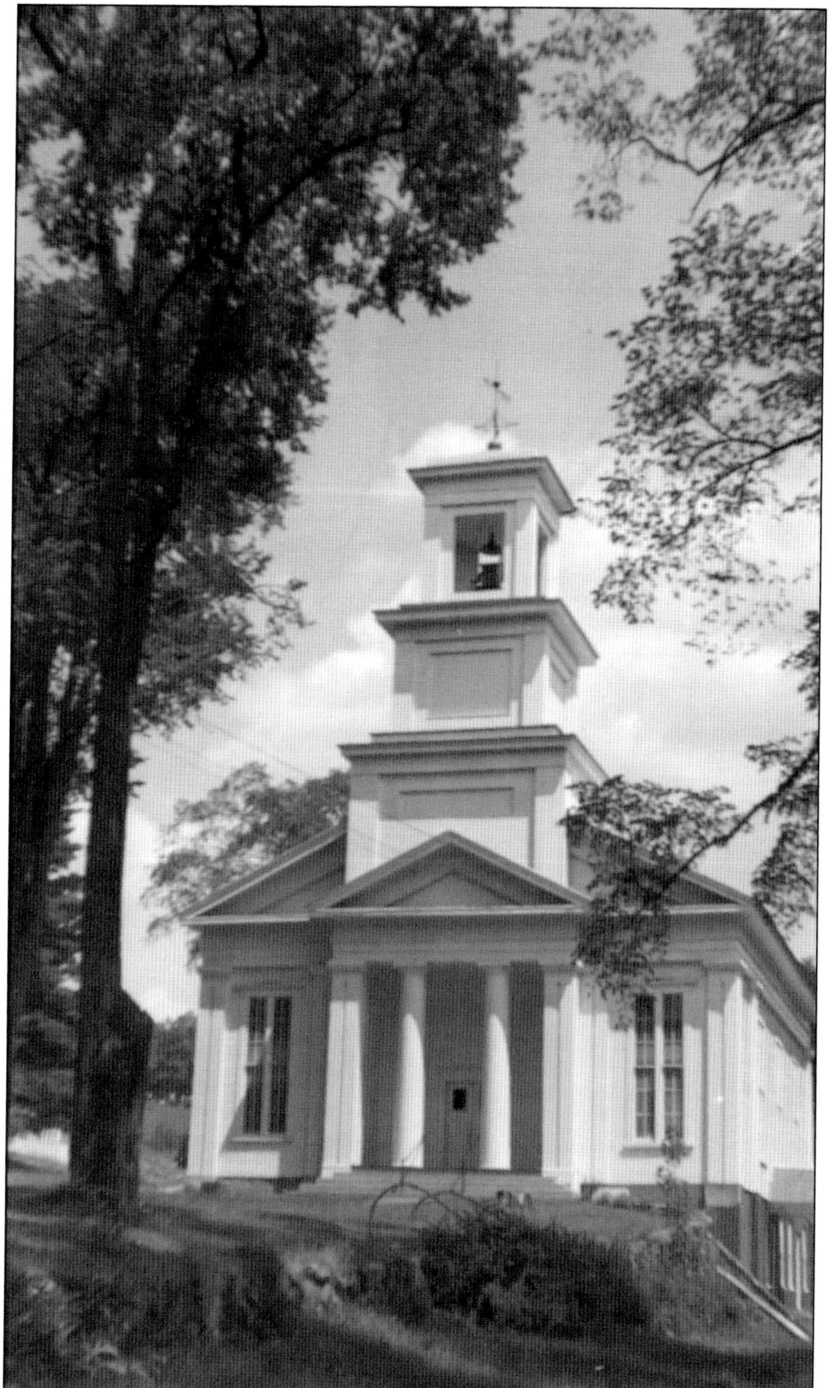

In 1854, when the Meredith and New Hampton Freewill Baptist Society was organized in the Pinnacle neighborhood of New Hampton, it united with the Fisk, or Second Freewill, Baptist Church of Meredith. The congregation built what is now the Community Church in the village. It remained as a Freewill Baptist society until 1951, when the church was reorganized as a nondenominational church with Baptist affiliations. (NHHS.)

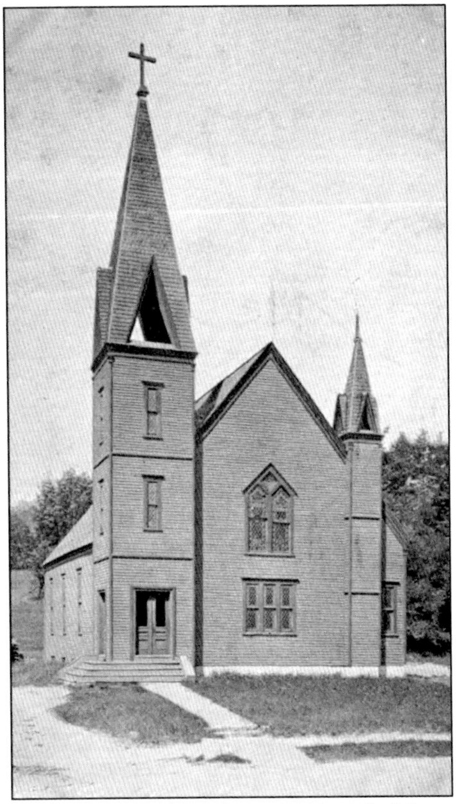

Seen here are the Christian church (above) and the Congregational church (right). The first church in Hill village, located on the floodplain, was dedicated in early 1822 and became known as the East Meetinghouse. By 1856, however, due to the difficulty in raising funds to support a long-term minister and its diminishing number of worshippers, the church was being shared by members belonging to two groups: the Congregationalists and the Christians. After Hill's only church was destroyed by arson in 1887, two new churches were built—the Christian church in 1888 and the Congregational church in 1889, each costing about $5,000. (HHS.)

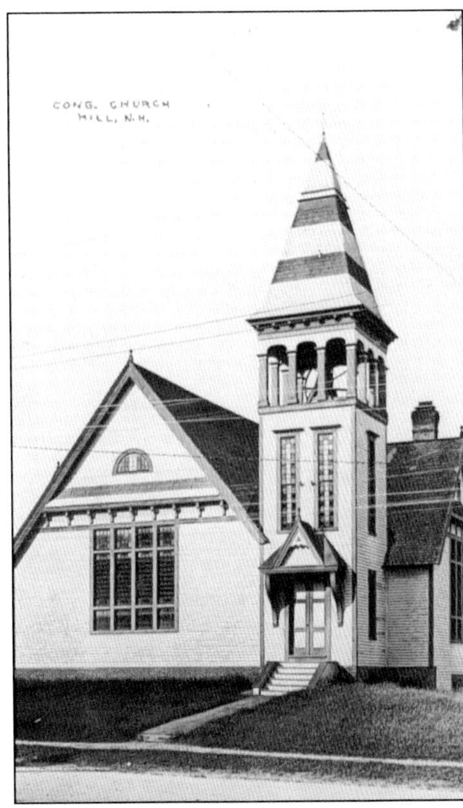

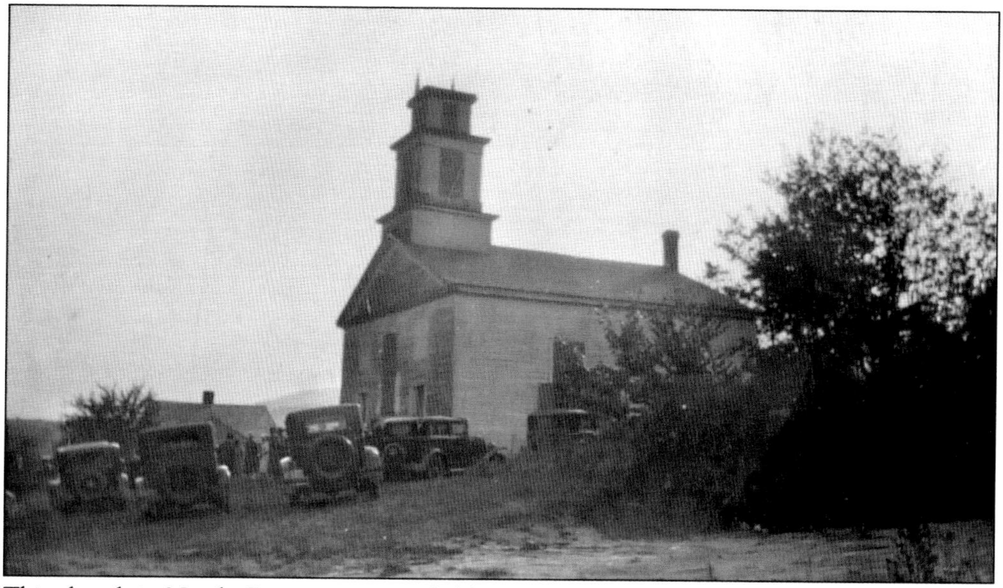

This church in North Groton was attended by Mary Baker Eddy, the founder of the Christian Science Church, in the late 1850s. It is now owned and maintained by the Longyear Foundation. (GHS.)

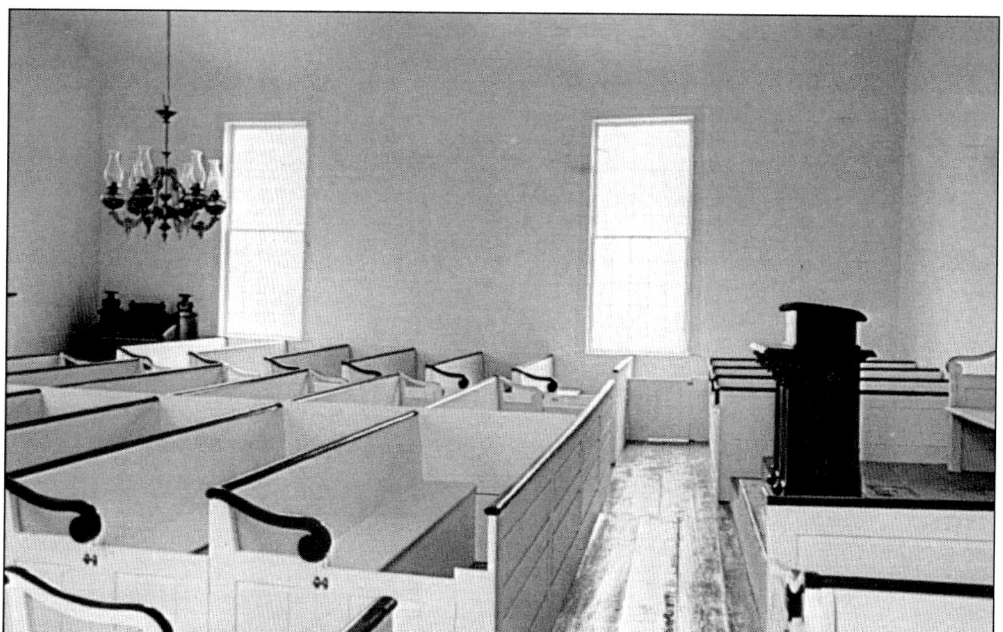

This is an interior view of the North Groton church showing the lovingly maintained pews and altar. (GHS.)

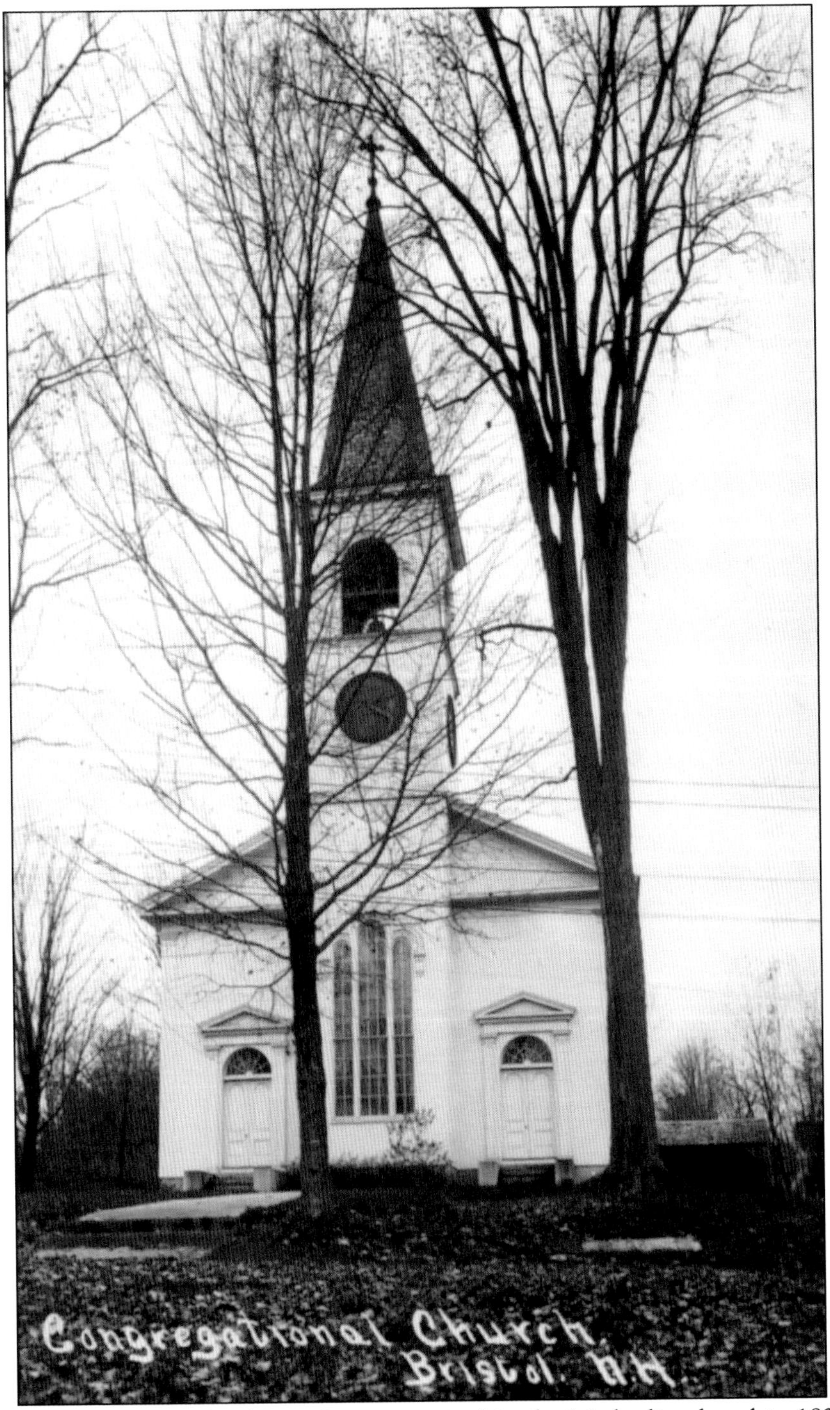

The Congregational church of Bristol was organized in the Methodist chapel in 1826 under the name of the First Congregational Church of Christ of Bristol, and the meetinghouse was built in 1827. In 1844, the meetinghouse was remodeled. The windows of the two stories were extended to unite, the gallery was removed, and the pew boxes were replaced with modern slips, but the pew doors were retained. It is a remarkably beautiful church. (MW.)

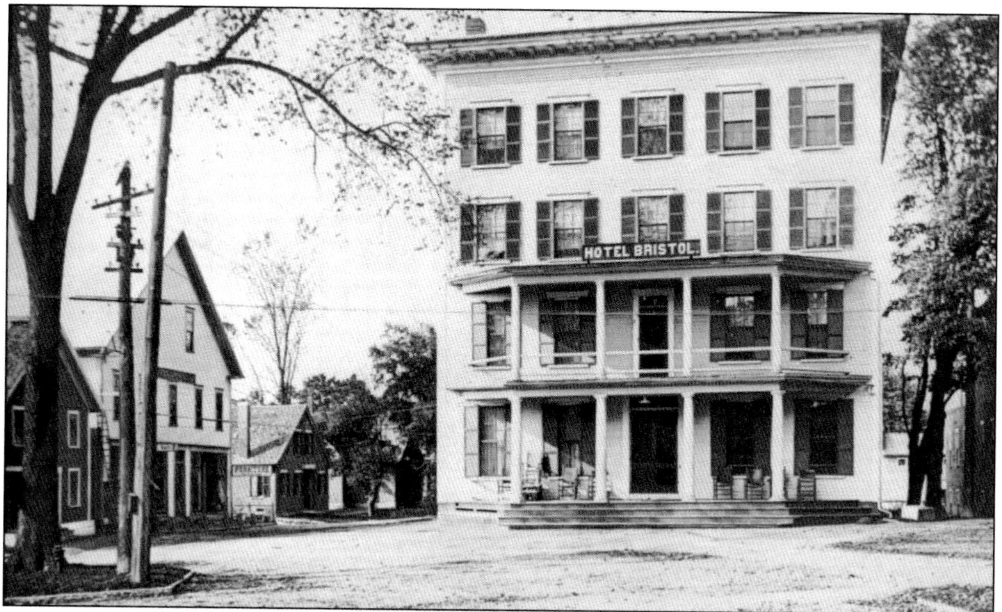

On this site in Central Square, prior to 1836, was the dwelling house of Edmond Brown. In that year, the house was sold to Joseph Malvern, who removed it and erected a two-story hotel. After a succession of owners, Otis K. Bucklin purchased and removed the old buildings and built the four-story hotel seen here. Containing 41 sleeping rooms, the Hotel Bristol was a favored destination for travelers. Seen here, from left to right, are the railroad baggage house, the G. Wheeler Block, the Westfall Restaurant, and the library. (MW.)

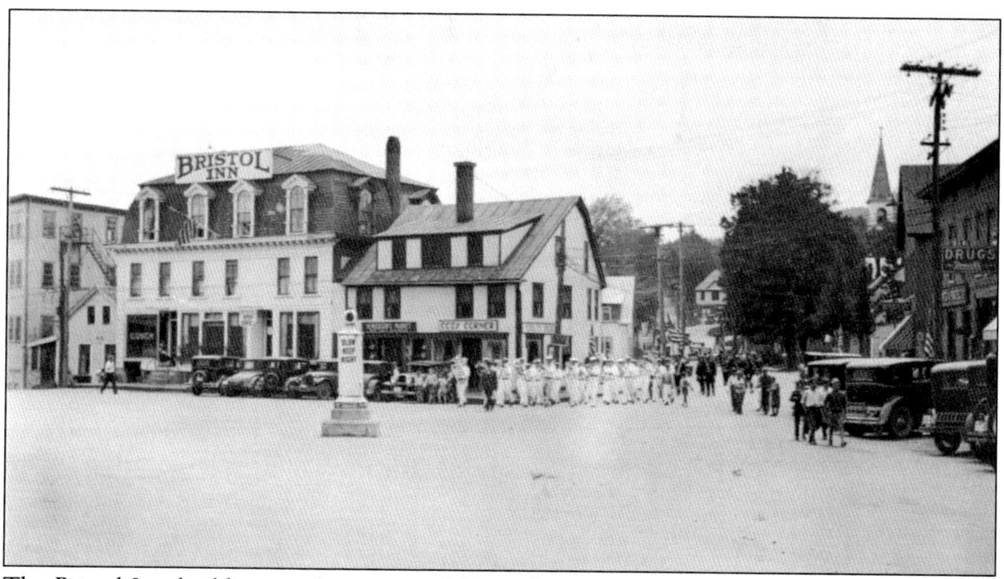

The Bristol Inn building, at the corner of Central Square and Spring Street, was built in the 1800s and has continually provided space for merchants of a wide variety of goods. It remains a charming landmark on the square. (MW.)

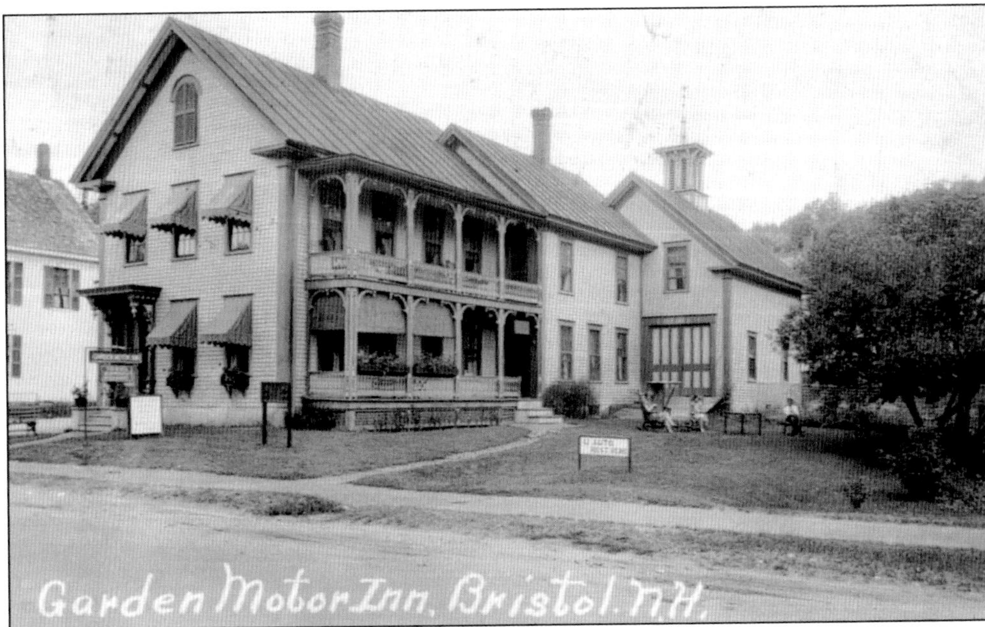

This magnificent Victorian structure with gingerbread-laced piazzas was operated as an inn in the late 1890s. It is located on Lake Street and is a private home today. Upon viewing the exterior, one can only imagine the elegance of the interior. As though its appearance is not inviting enough, the sign to the right-center of this view states: "U Auto Rest Here." (MW.)

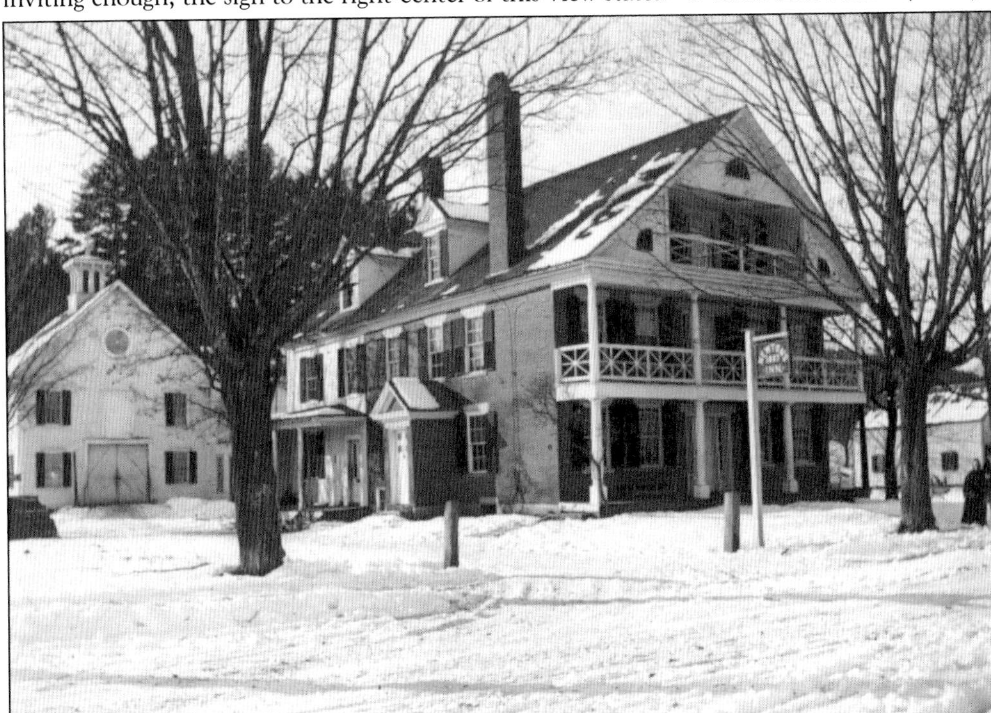

Newton's Inn, c. 1897, was located on Main Street in Hill village. It was a fine brick building that was owned by Dr. William T. Vail from 1859 to 1870. It was known far and wide as "Dr. Vail's water cure." Mary Baker Eddy frequently came to drink of this "cure for all ills." (HHS.)

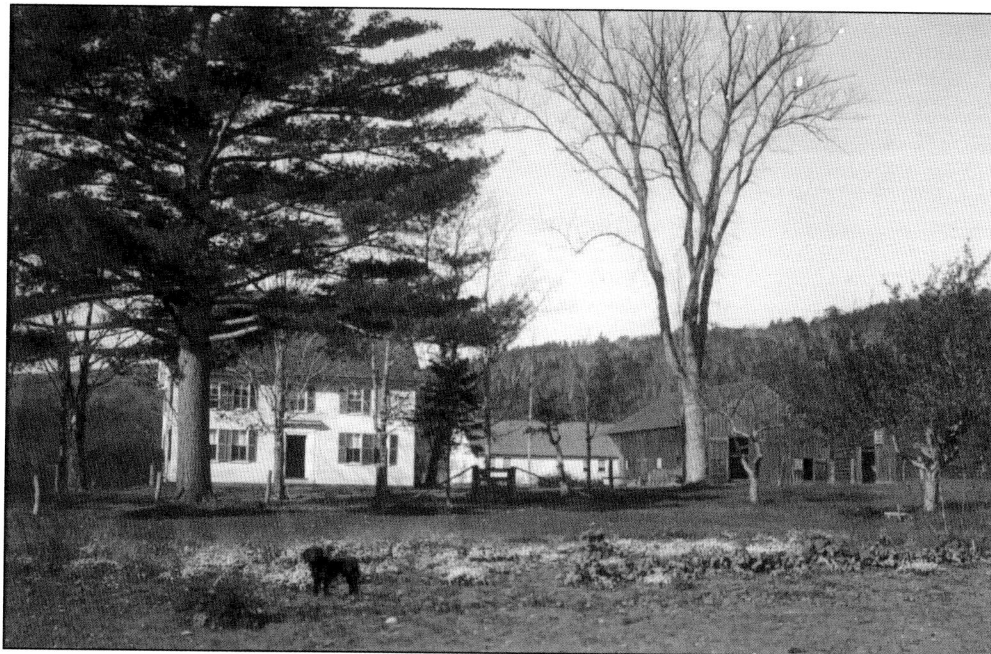

The Webster Tavern, at Webster Farm in Bridgewater, was built in 1806. This tavern, not unlike all taverns of its era, offered travelers a sleeping room on the second floor, a gentleman's parlor adjacent to the bar, and a lady's parlor opposite the front entry. The rooms and original architectural features remain today. Noted visitors to this house were Robert Frost, Daniel Webster, and Ralph Waldo Emerson. (WF.)

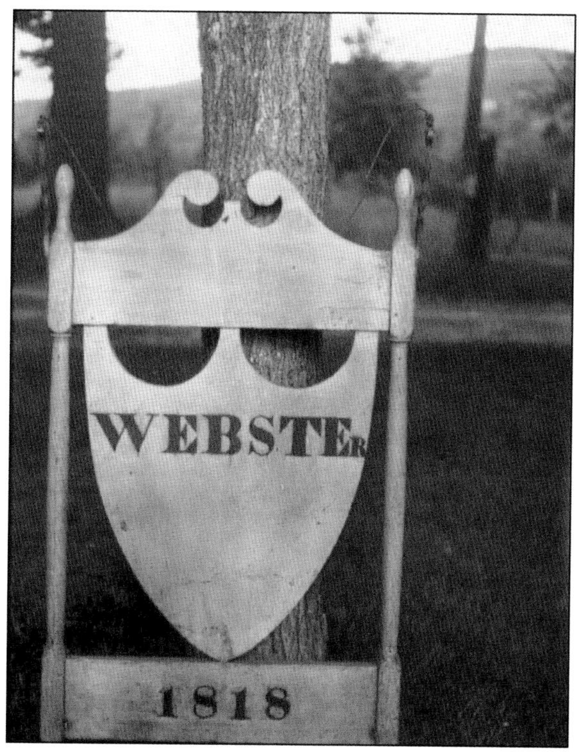

This shows the Webster Tavern sign.

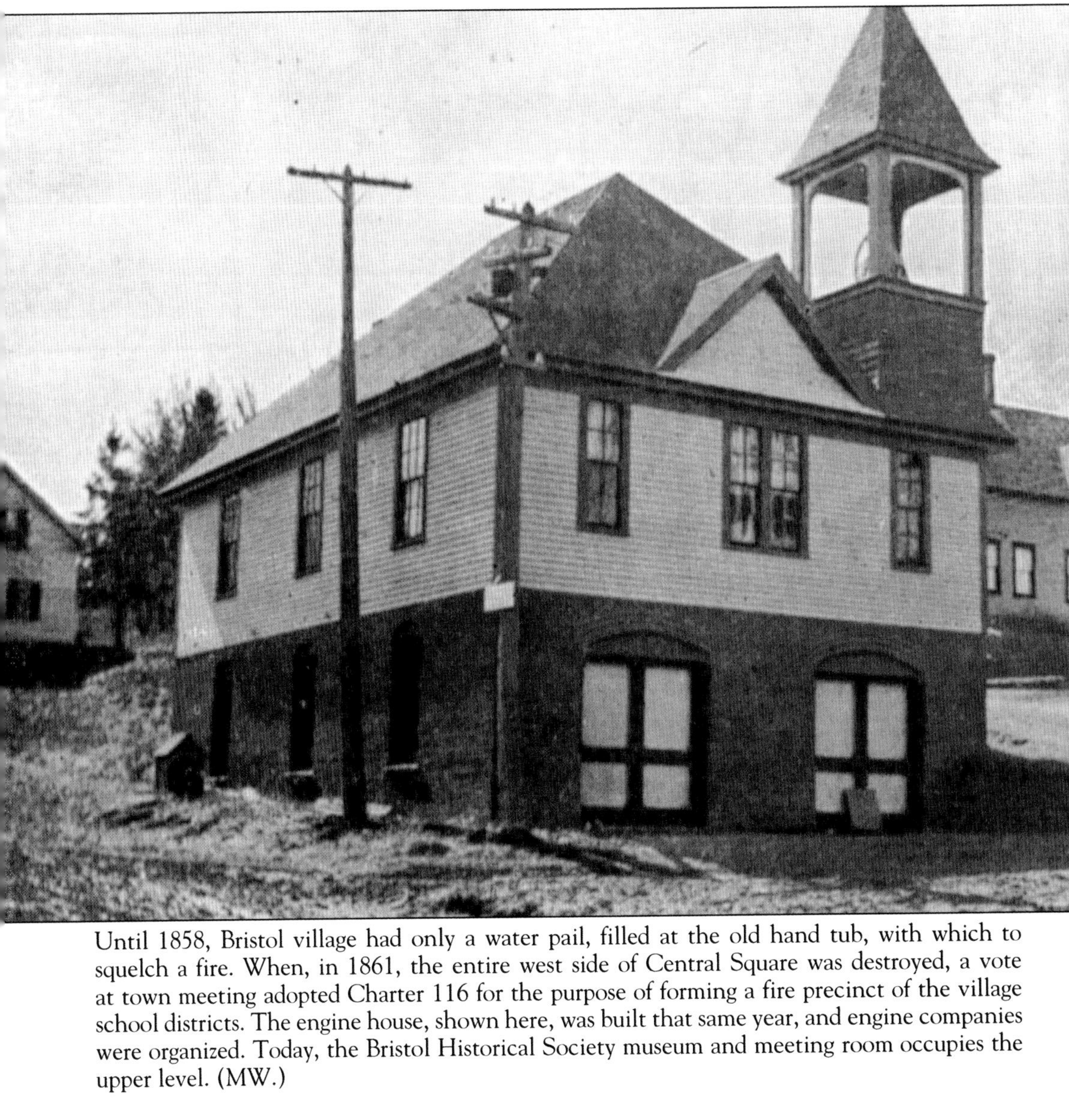

Until 1858, Bristol village had only a water pail, filled at the old hand tub, with which to squelch a fire. When, in 1861, the entire west side of Central Square was destroyed, a vote at town meeting adopted Charter 116 for the purpose of forming a fire precinct of the village school districts. The engine house, shown here, was built that same year, and engine companies were organized. Today, the Bristol Historical Society museum and meeting room occupies the upper level. (MW.)

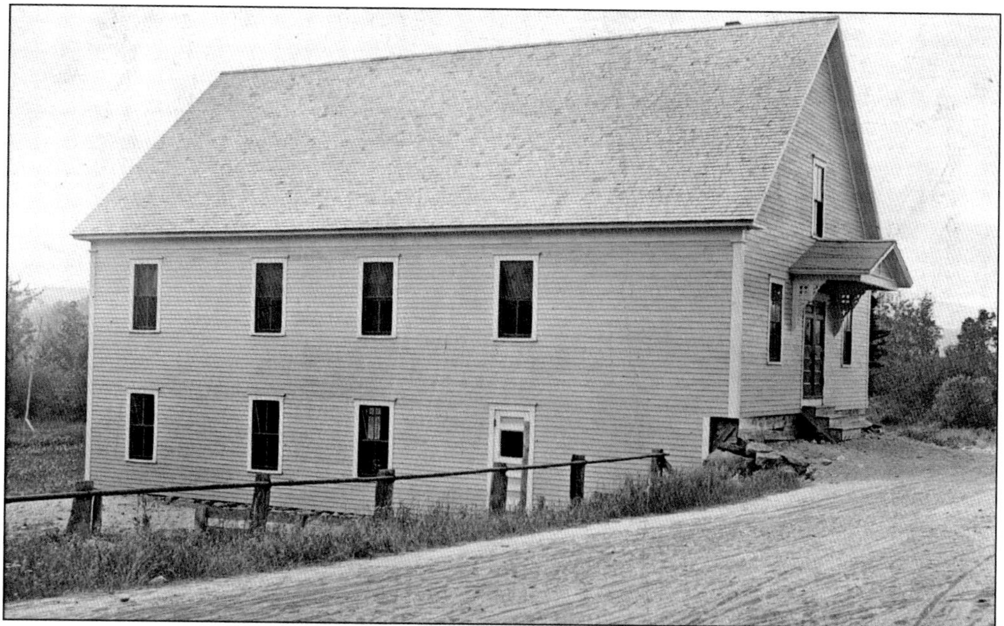

The Grange Hall in most communities would accommodate large groups of people for various social functions. The Danbury Grange Hall, pictured here, was no exception. At a box party and dance held here in the 1890s, dancers enjoyed the promenade, the waltz, the old Zeb Coon, the polka, the tempest, the galop, and the two step, as well as the Portland fancy and the Virginia reel. During intermission, the sale of boxes took place. (JP.)

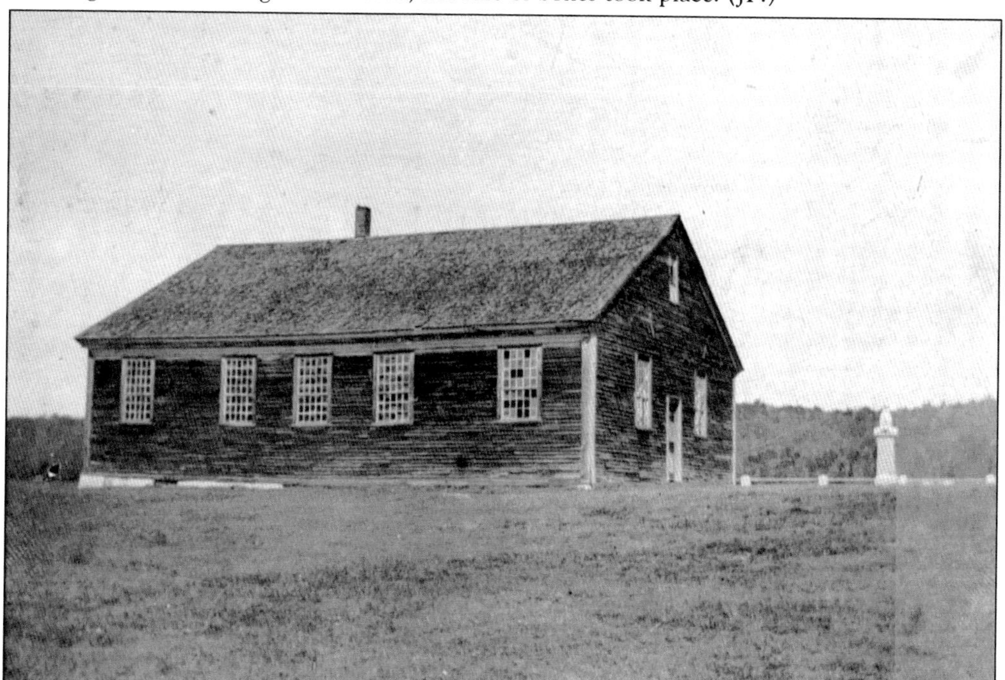

Originally, the North Groton Town House was a two-story building that accommodated the business of the town government as well as worship services. It is located about one mile south of the village. This photograph was taken *c.* 1903. (GHS.)

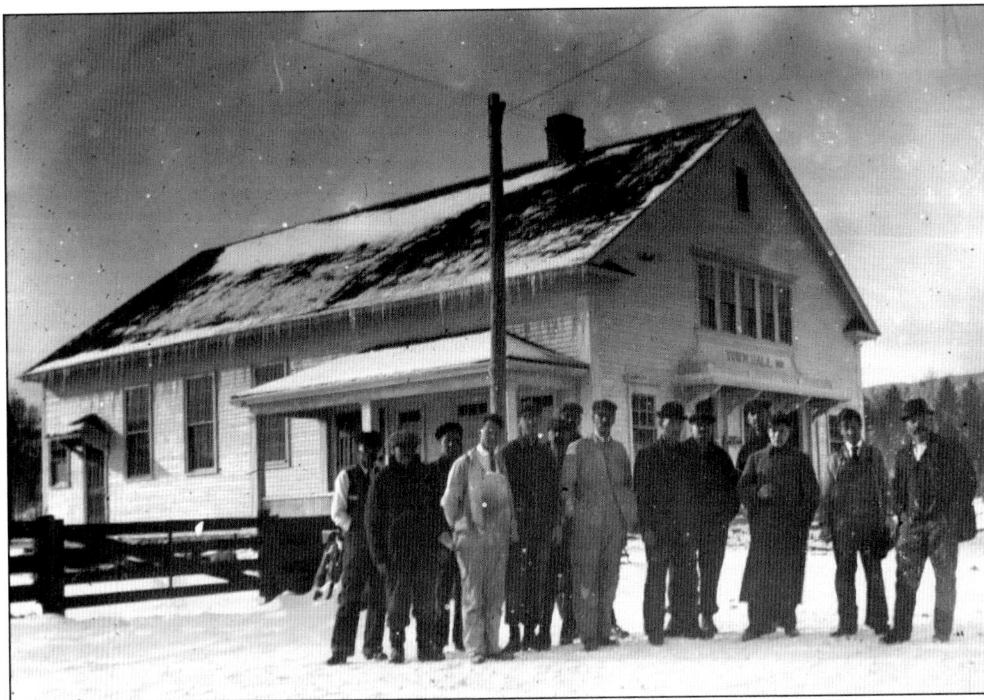

The spacious town hall in Alexandria underwent extensive renovation in 1913. It is believed that the men pictured here were the carpenters who did the work. (AHS.)

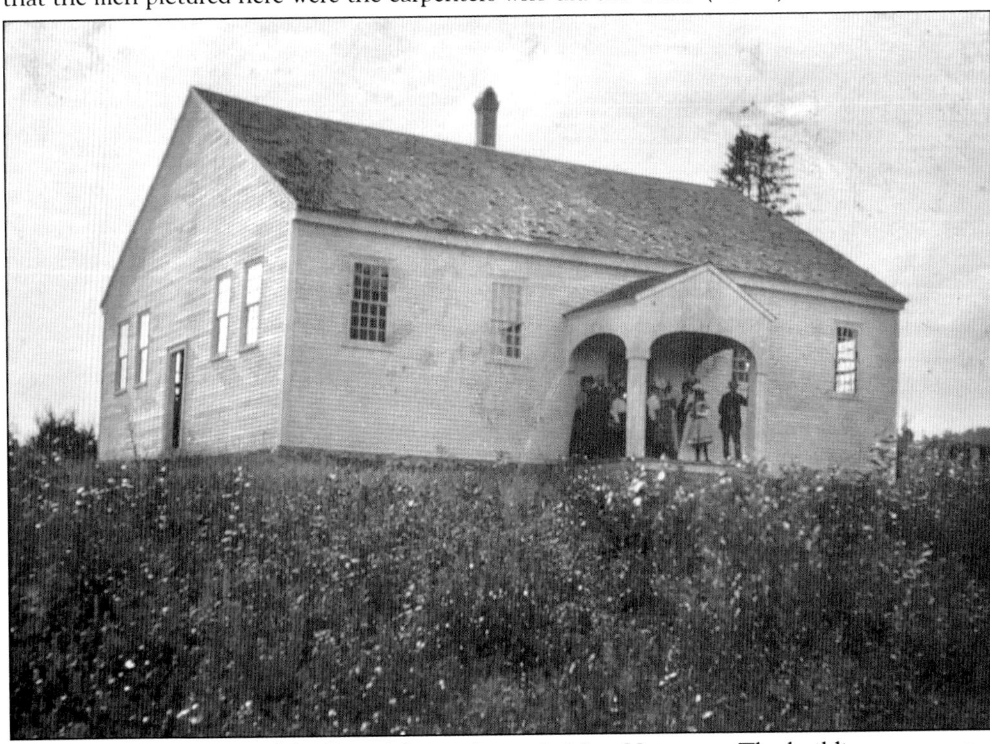

This is an exterior view of the Dana Meetinghouse in New Hampton. The building was erected in 1800. (NHHS.)

Three

DOING BUSINESS

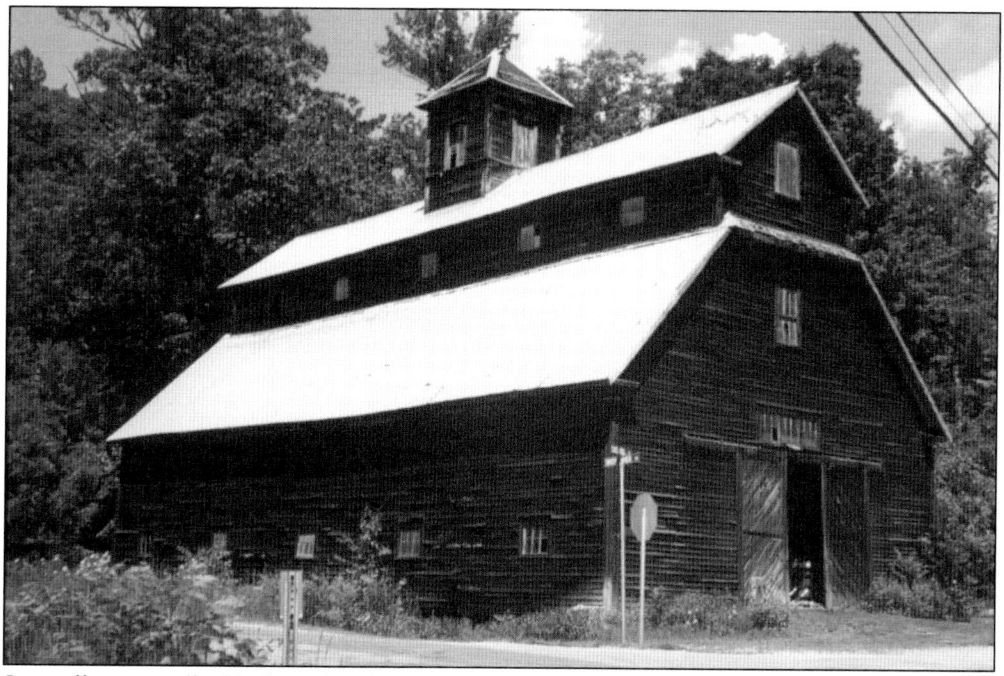

Sawmills, gristmills, blacksmith's shops, and tanneries were the industries of necessity during the early days of the region's settlement. For mining, forestry, and agriculture, the natural elements indigenous to an area dictated the lifestyle and employment of the early settler as well. In the early 19th century, large mills came into production. These factories—producing textiles, pulp, paper, and wooden novelties—became common along the rivers and streams. In the villages, shops were opened in which merchants provided necessary products to the consumer. Cass Mill was named for Nason Cass, who settled Lot 81 at Smith's River in New Chester. It is not clear whether the mill was located across the road on the river or was operated from within this wonderful old barn, using an overshot wheel for power. Over several decades, the building served as a gristmill, carding mill, clothing mill, sawmill, and a cabinet shop. (BML.)

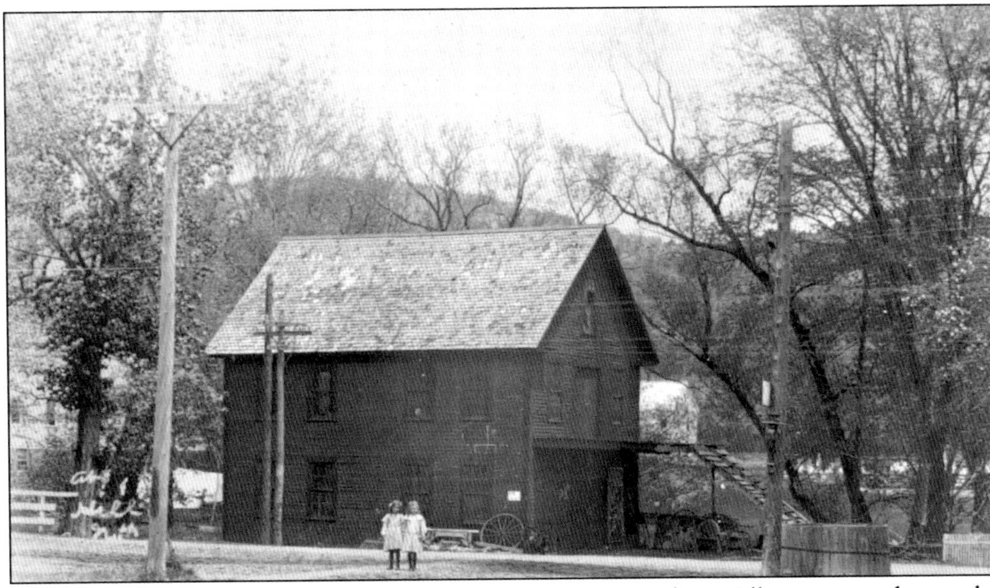

Verne Straw's blacksmith and carriage-painting shop, located in Hill, was carried away by floodwaters on May 29, 1918, when the Woodward Mill dam broke. This photograph was taken c. 1907. (HHS.)

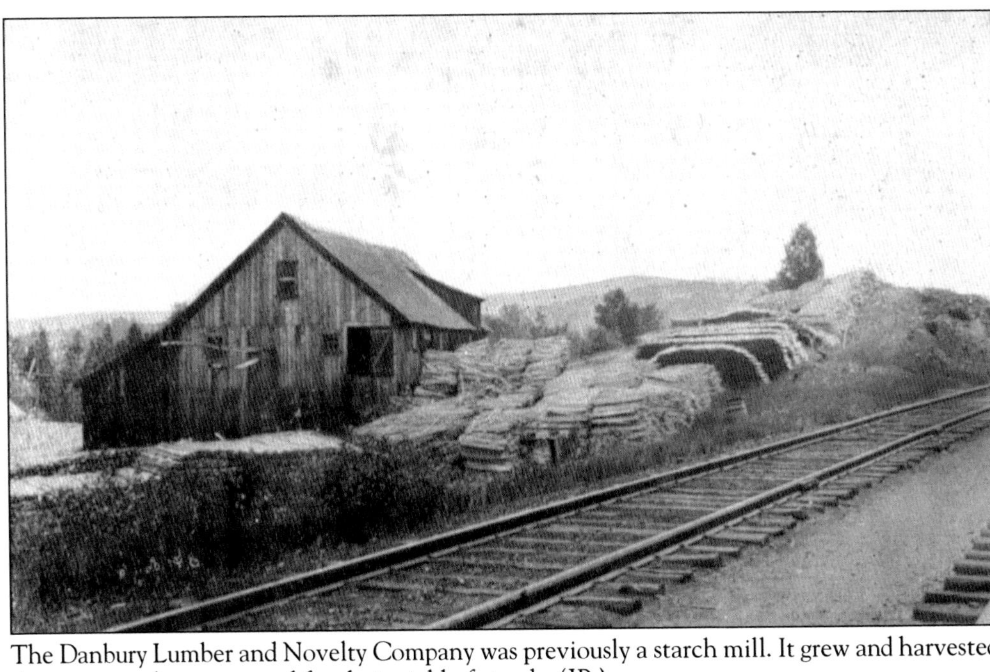

The Danbury Lumber and Novelty Company was previously a starch mill. It grew and harvested the potatoes that were used for their yield of starch. (JP.)

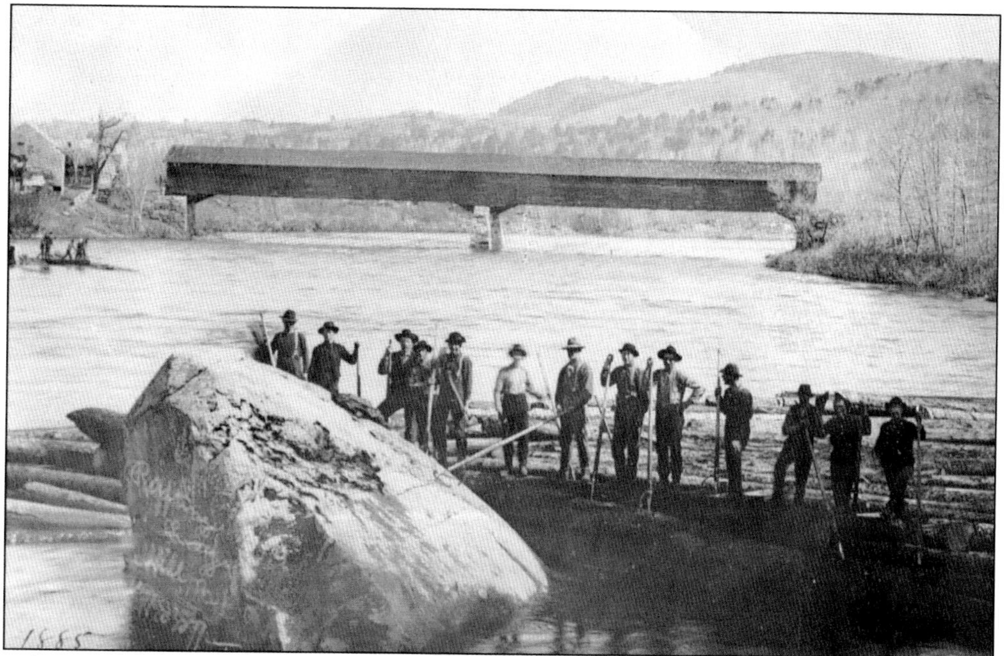

A logging crew, with peaveys in hand, prepares to float a raft of logs down the Pemigewasset River at Hill. This is a *c.* 1885 photograph. (HHS.)

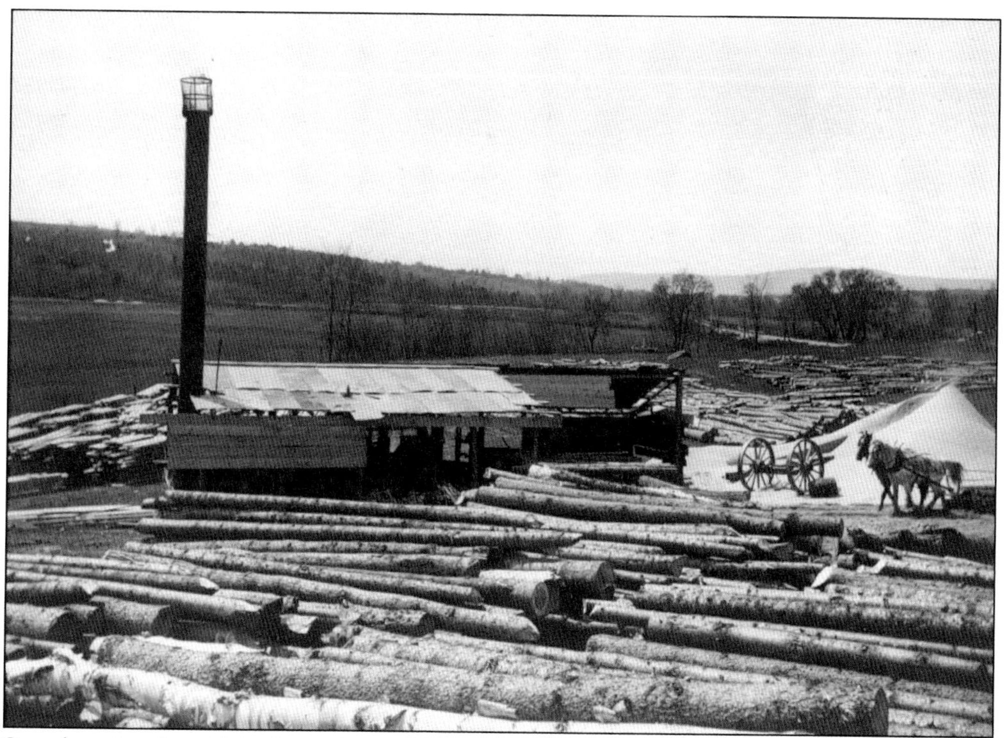

Seen here is a flourishing Bristol sawmill along the Pemigewasset River, *c.* 1890. (BHS.)

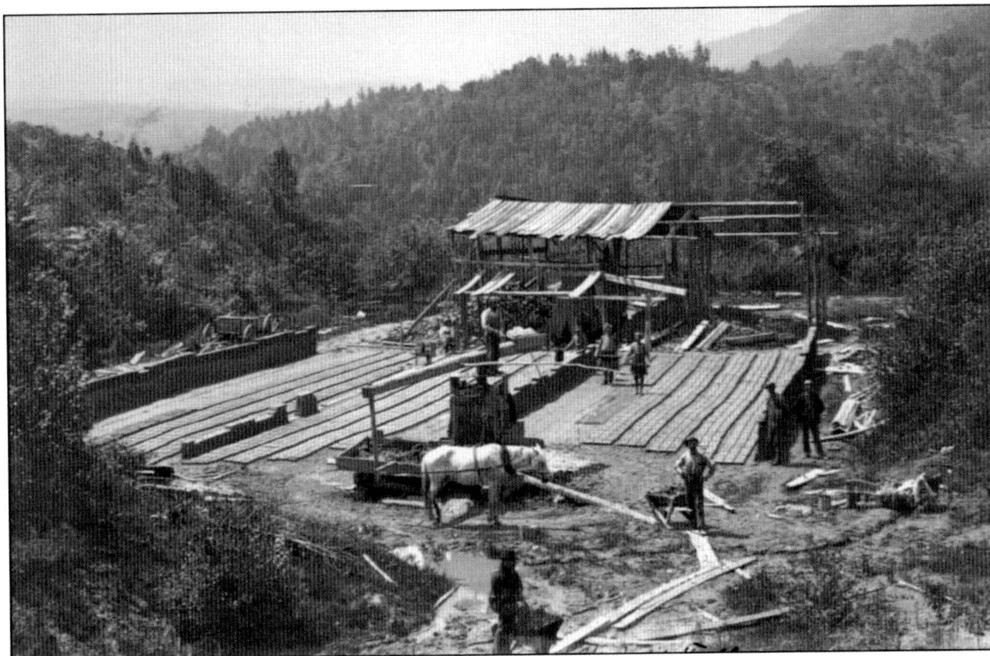

A makeshift roof of sawn timber helps to keep the hot sun at bay at this sawmill at Profile Falls in Hill. This photograph was taken *c.* 1904. (HHS.)

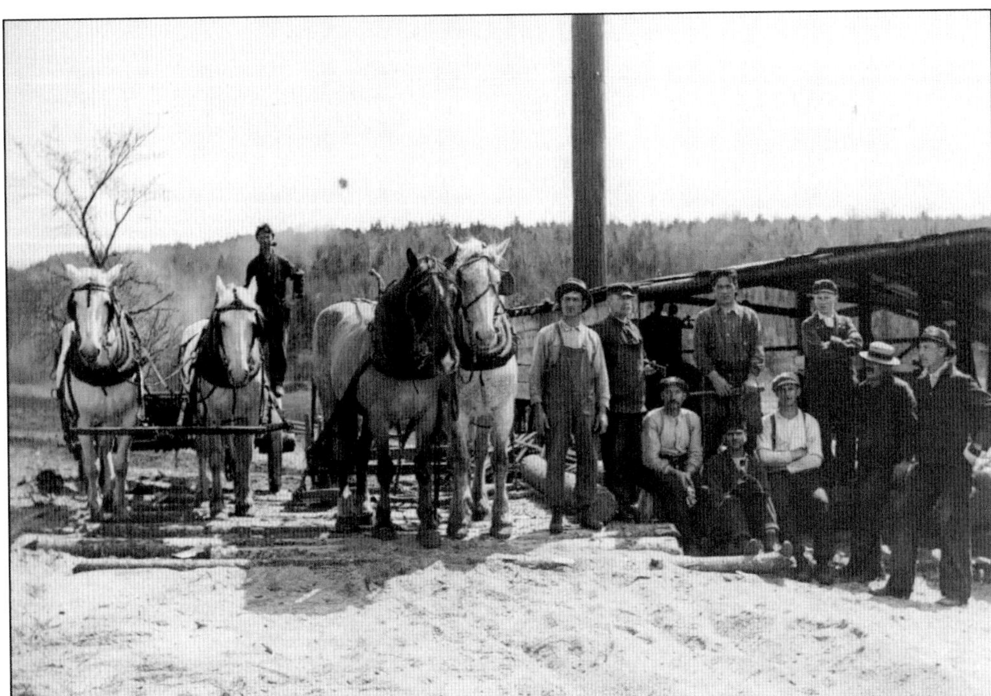

Even the horse teams are ready to take time out from their labors to pose for this photograph, which was taken at the Bristol sawmill. (BHS.)

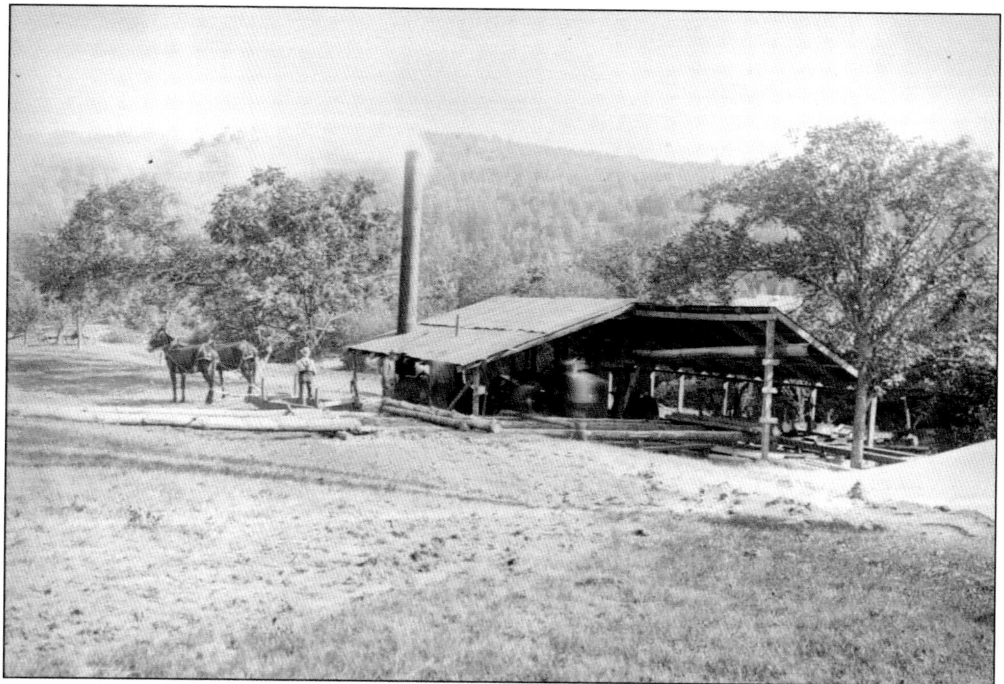

Seen here is the Garrattson's Mill in Hebron *c.* 1910. (HBHS.)

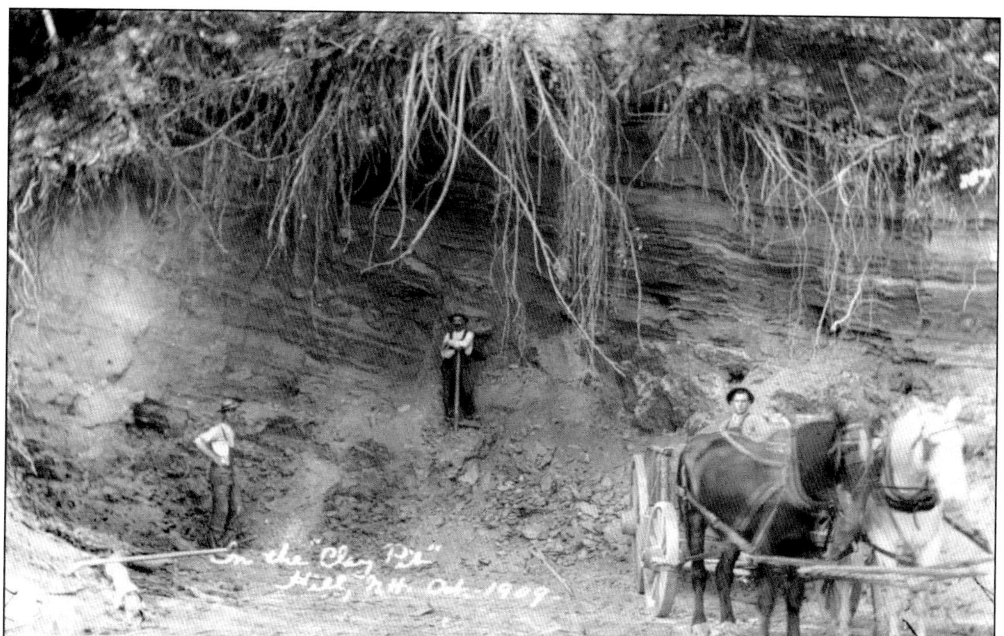

James Clark, John Straw, and Ed Tebo use a team to haul clay from the clay pit near the Franklin town line in October 1909. (HHS.)

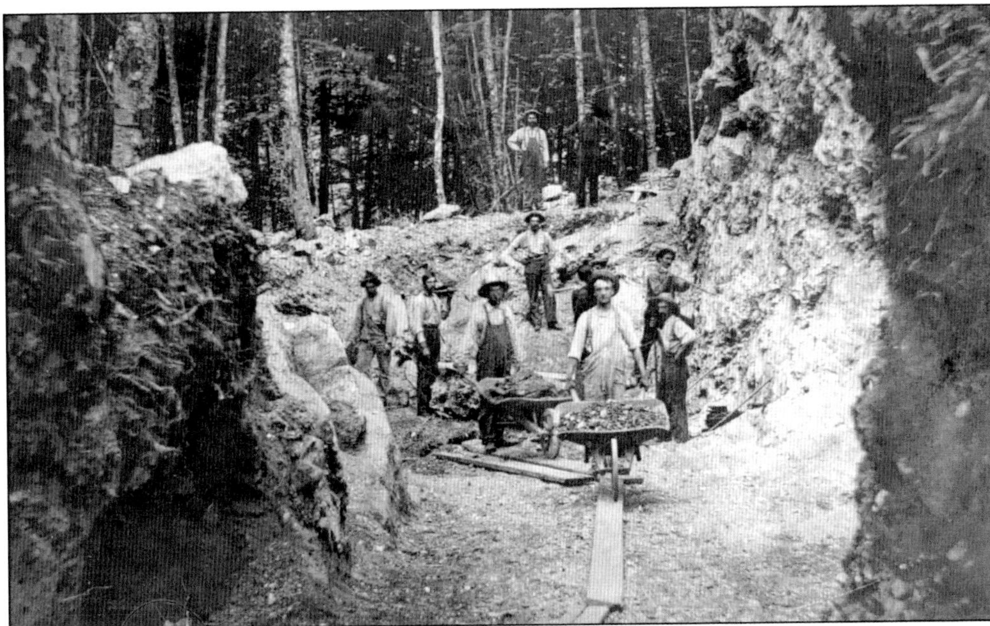

North Groton was primarily a thriving farming town in the early 1800s before the first evidence of mica was discovered here between 1840 and 1860. Mining then began for this highly sought mineral, which was used for stove windows and lamp shades at that time. When, in 1868, competition from other states and foreign countries reduced the profitability of operating the mines, North Groton mining became sporadic. Then, shortly after 1900, the General Electric Company purchased the mineral rights to the area's mines and used the mica as electrical insulation. Feldspar and beryl were also mined here. Beryllium, from beryl, was used in containment vessels in the Manhattan Project, secret research undertaken in 1942 with the ultimate aim of producing an atomic bomb. (GHS.)

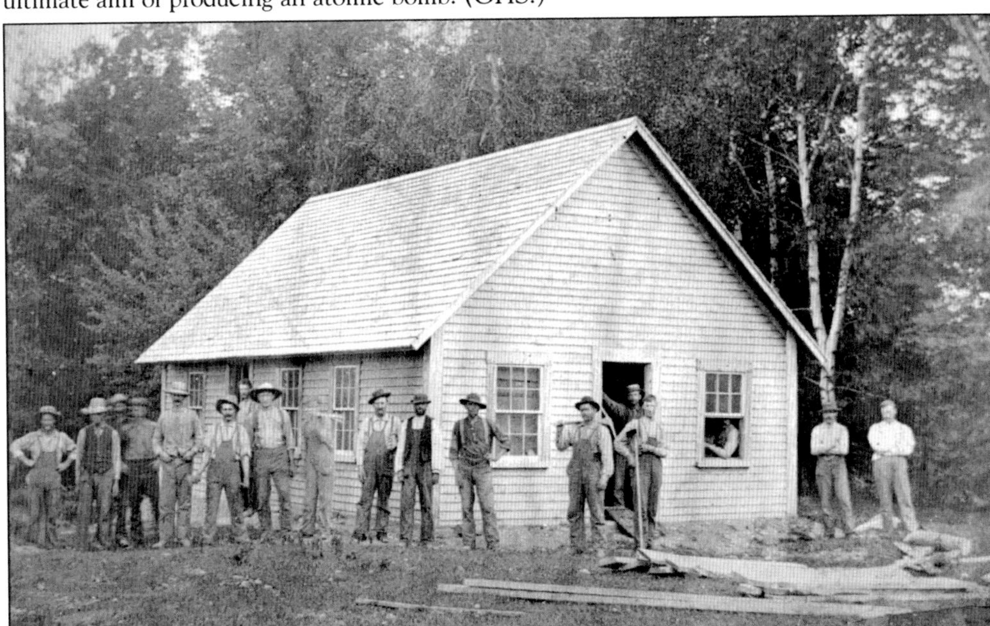

Seen here are miners at the Palermo mine camp in North Groton c. 1850. (GHS.)

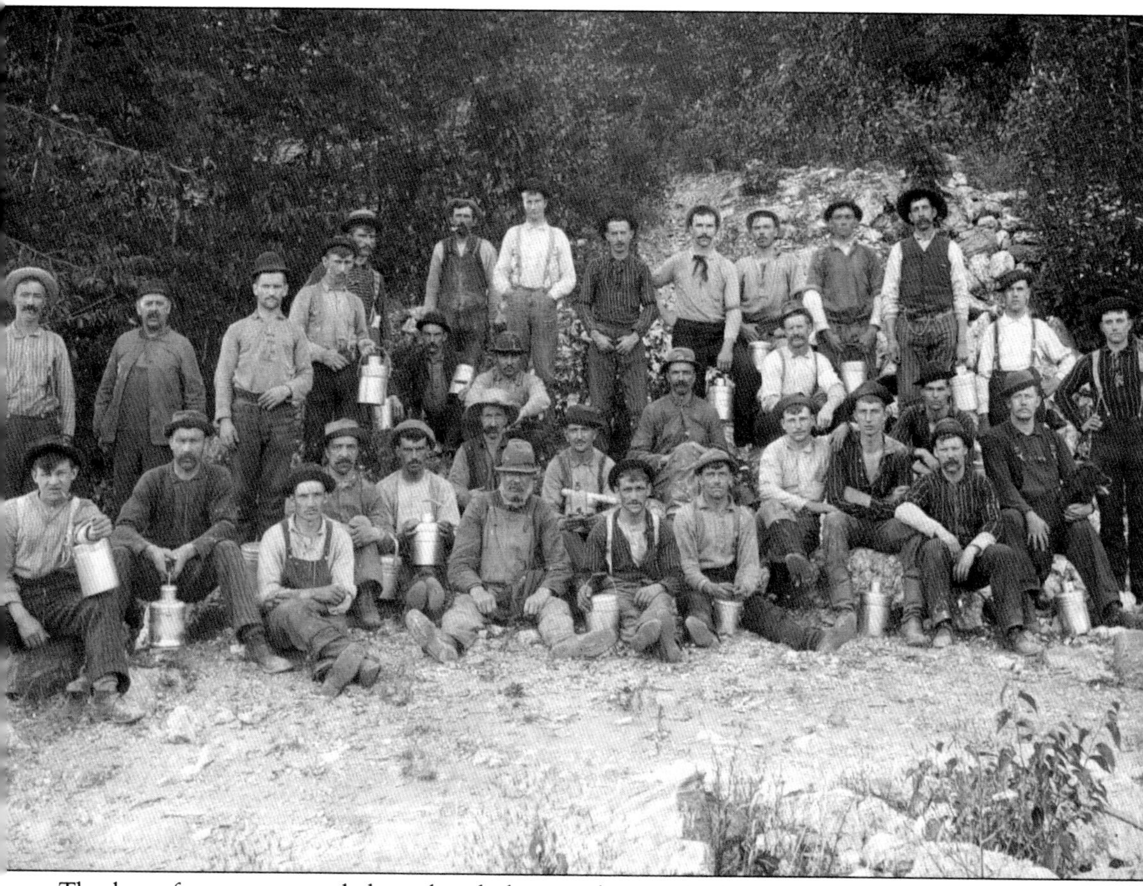

The loss of manpower and the cultural changes that resulted from the Civil War caused a decline in farming as a means of family support. Farmers were encouraged to seek other means of employment. In Alexandria, as in the surrounding towns of the region, men turned to mica mining. Perhaps the large crew of miners shown here worked at Ruggles Mine in nearby Grafton or at the mines in North Groton. (AHS.)

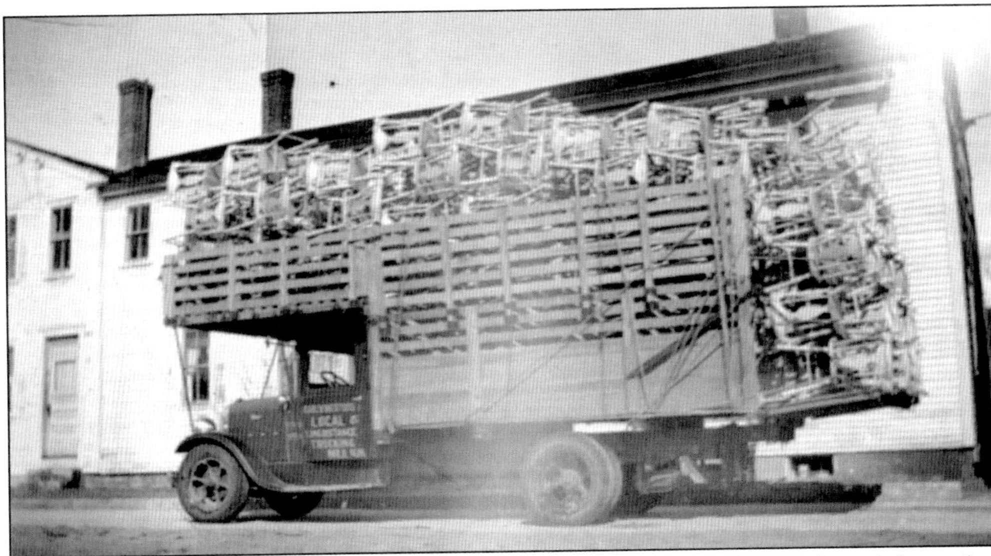

Using this view, it would be extremely difficult for one to estimate the number of chairs that were carefully loaded onto this early-model delivery truck. The chairs were manufactured at the Hill Chair Factory *c.* the 1930s. (CR.)

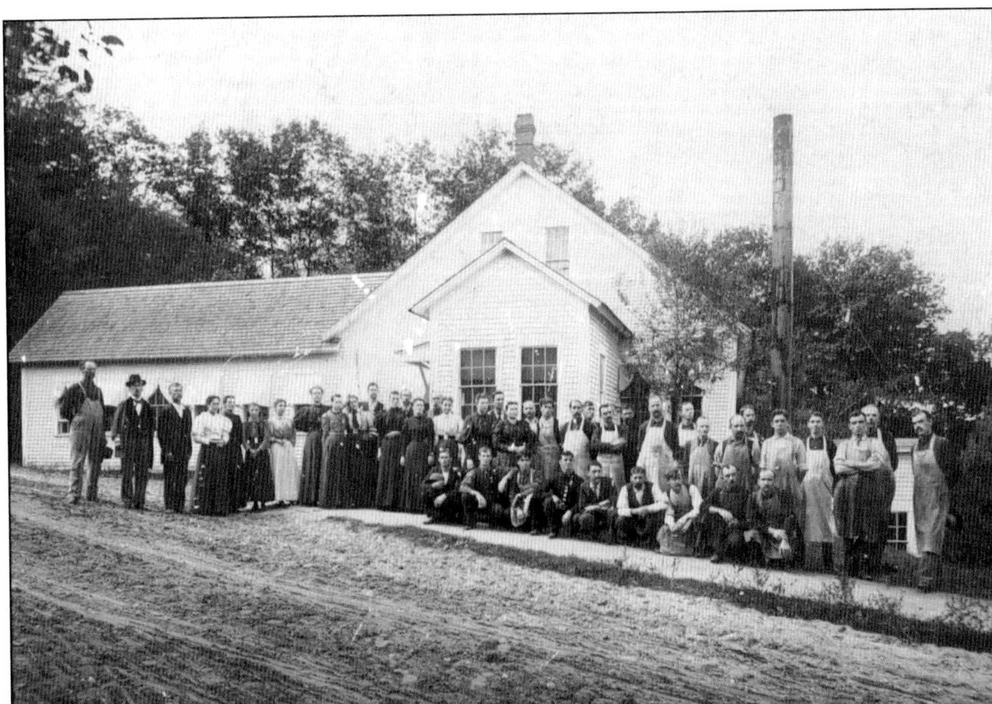

In this 1896 photograph are the employees of the Adams Needle Shop in the old village of Hill. (HHS.)

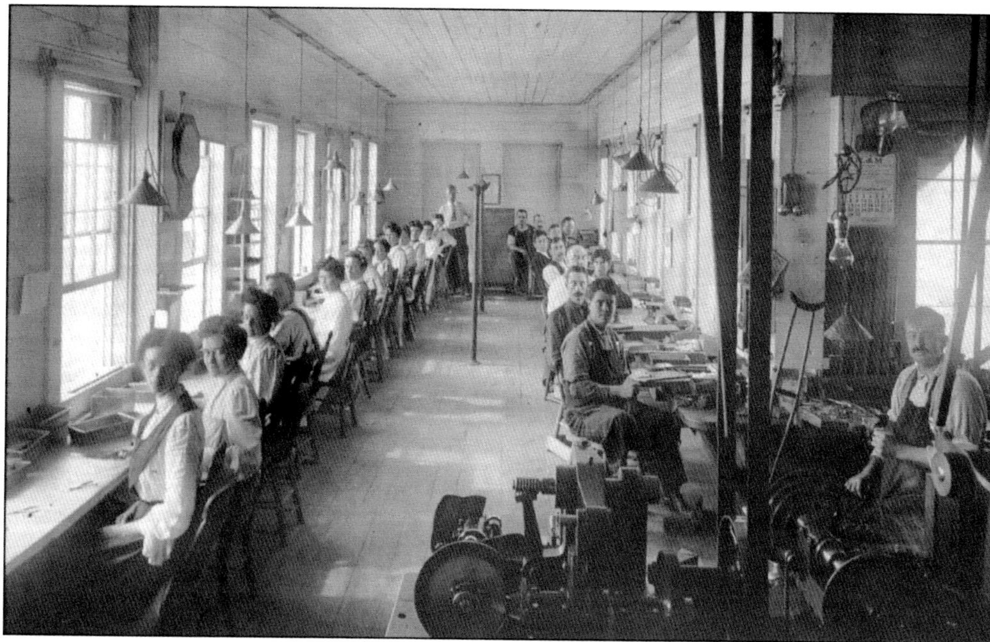

An important industry to Hill during the second half of the 19th century and into the 20th century was the Adams Needle Shop. The shop was located on Mill Brook, which was later known as Needle Shop Brook. Employees made curved latch needles for the manufacture of hosiery, sail making, carpet sewing, upholstery, and mattress making. When the dam broke at Woodwards Novelty Shop in 1918, a section of the Needle Shop was washed away. It was replaced with an even larger addition. In 1925, the company moved to Franklin, and Alvah Carr used the mill as a dowel shop until 1941. These photographs were taken c. 1920. (HHS.)

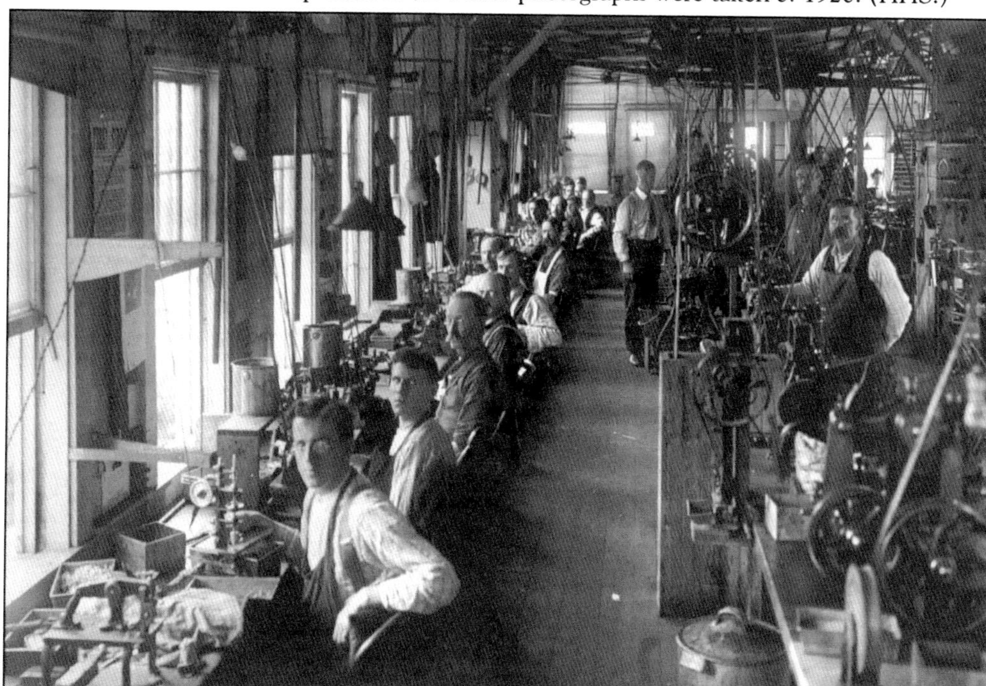

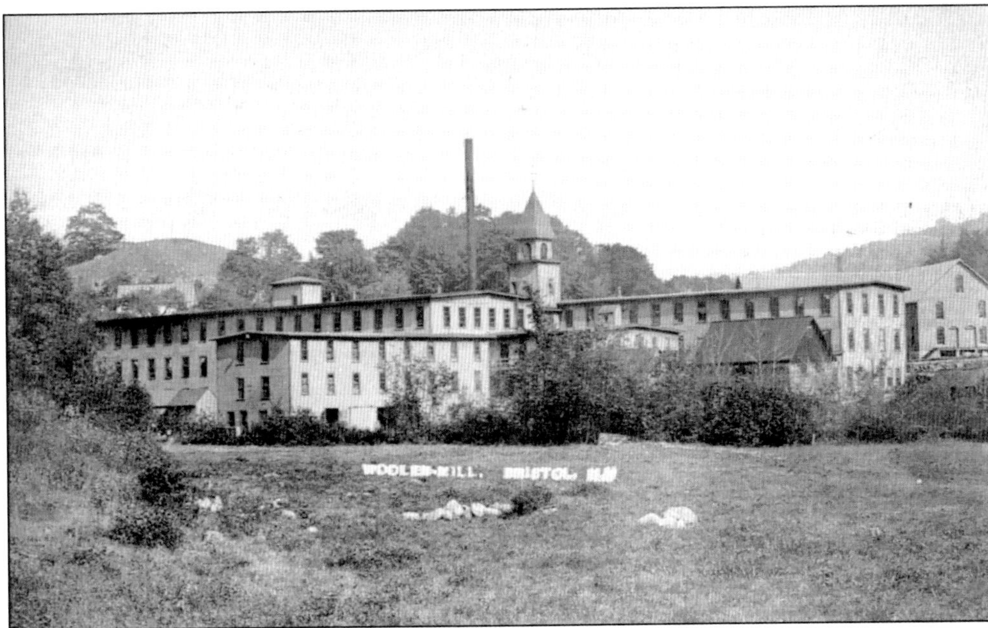

The Dodge-Davis Woolen Mill was started in the former D&DS Mason & Company paper mill building on Lake Street in Bristol. By 1900, the building had been enlarged to 60,500 square feet with 11 sets of machinery and a complete electric lighting plant, all driven by a 200-horsepower waterwheel. Other improvements included a repair shop, an interior sprinkler system, 17,300 feet of storehouse space, and houses with eight tenements for employees. (DP.)

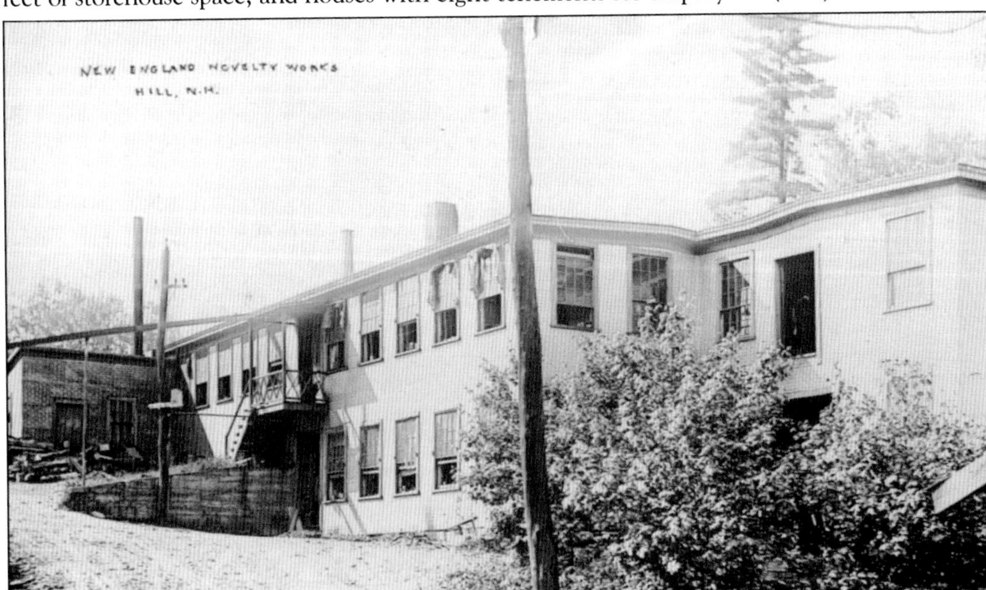

New England Novelty Works, located in Hill, was started by Frank R. Woodward, a clever man of invention. In 1875, Woodward had patented his Wizard, an inexpensive glass-cutter. A later invention was a diverse tool that performed six functions, including opening cans, sharpening knives, and lifting wood stove lids. The Novelty Works employed 30 to 50 people and became Red Devil Incorporated in the late 1920s. In 1933, the business moved to New Jersey and the Hill Chair Factory took over the building. This is a c. 1914 photograph. (HHS.)

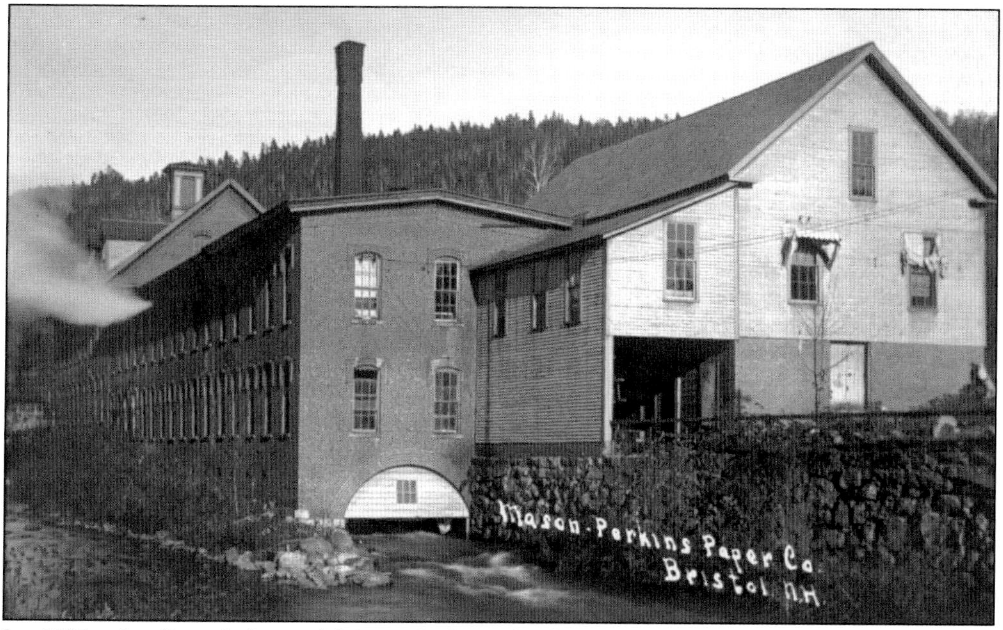

In 1871, the Bristol firm of Mason-Perkins & Company was formed, and in 1872 the brick mill was built and began the manufacture of paper. By 1891, the mill had expanded. It had a total floor space of 36,000 square feet. During its heyday, this mill was equipped with the most modern machinery and automated systems, and produced from five to six tons of paper per day. (MW.)

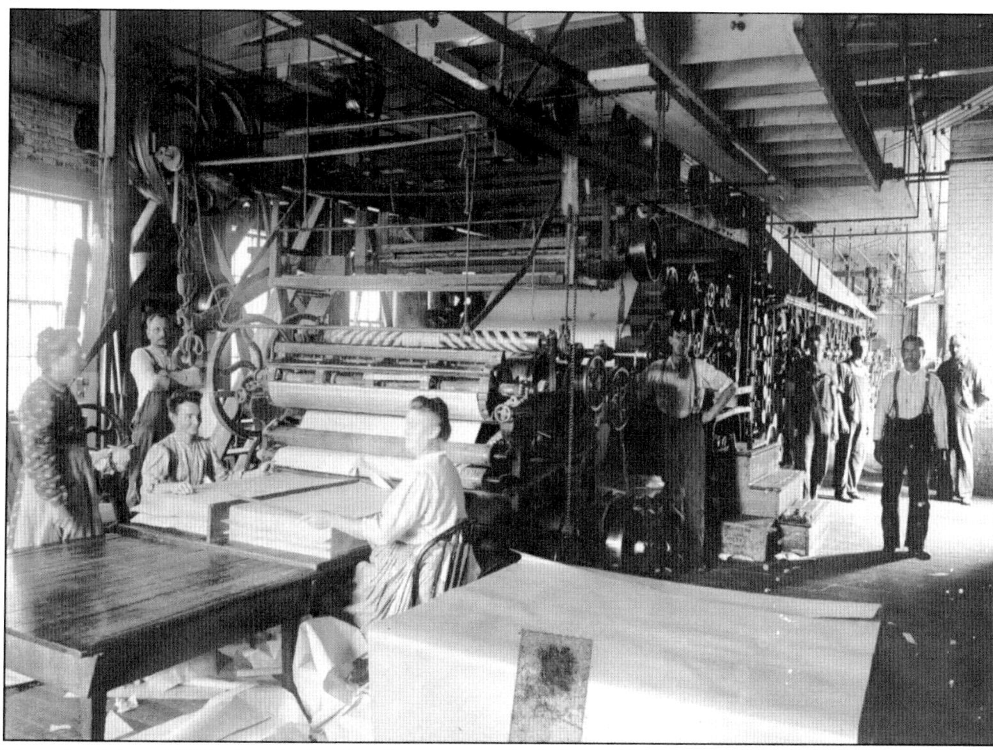

Seen in this *c.* 1904 view is the finish room at the Mason-Perkins Paper Mill. (BHS.)

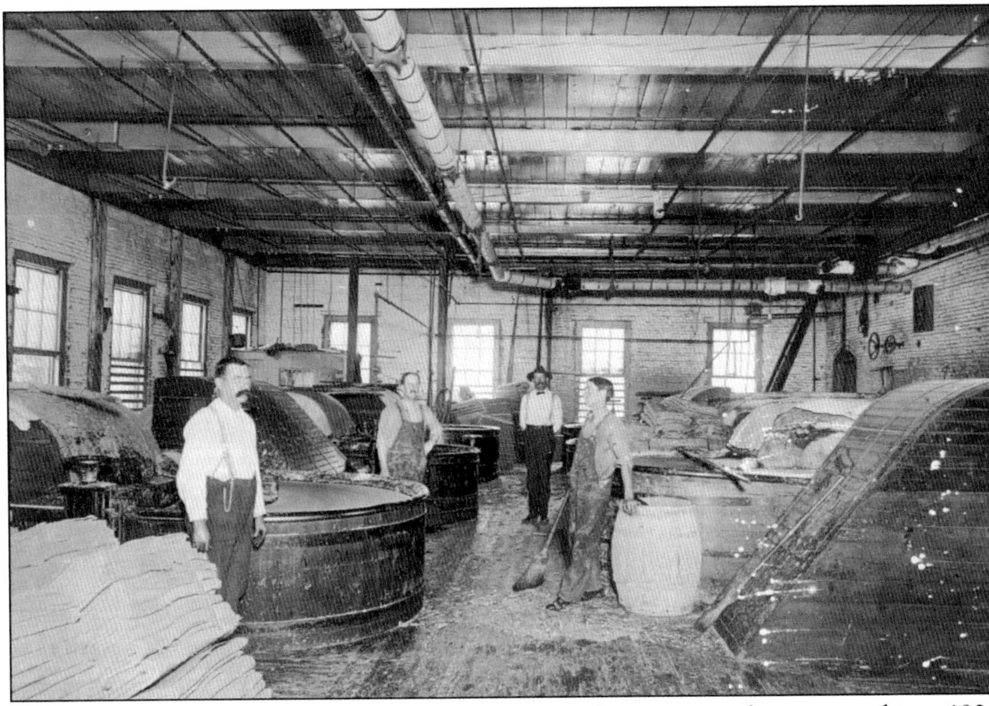

The Mason-Perkins Paper Mill beater room, where stock was prepared, is seen in this *c.* 1904 photograph. (BHS.)

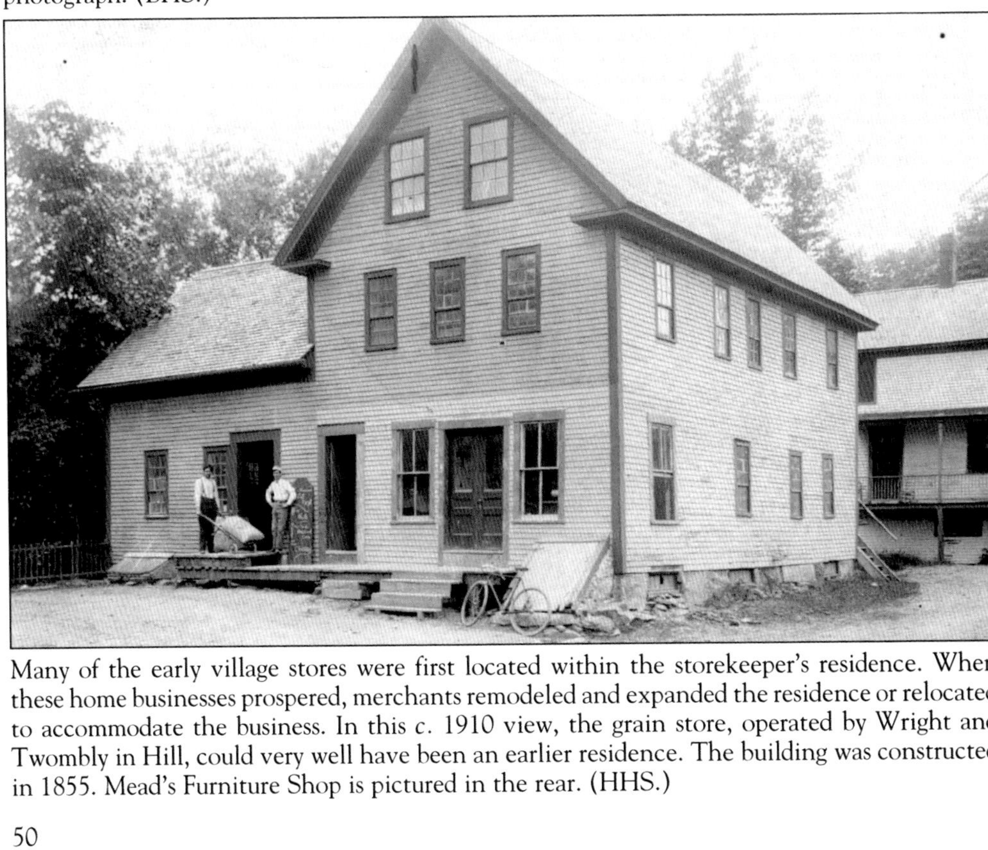

Many of the early village stores were first located within the storekeeper's residence. When these home businesses prospered, merchants remodeled and expanded the residence or relocated to accommodate the business. In this *c.* 1910 view, the grain store, operated by Wright and Twombly in Hill, could very well have been an earlier residence. The building was constructed in 1855. Mead's Furniture Shop is pictured in the rear. (HHS.)

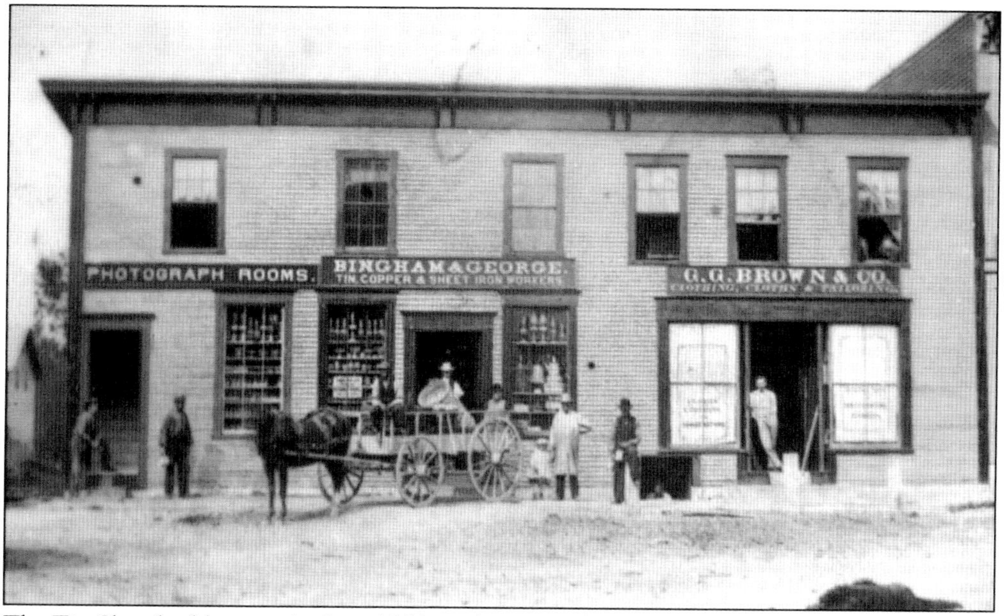

The Tin Shop building was built in 1850 on the west side of Central Square in Bristol. A dealer in stoves and tinware, Hiram W. Kendall was probably the first merchant to occupy the main lower story. The second-story rooms were used as a photographer's studio. This is a *c.* 1867 photograph. (BHS.)

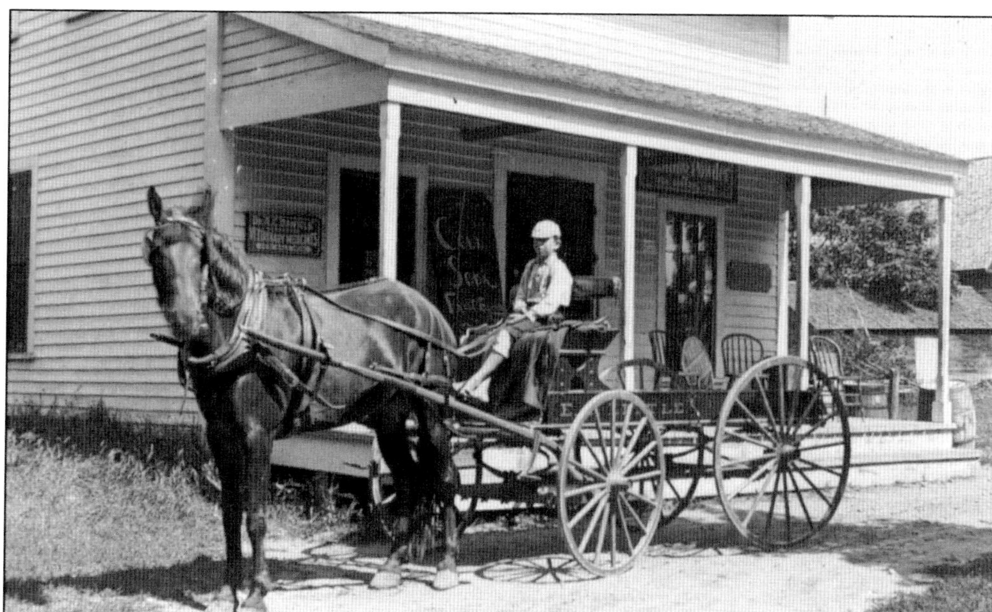

Young Ted Colby tends to the horse and wagon while his grocery order is being prepared by storekeeper Moses F. Little in Hill. Later, the building was converted to a rental dwelling. This photograph was taken *c.* 1900. (HHS.)

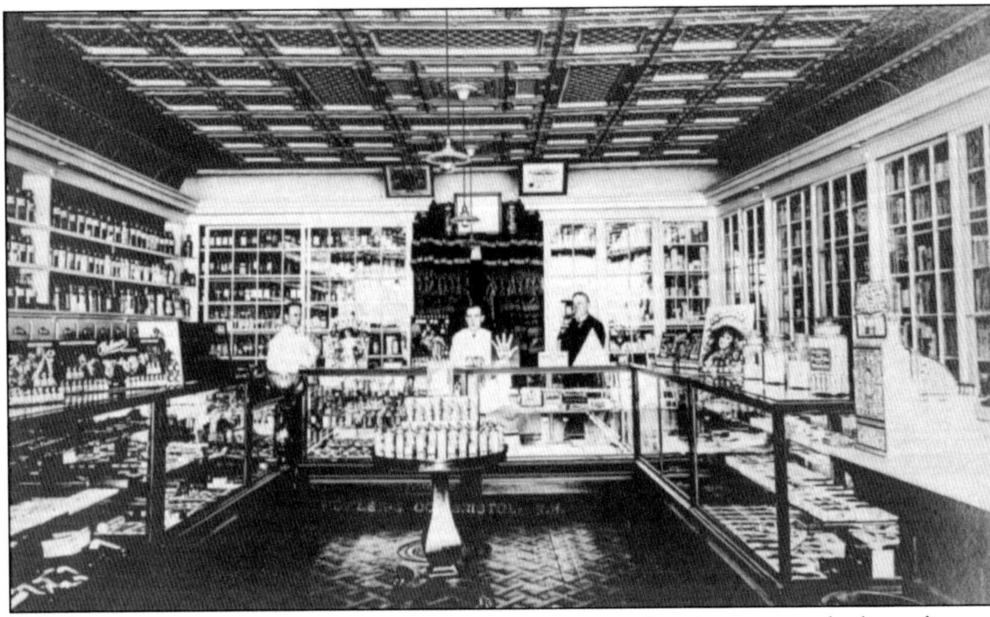

This *c.* 1900 photograph reveals an early interior view of Fowler's Drugstore, which was located next to the Rollins Block on Central Square in Bristol. Note the embossed tin ceiling and gleaming ceramic flooring. (MW.)

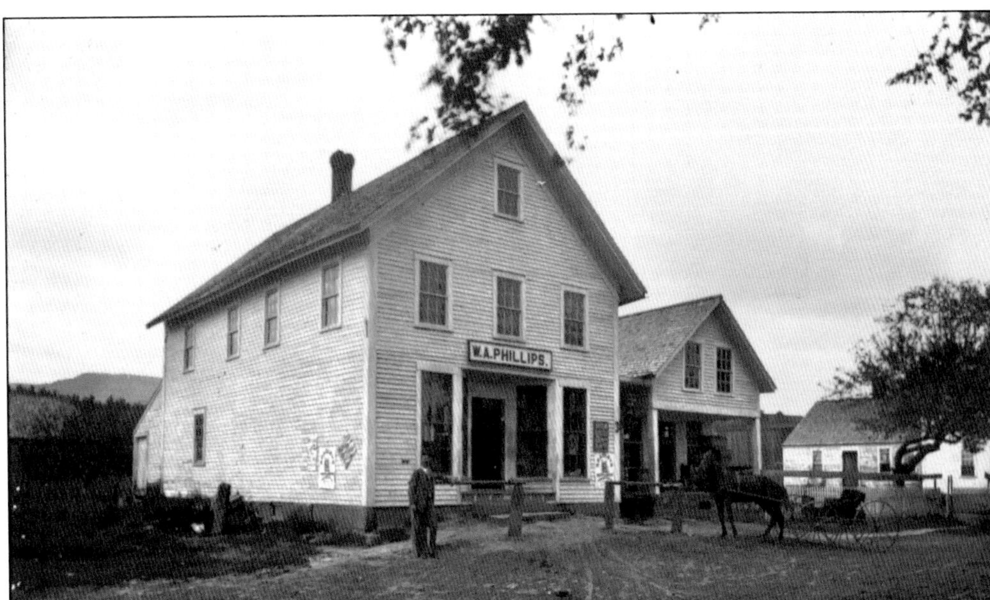

This view shows the Alexandria Village Store in the late 1800s. At that time the proprietor was W.A. Phillips. The building was destroyed by fire in the early 1900s. (AHS.)

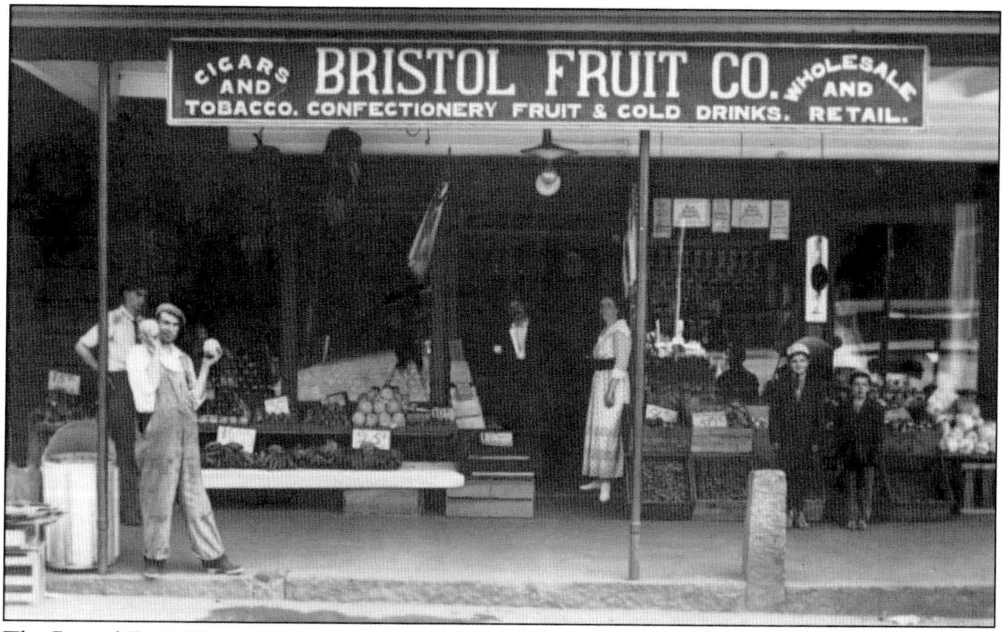

The Bristol Fruit Company was located on Central Square in Bristol. The fresh fruit in this view looks quite enticing. (BHS.)

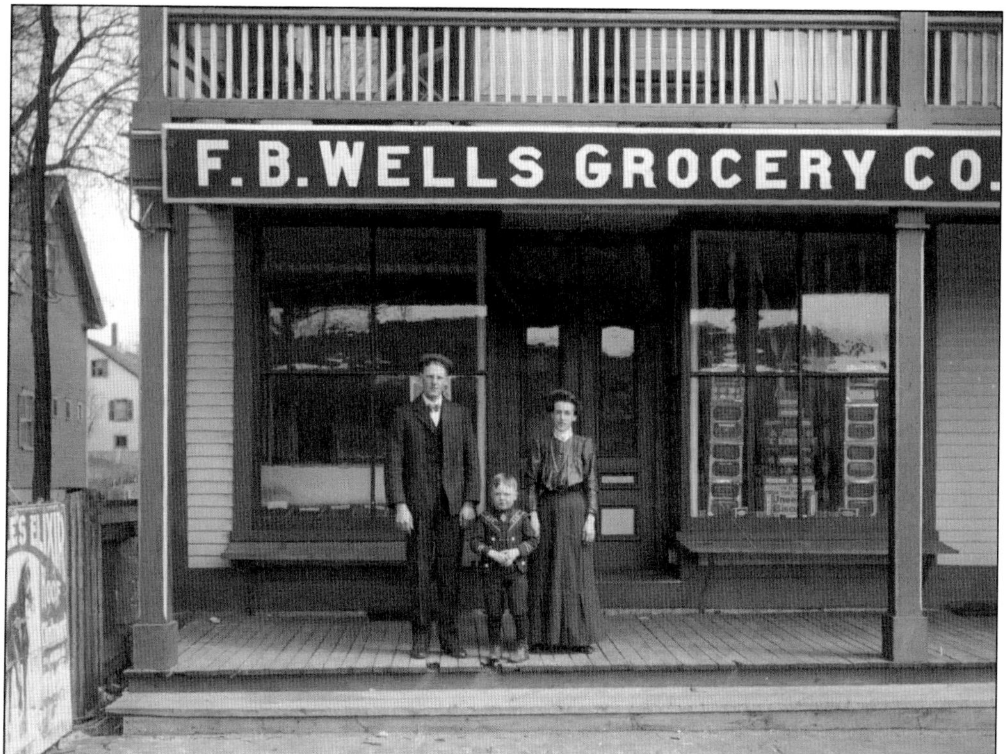

Frank B. Wells owned and operated this grocery store, on Central Square in Bristol, during the second half of the 19th century. Later, he sold the business, worked in carpentry, and started the manufacture of house finish. (BHS.)

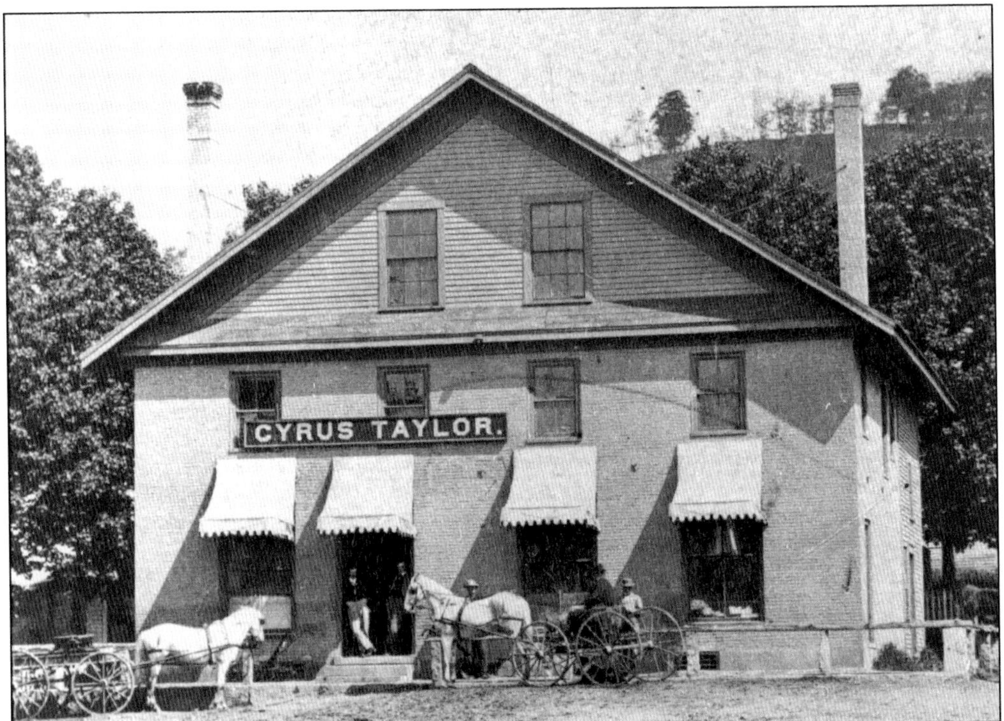

Cyrus Taylor had been a clerk at this store for six years when, in 1842, he bought into the partnership with Ichabod Bartlett. In 1860, Taylor became the sole owner of the store and conducted business here until 1892, when he sold out. He gave continuous service here for 56 years. (DP.)

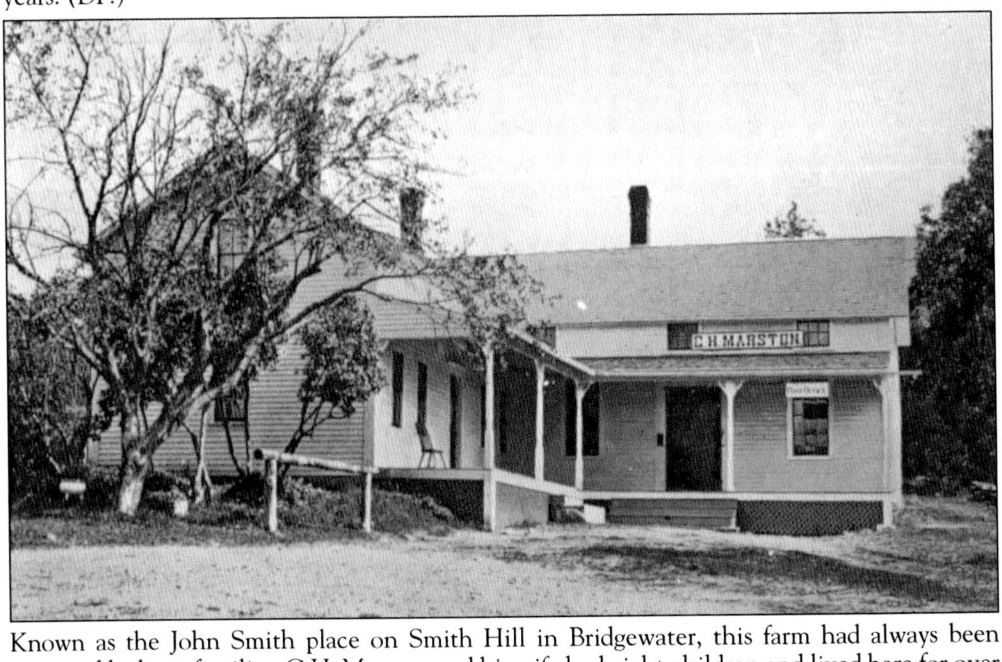

Known as the John Smith place on Smith Hill in Bridgewater, this farm had always been occupied by large families. C.H. Marston and his wife had eight children and lived here for over 50 years. In the 1890s, Marston operated this store and post office. (BWHS.)

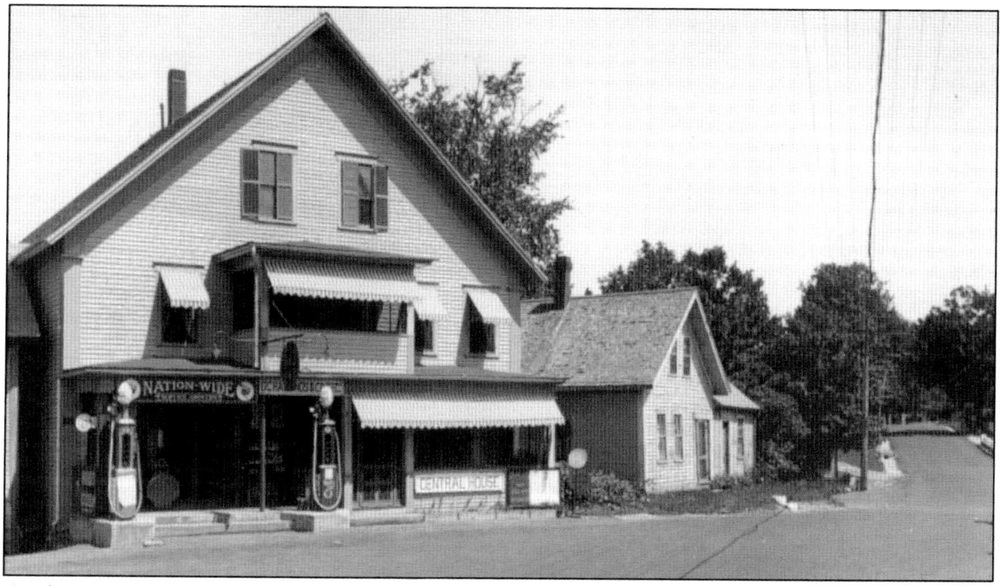

At the junction of Routes 4 and 104 in Danbury, this store is still in operation today. (JP.)

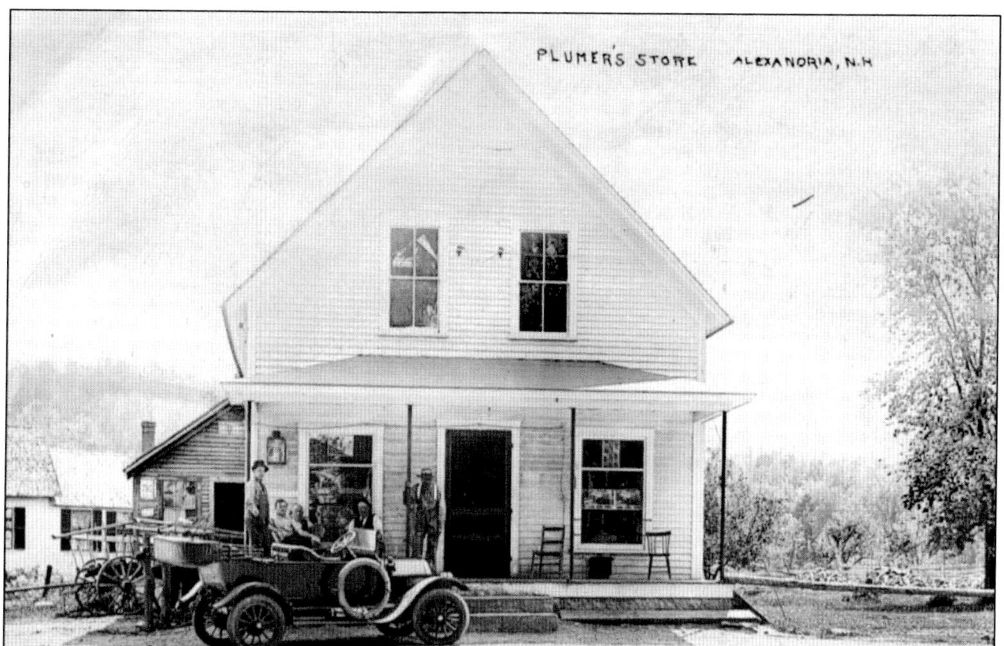

At Plumber's Store, in Alexandria, several men discuss either the current affairs of the world or the number of miles per gallon that the classy automobile gets. (AHS.)

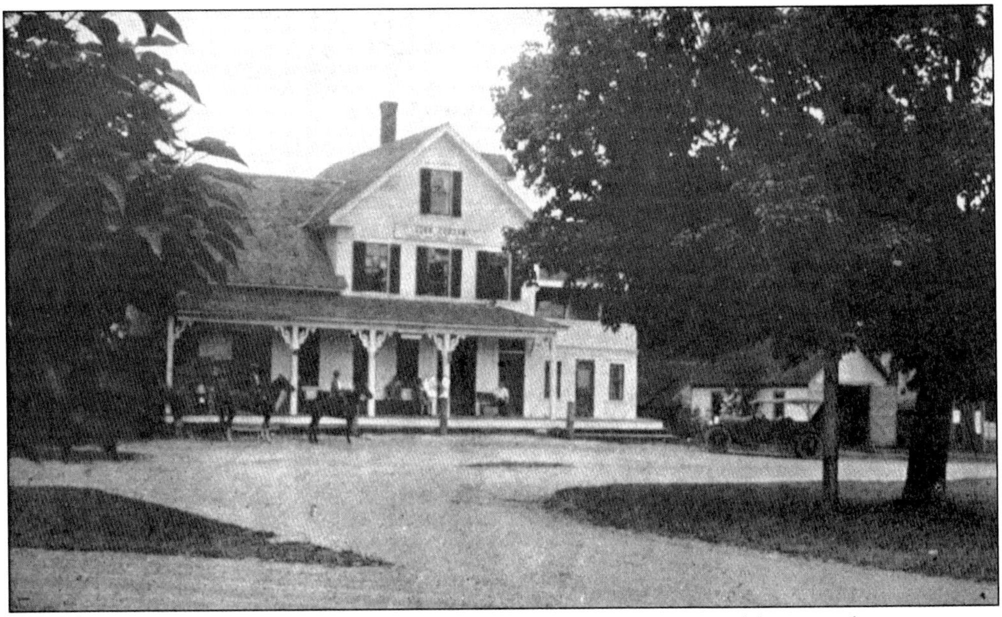

John Cordon of Franklin bought Hebron's Village Store in 1909 and became the postmaster that same year. He was the storekeeper and postmaster until his death in 1939. A disastrous fire in the spring of 1945 destroyed this building, along with the old Union Congregational Church, which was located next door. (HBHS.)

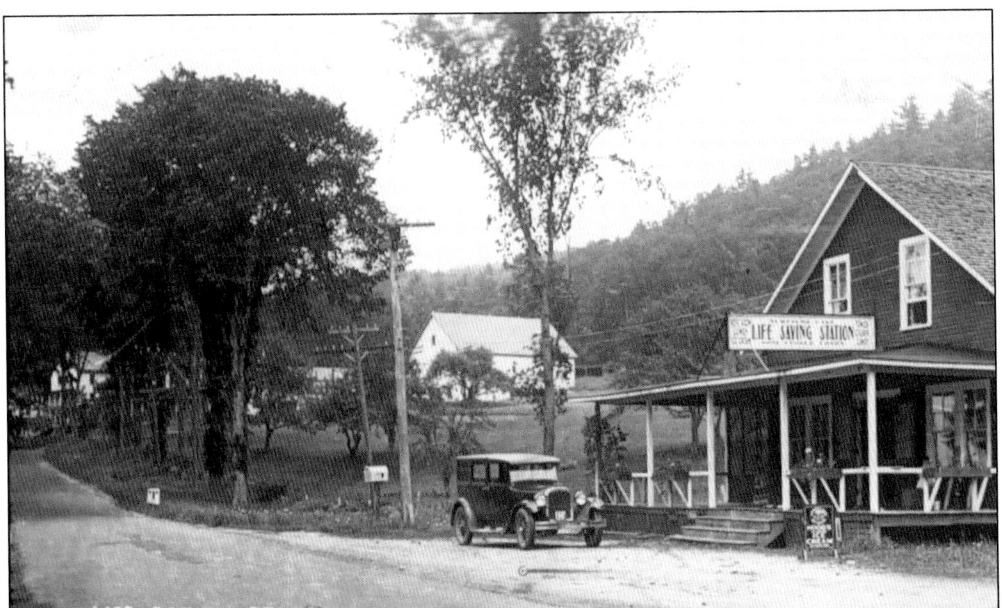

The Life-Saving Station, which was located on Route 3A near Newfound Lake, provided convenience foods and snacks for vacationers and summer residents. This photograph was taken c. 1935. (MW.)

Four

A Proper Education

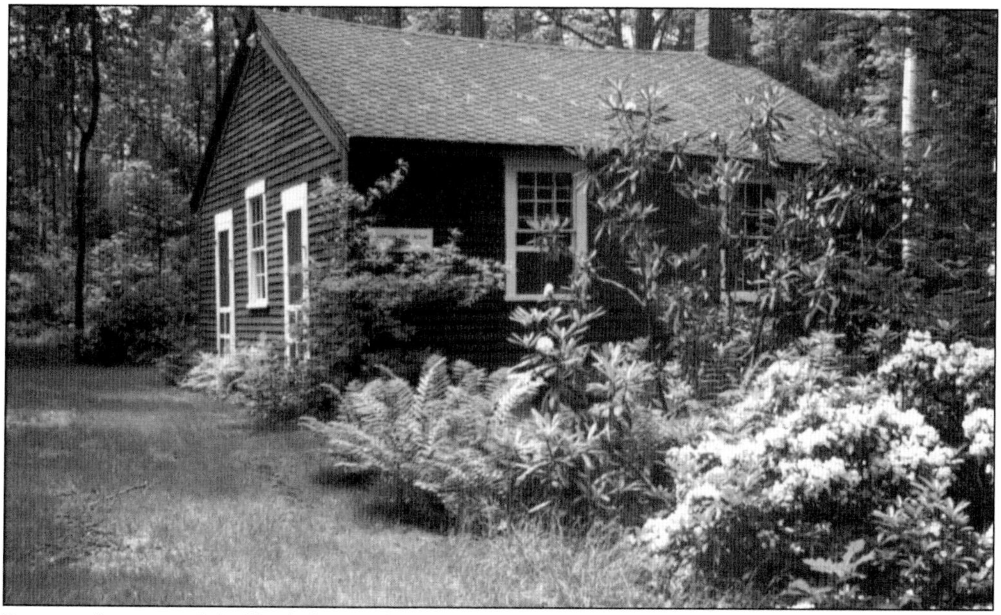

During the second half of the 18th century, when most of the towns in the region were settled, New Hampshire had mandated a law saying that towns with 50 or more freeholders should employ a schoolmaster to teach reading and writing. Larger towns with more than 100 freeholders were required to provide a grammar school. Towns were divided into self-governing school districts, where schoolhouses—usually small, one-room structures—were built. District boundaries changed over the years. These changes often depended upon the number of students in a district. The school year was divided into two or three terms. Teachers usually boarded with the family of a student. Children walked to school without regard to distance or weather conditions. By 1900, a number of the small schools had closed. They were either left to deteriorate or put to new use. Shown is the Dickerson Hill School, located in New Chester. Built c. 1810, it was in District No. 3 on Murray Hill. It provided a proper education for about 30 students. Called Murray Hill School after 1904, it was closed in 1910, after 77 years of continuous use. The school was restored in 1983. (HHS.)

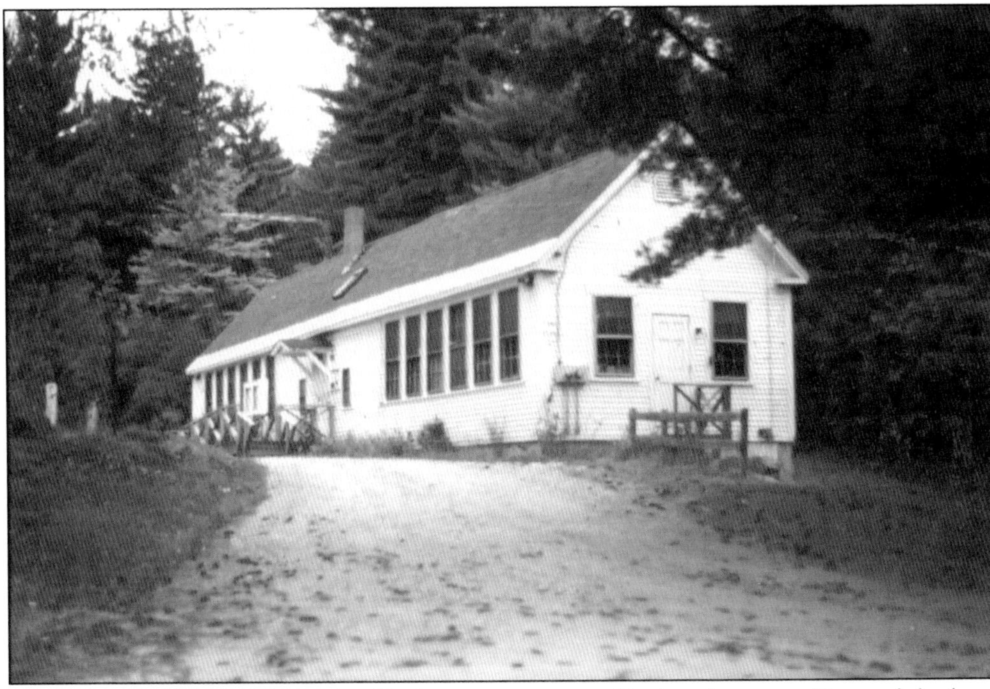

The River Road School, located in Bridgewater, is now utilized as the town office and the local historical society's museum and meeting room. (BWHS.)

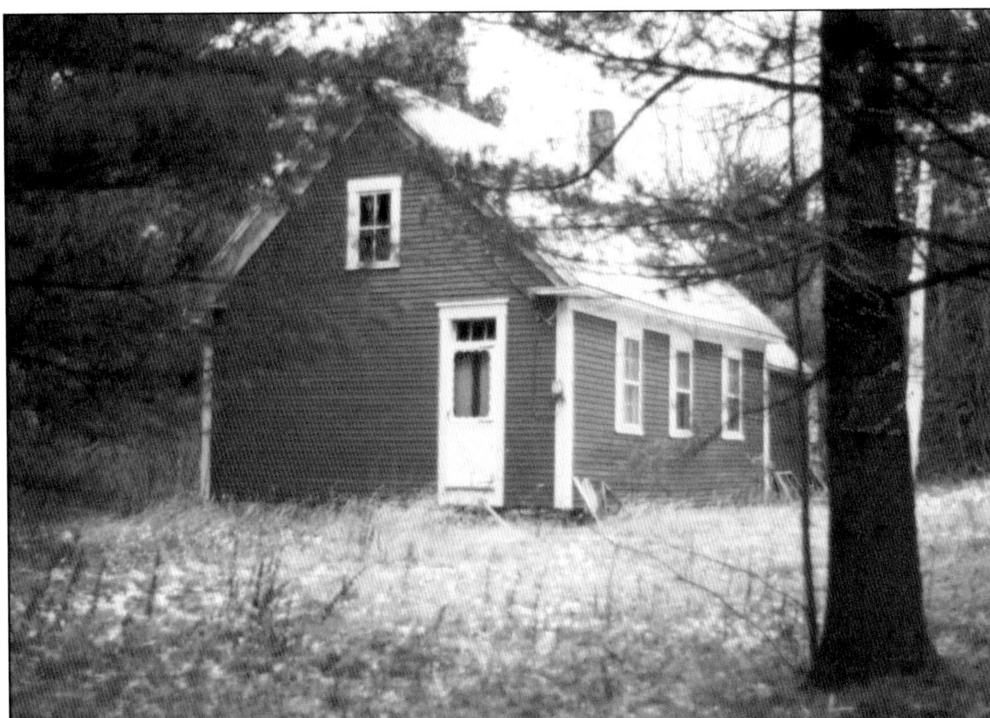

This one-room schoolhouse, on Bridgewater Hill in Bridgewater, is a fine example of the post-and-beam construction typical of the early district schools. (BWHS.)

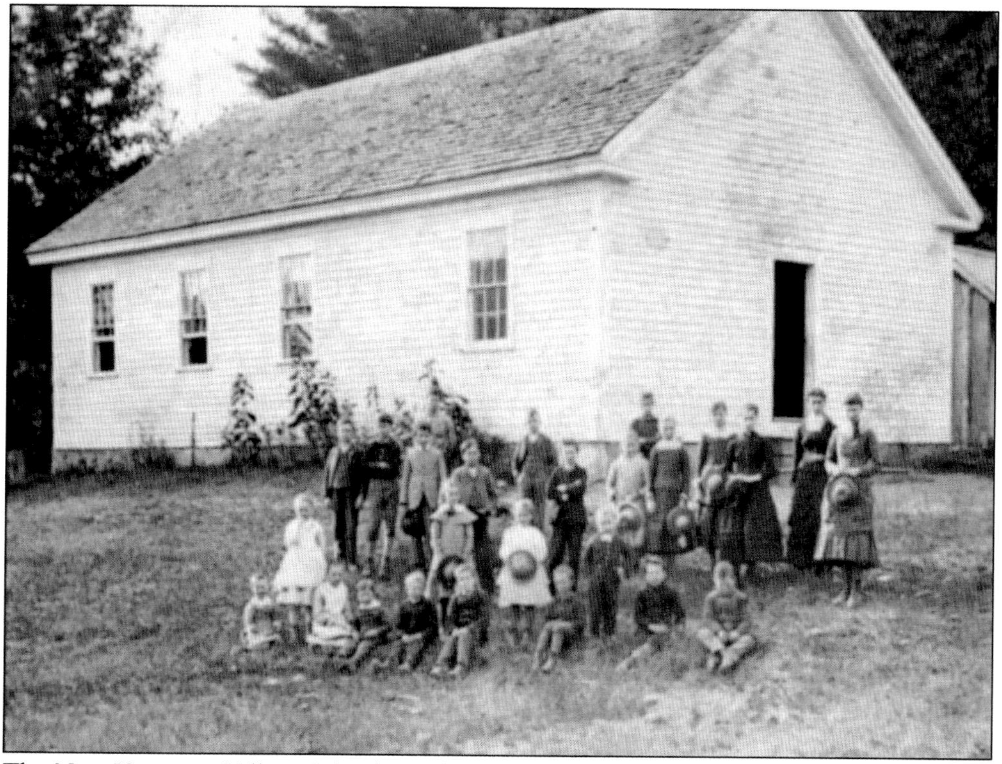

The New Hampton Village School was built in 1821. This *c.* 1880 view shows almost two dozen scholars and three teachers. (NHHS.)

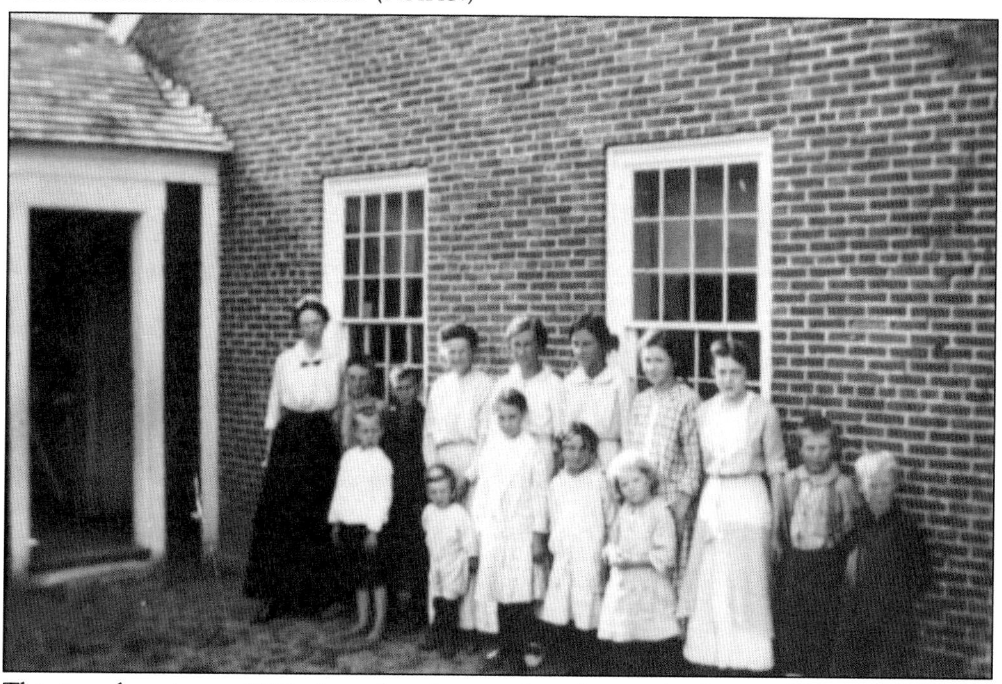

This is a charming *c.* 1916 view of students and teacher at the District No. 1 schoolhouse, which was known as the Institution School in New Hampton. (NHHS.)

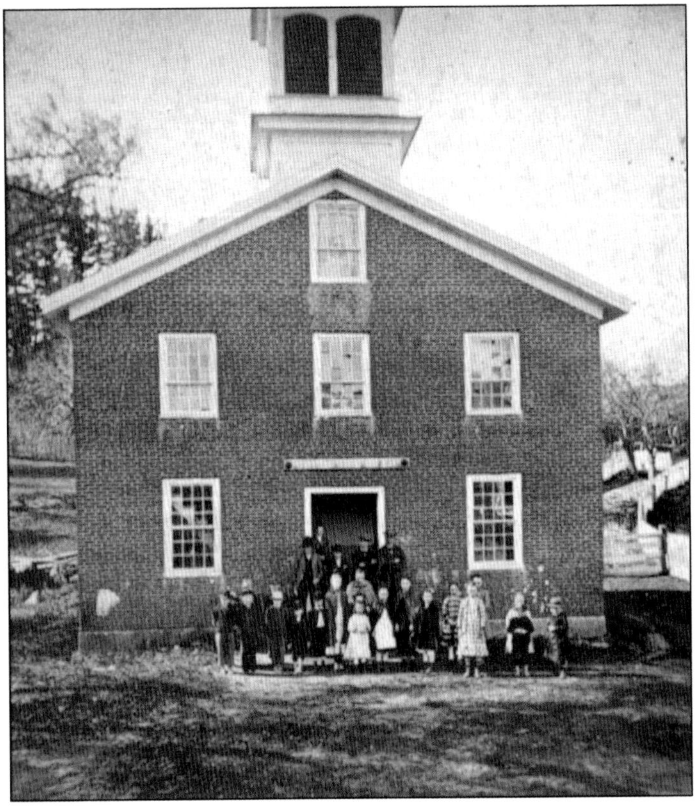

Built c. 1832, this brick building was known as the Academy or the Village School in Hill. In 1909, a new two-room school was built and, until 1941, when the village was relocated, the first floor of this building was used as the selectmen's offices and the Hill Public Library, and the second floor was the location of Hill Town Hall. (HHS.)

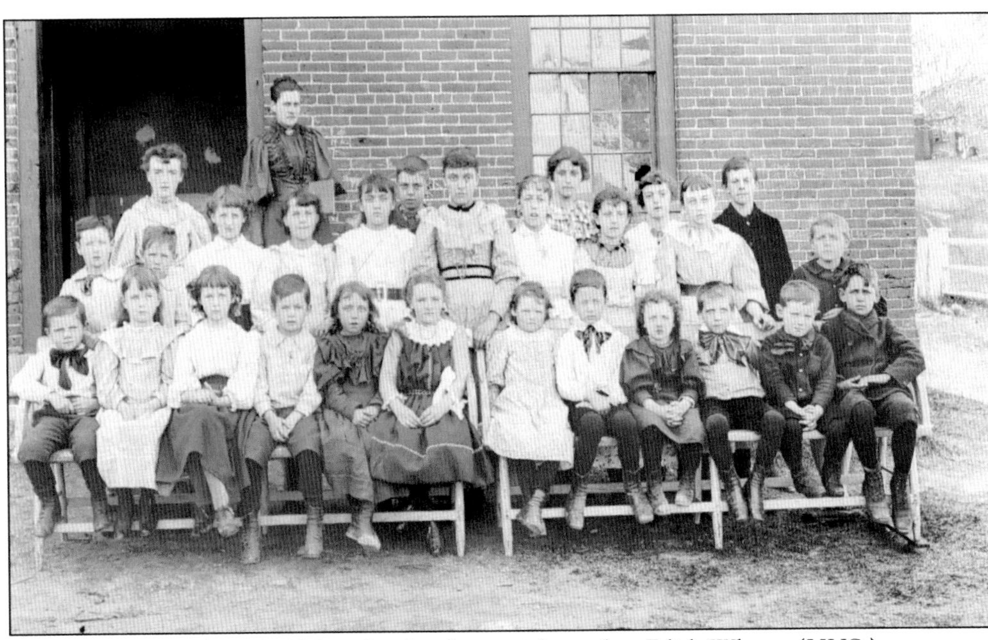

Seen here is the Class of 1904 at the Academy with teacher Edith Wheet. (HHS.)

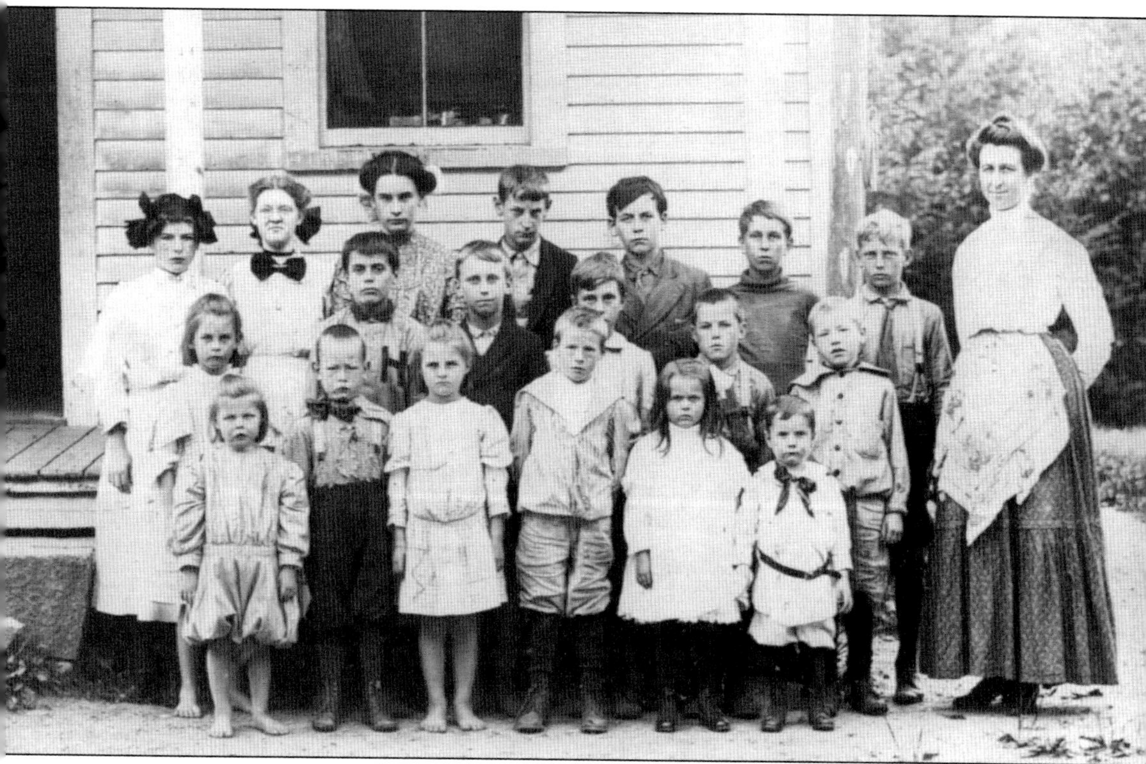

Tiny toes are showing in this wonderful *c.* 1910 view of students at the East Hebron School, with their teacher Lola Coolidge. Pictured here, from left to right, are the following: (front row) Lillian Hamilton, Wesley Merry, Violet Hamilton, Robert MacDougall, Melva Adams, and Milan Adams; (middle row) Ivy Hamilton, Max Adams, Fred Morse, Manson Smith, George Merry, and Norman MacDougall; (back row) Edith Merry, Irene Hartford, Vera Adams, and Harold Adams. (HBHS.)

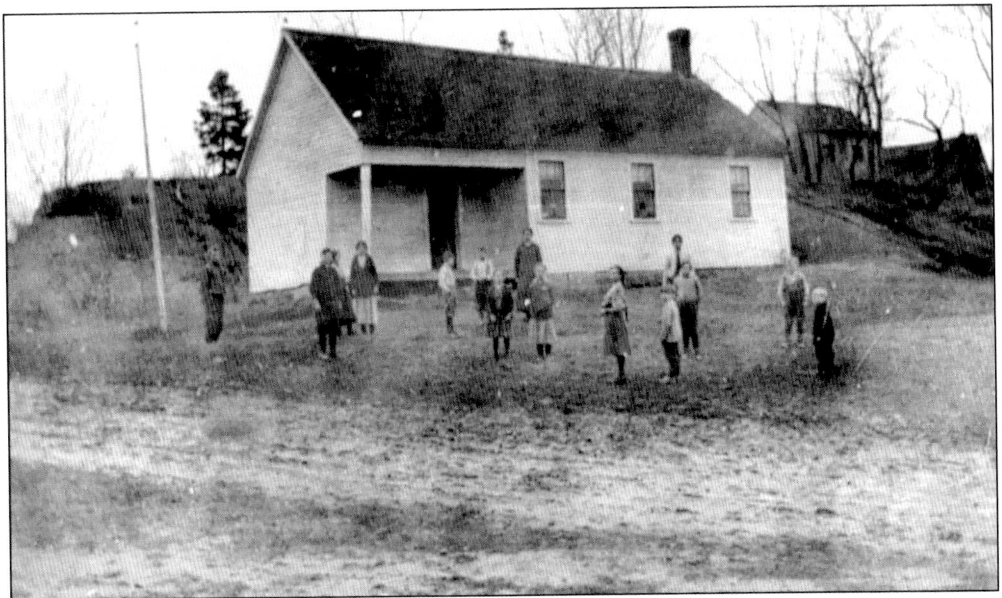

The North Groton School is situated on a knoll with a captivating view of the village. Today, it is in the process of being restored, after many years of vacancy and neglect. (GHS.)

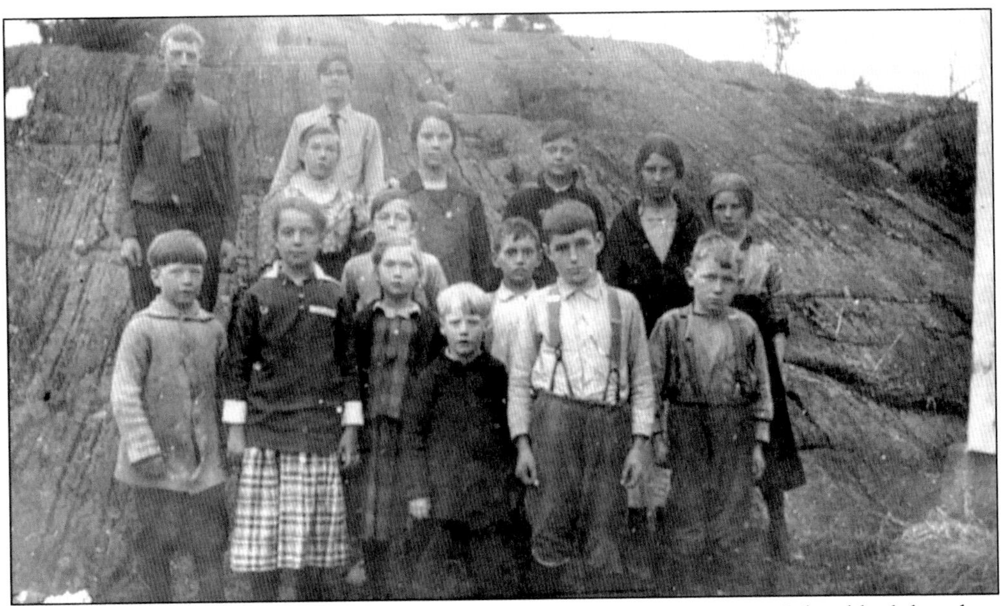

In this c. 1911 photograph, the students and teacher of the North Groton School look less than delighted to pose for the camera. Seen here, from left to right, are the following: (front row) Joe Stevens, Viola Davis, Marjorie Parris, Walt Stevens, Burton Merritt, and unidentified; (middle row) Violet Parris, Daniel Davis, and Max Parris; (back row) Clayton Eastman, Chestley Parris, Erville Davis, Pearl Cross, Georgie Brayley, and unidentified. (GHS.)

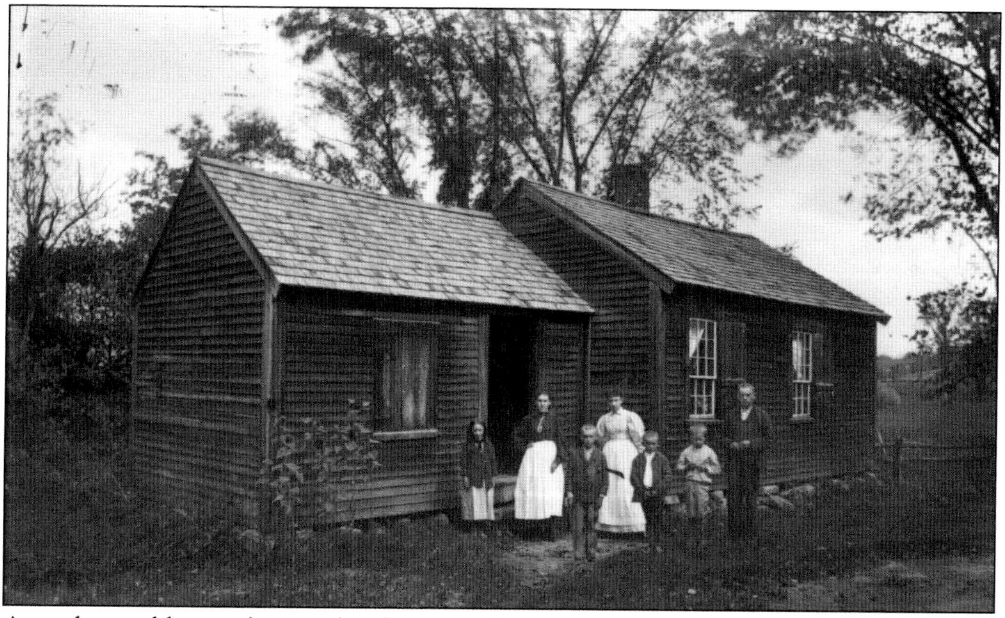

A teacher and her students gather for a *c.* 1890 class photograph next to their schoolhouse, which was known as the Bog School of District No. 3 in Alexandria. (AHS.)

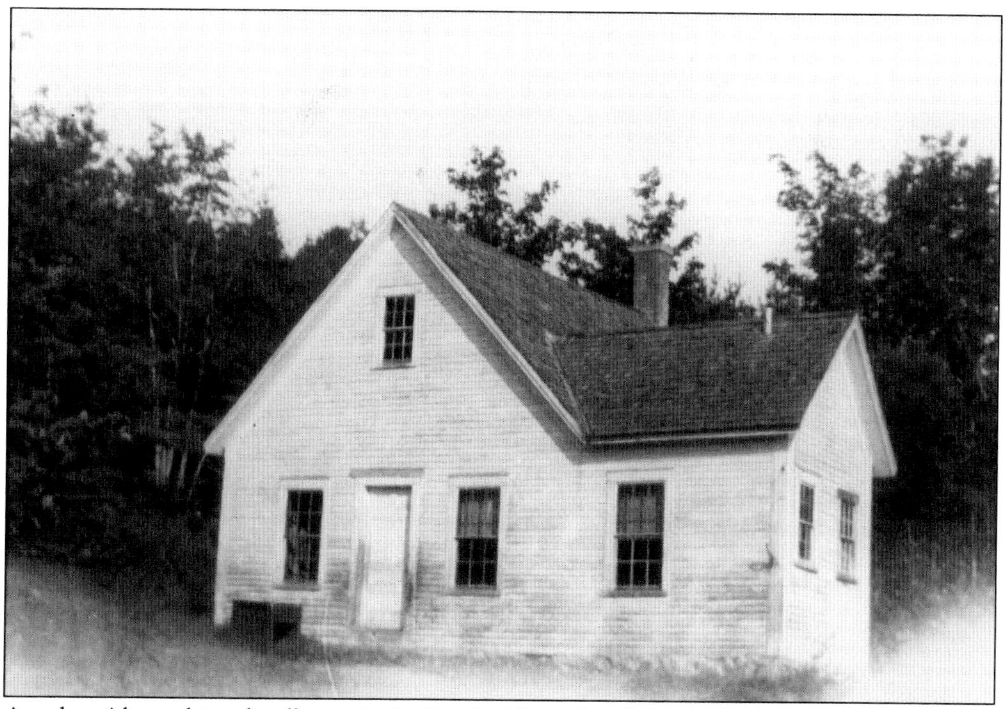

Another Alexandria schoolhouse is the South Alexandria School of District No. 1, located on Route 104. Several years ago, the schoolhouse was renovated and is now a private residence. This photograph was taken in 1931. (AHS.)

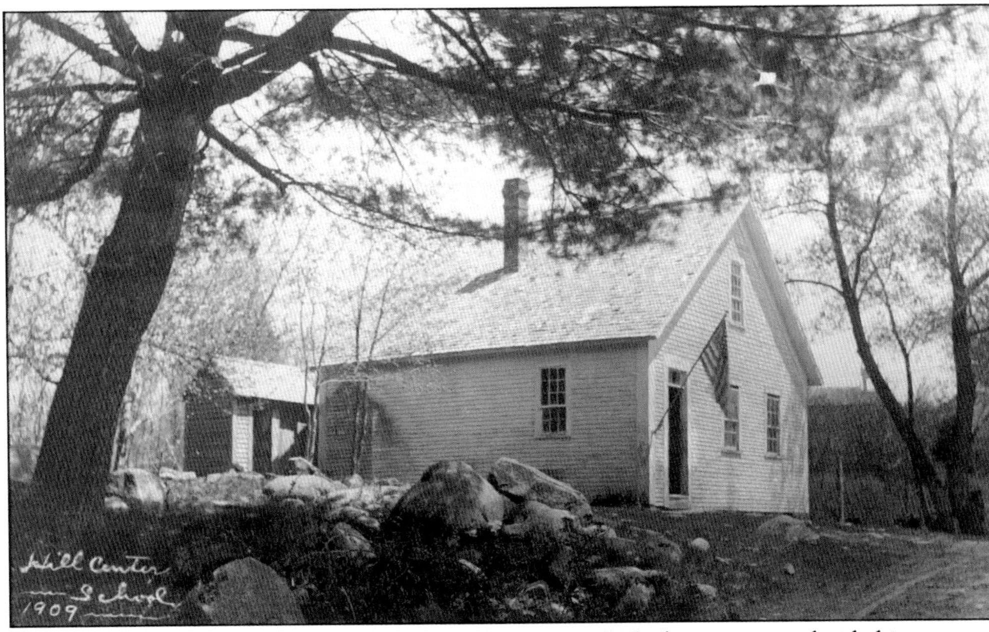

When school districts were formed in New Chester in 1795, the town was divided into seven districts. Shown in this 1909 photograph is Hill Center, which was located in District No. 5, where this one-room schoolhouse was built in 1816. It operated as a school until it closed in 1923. Later, the building was moved to the south side of Murray Hill Road and became a private residence. (HHS.)

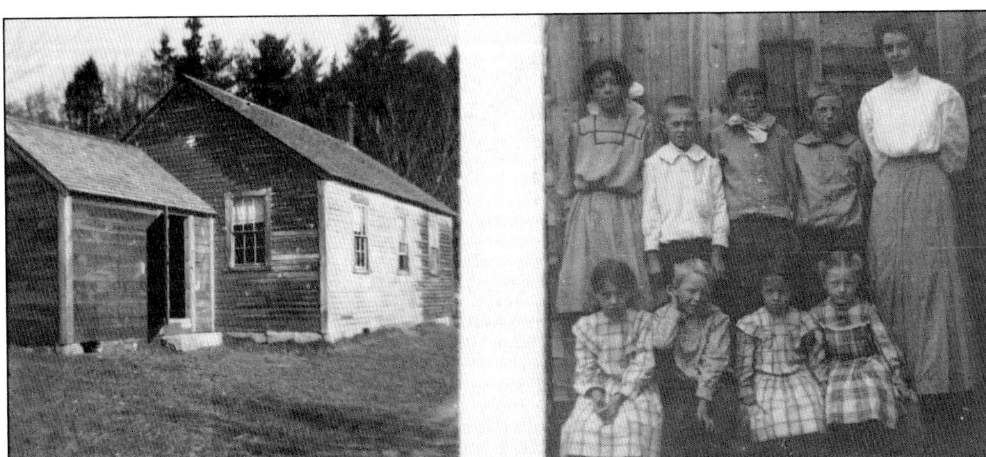

This schoolhouse was built in Bristol's District No. 1 and was known as Foot of Mountain School. The students pictured in this 1908 photograph are, from left to right, as follows: (front row) Hazel Brown, Frank Patten, Edna Brown, and Arlene Kenney; (back row) Pearl Ballou, Charles Wallace, Walter Hamel, Fred S. Patten, and Mary Wells. (DP.)

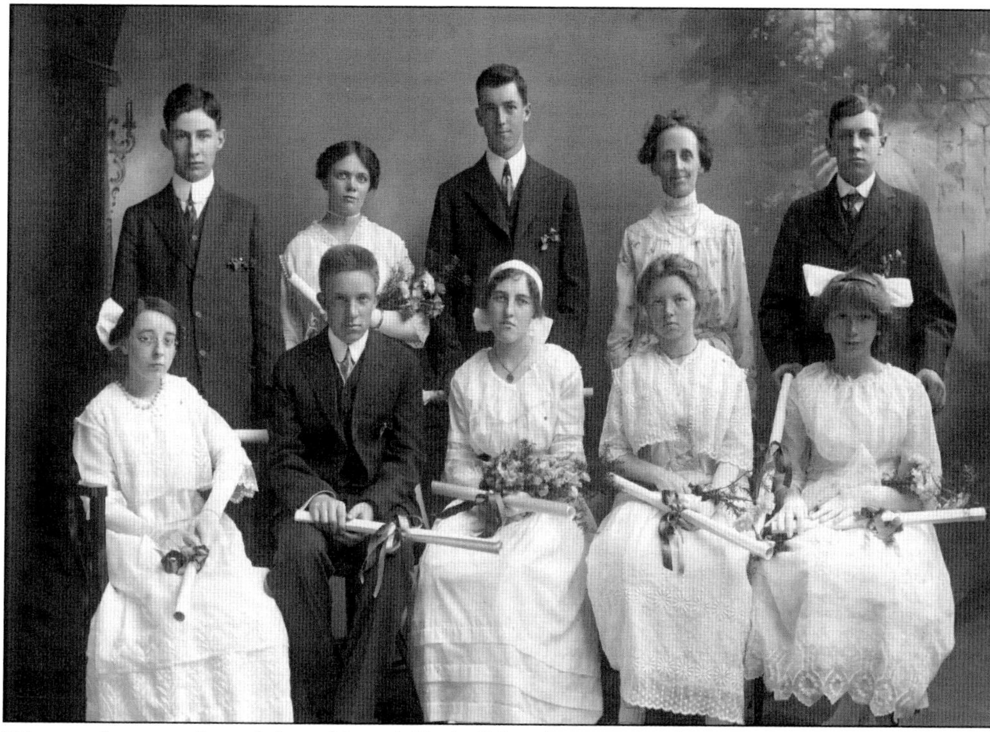

Nine students graduated from Bristol High School in 1915. They are, from left to right, as follows: (front row) Olive Woodman, Harry Littlefield, Ethel Southard, Flora Hazelton, and Alice Pope; (back row) Frank Higgins, Hilda Kenny, teacher Swain-Rensford Mitchell, and Elwin Verrill. (BHS.)

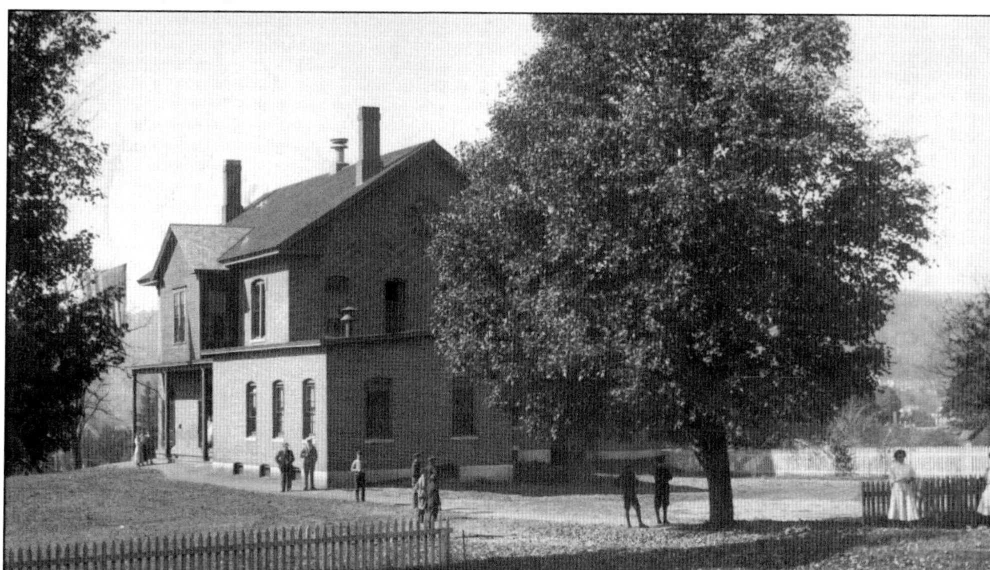

In Bristol, the Union School District was formed of Districts No. 2, No. 10, and No. 11 in 1864. A new brick schoolhouse was needed to accommodate the three districts. As voted upon, the schoolhouse was to have been built within a year at a cost of $3,500. Three years later, at an estimated cost of $16,000, the school opened. (MW.)

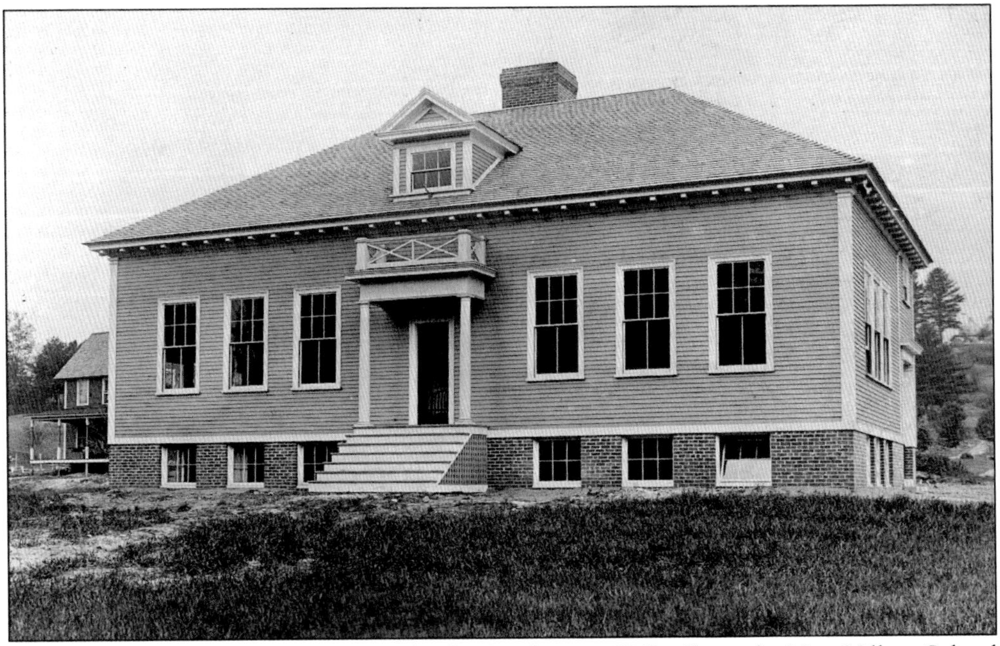

When students became too numerous for the Academy in Hill village, the New Village School was built. Jennie Dickerson Blake, a beloved teacher, taught at this school for more than 50 years. Teachers Ruth Merrill Rounds and Elsie Fowler Jefts each taught at the school for 23 years. This photograph was taken in 1909. (HHS.)

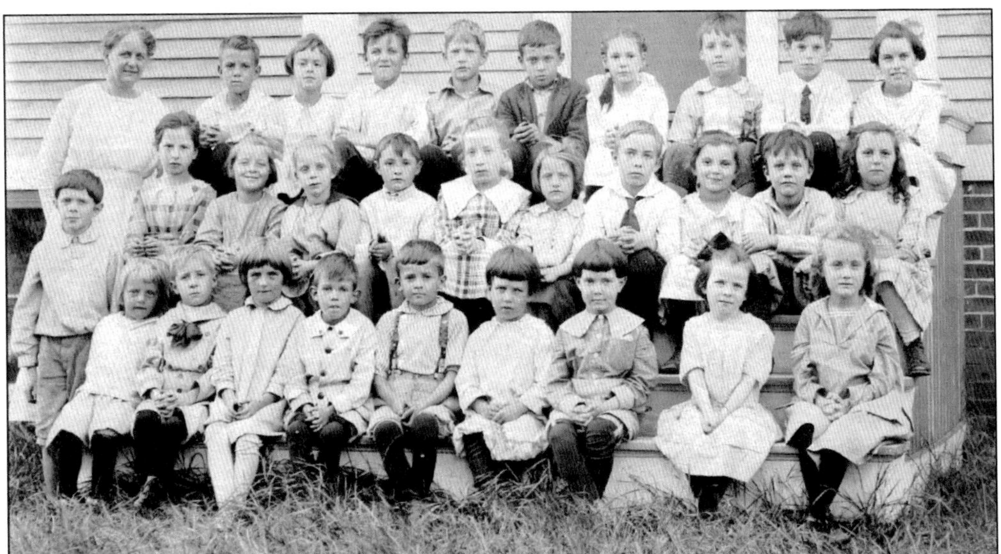

In this view, students are seated on the steps of the New Village School, located in Hill. With them is teacher Jennie Dickerson Blake, for whom the school in the new village is named. (HHS.)

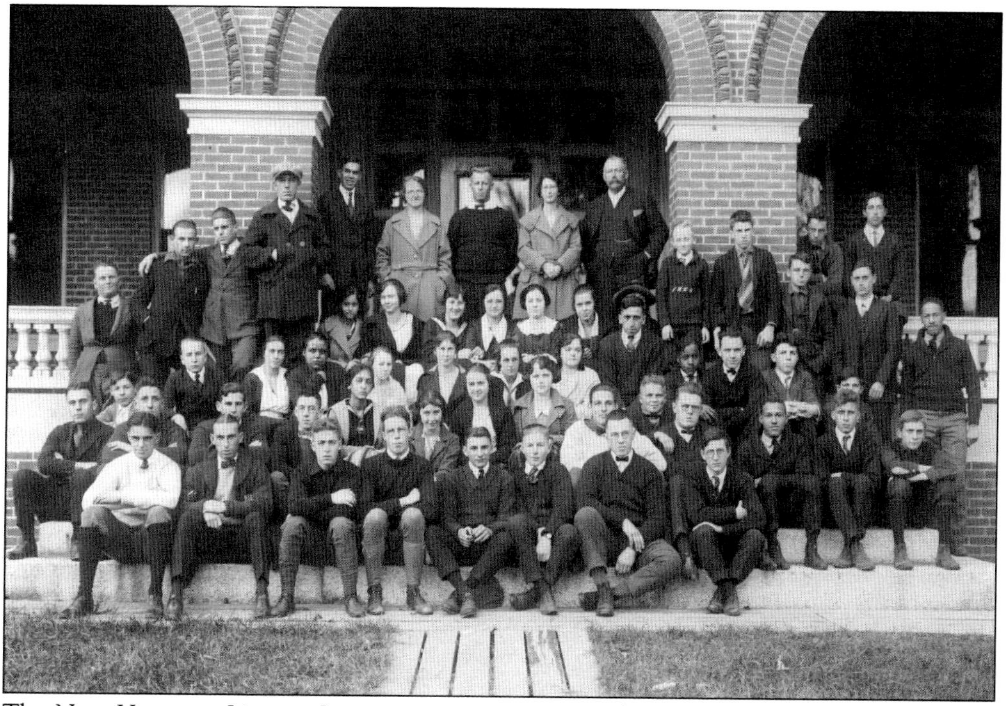

The New Hampton Literary Institution was incorporated in 1821 and was a coeducational school until 1826. At that time, the institution was reorganized as the New Hampton Academical and Theological Institution under Baptist auspices and became a male institution. Here, the class and faculty gather for a photograph during the fall term of 1921. (BHS.)

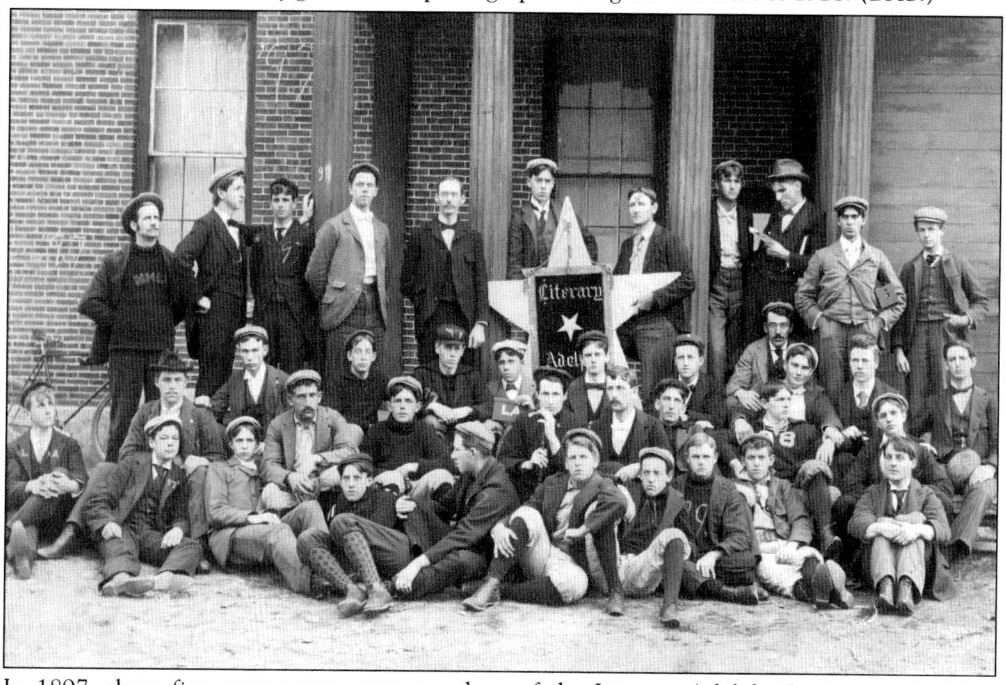

In 1897, these fine young men were members of the Literary Adelphi Society at the New Hampton Literary Institution. This society was founded in 1827. (NHHS.)

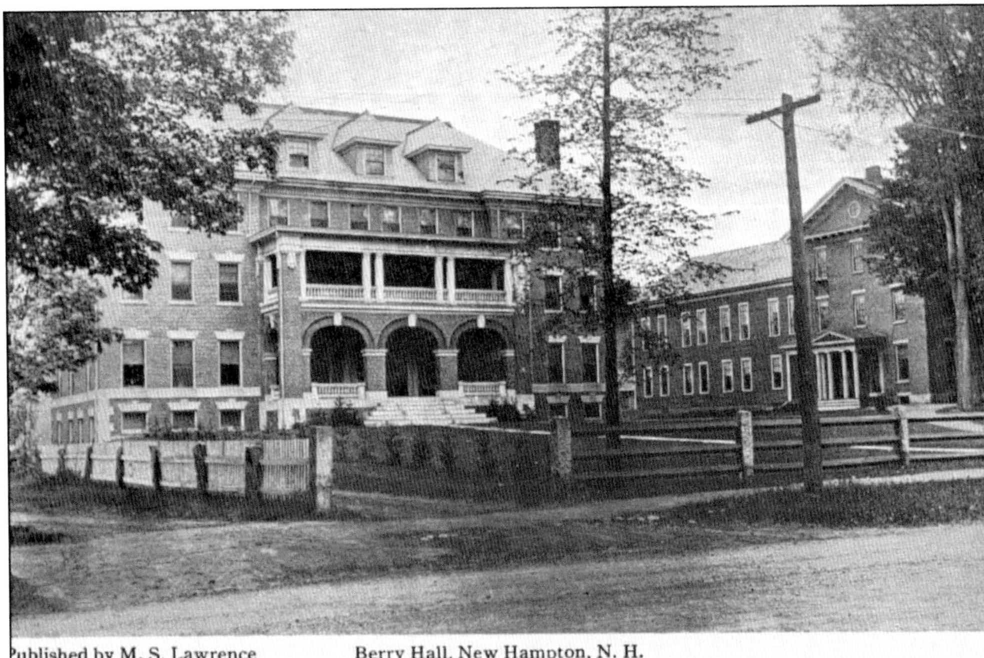

The beautiful Berry Hall at the New Hampton Literary Institution was built in 1911 as a dormitory for girls. (NHHS.)

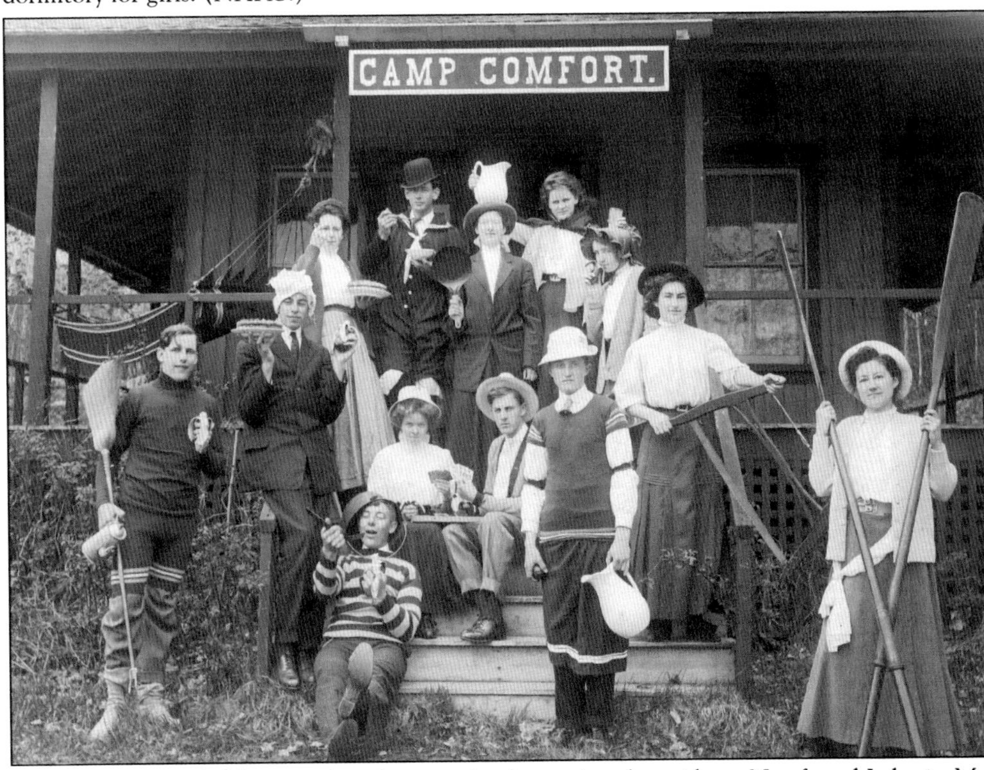

As evidenced by the faces in this photograph, the senior class ride to Newfound Lake in May 1909 was a joyful outing. The class attended the New Hampton Literary Institution. (NHHS.)

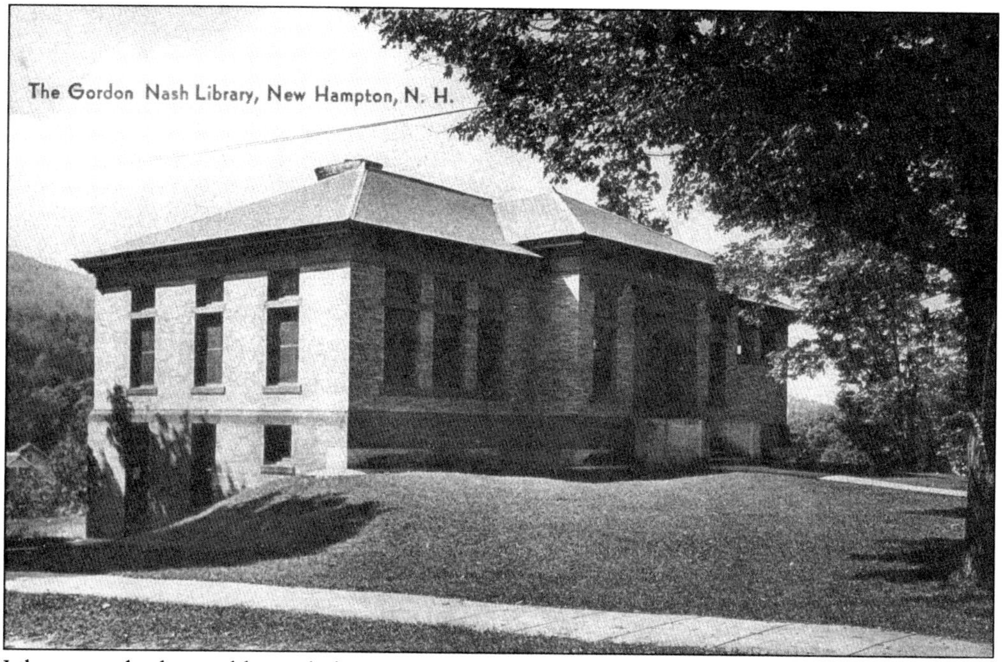

Libraries, whether public or belonging to schools, have been and remain inextricably tied to the education of children. The Gordon-Nash Library, in New Hampton, was built in 1895 with funds given by the will of Judge Steven Gordon Nash. Nash was a native of the town and a direct descendent of Enoch Gordon, one of the earliest settlers there. (NHHS.)

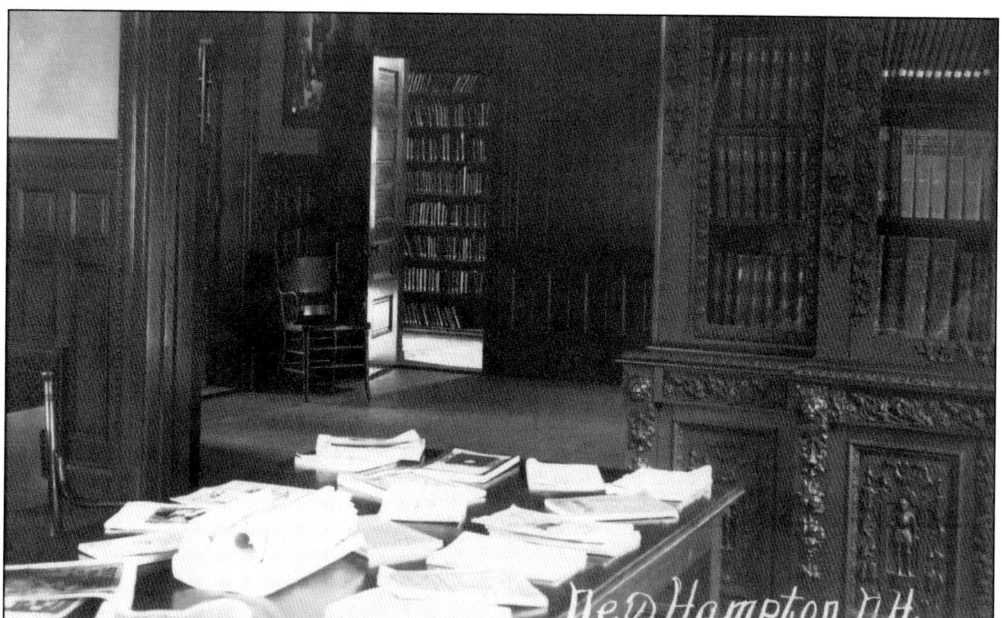

This interior view of the Gordon-Nash Library in New Hampton shows magnificent carved and paneled walls. (NHHS.)

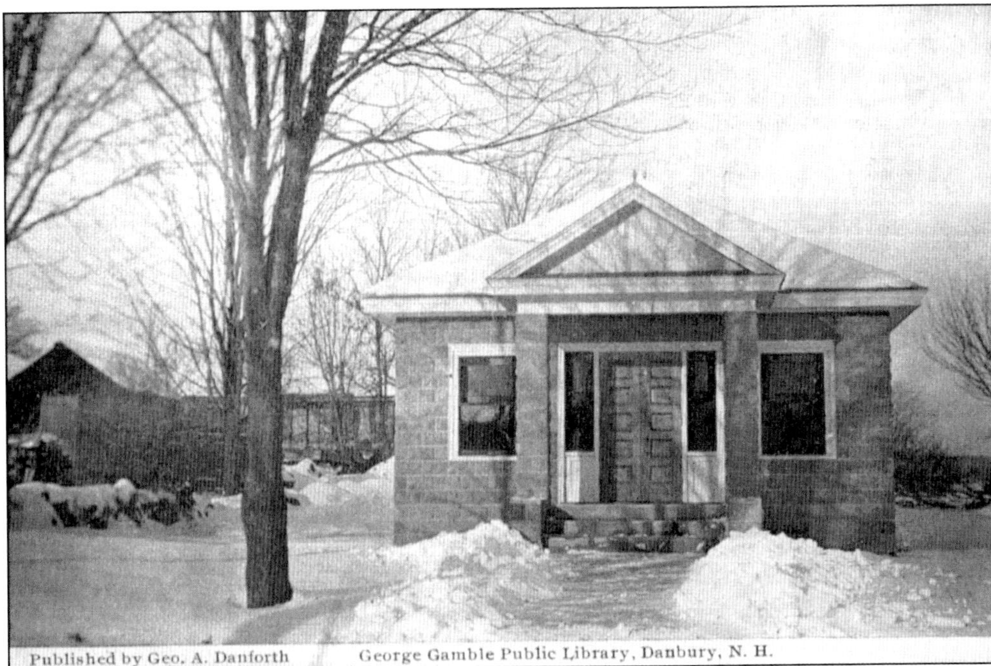

Shown after an early winter snowfall is the George Gamble Public Library in Danbury, which was built in 1911. (JP.)

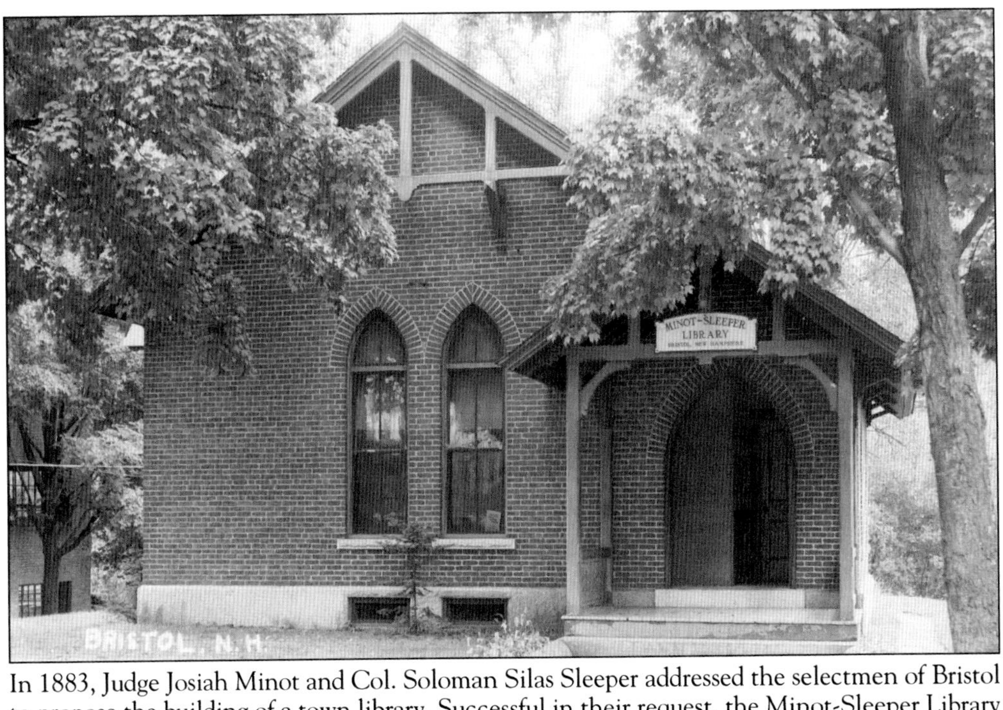

In 1883, Judge Josiah Minot and Col. Soloman Silas Sleeper addressed the selectmen of Bristol to propose the building of a town library. Successful in their request, the Minot-Sleeper Library was built in 1884 and opened to the public in 1885 with 900 volumes for circulation. (MW.)

Five

Newfound Rural

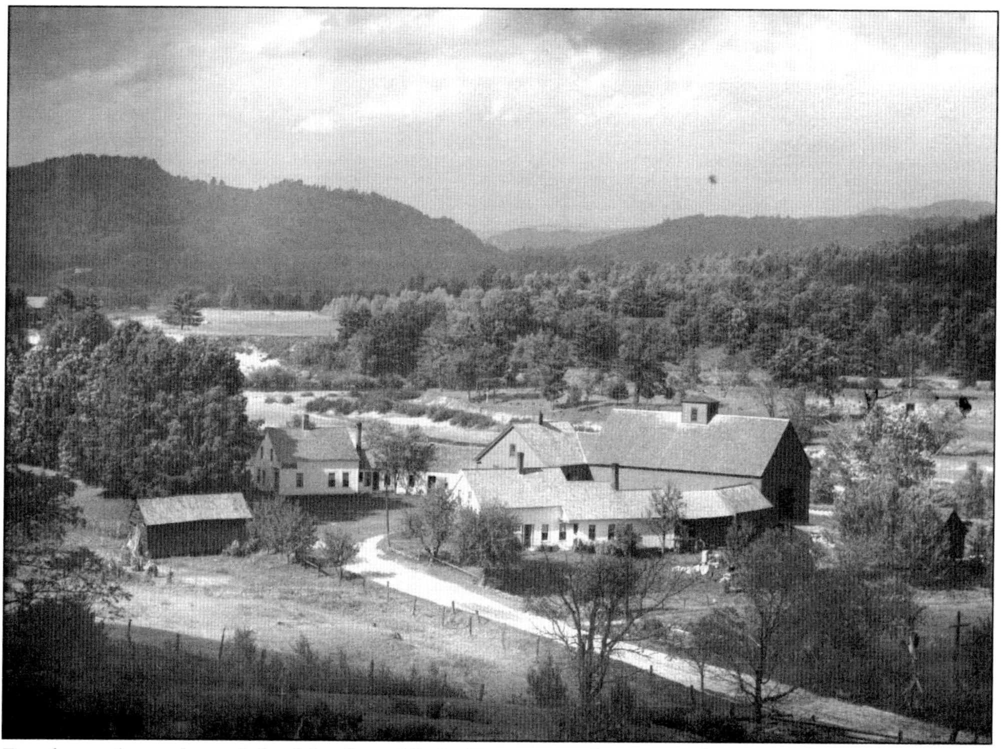

For the early settlers of the Newfound Lake Region, as for most of New England, farming was the dominant economic activity. Most farms consisted of many acres that would yield a full year's subsistence for the family and livestock. The farm buildings were large, with a series of attachments from house to barn. This view shows the Frank Foster Farm, located on the floodplain in Hill. It was on this site that New Chester's first settler, Capt. Cutting Favor, built a log cabin in 1766. The first white child born in New Chester was his son Isaac Favor, who was born at the farm. After building a sawmill, Captain Favor replaced his log cabin with a frame house in 1769. This photograph was taken in 1907. (HHS.)

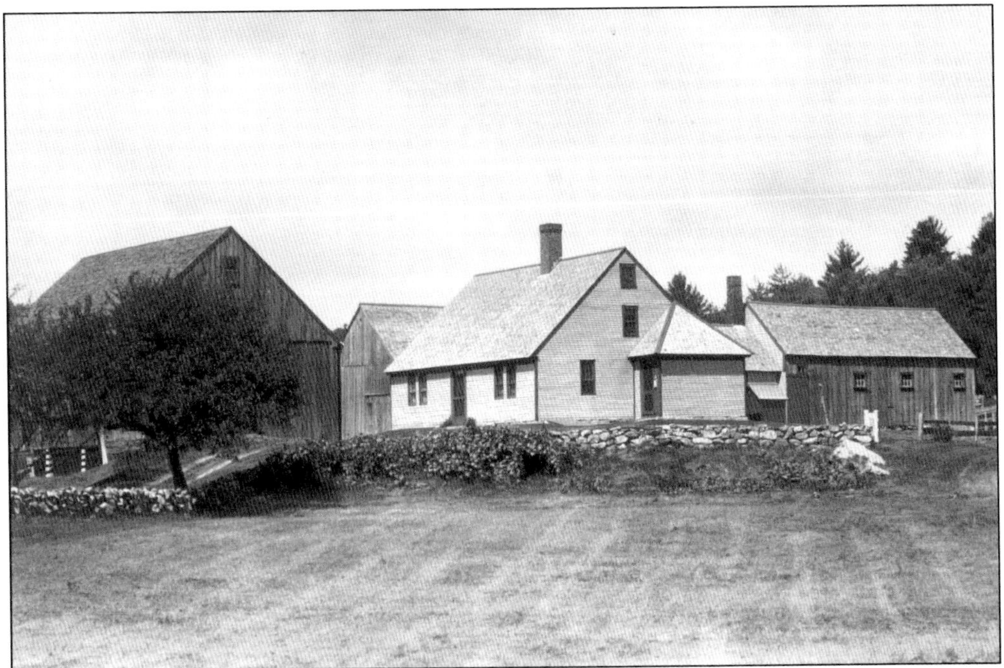

This beautifully maintained homestead, known as the Jewell Farm, is one of Hebron's earliest settlements. (HBHS.)

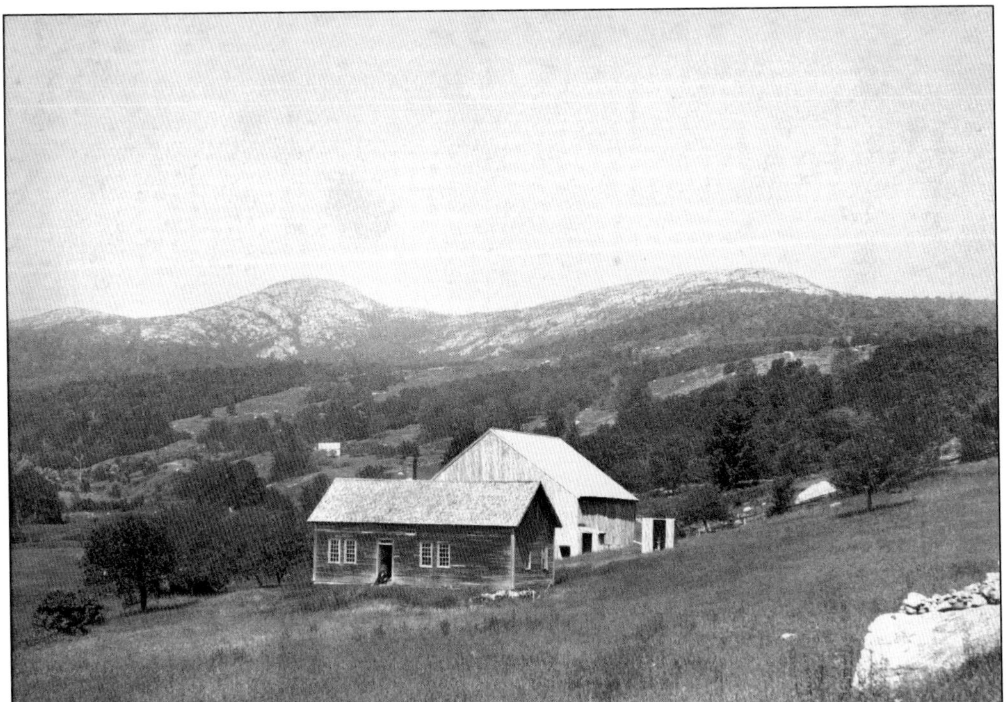

Information about this farmstead, which was probably located in Alexandria, is vague. However, the *c.* 1900 view of Mount Cardigan's rocky peak is striking. (BHS.)

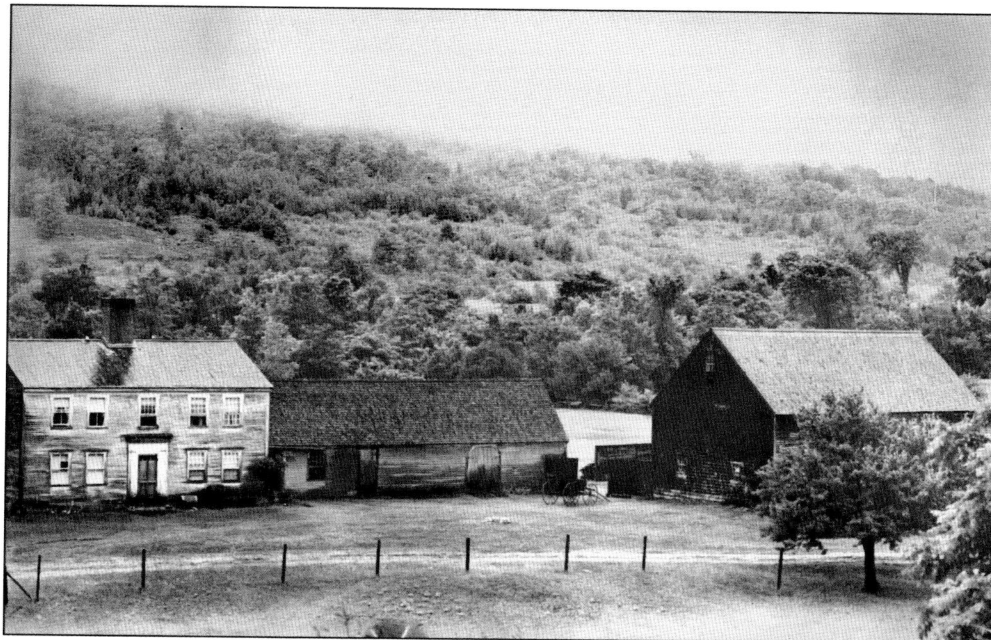

This view of the Hobart Farmhouse, nestled in a peaceful valley of Groton, is a wonderful reminder of the simple, albeit often stressful, times of the past. Unfortunately, this farm burned in 1910. (HBHS.)

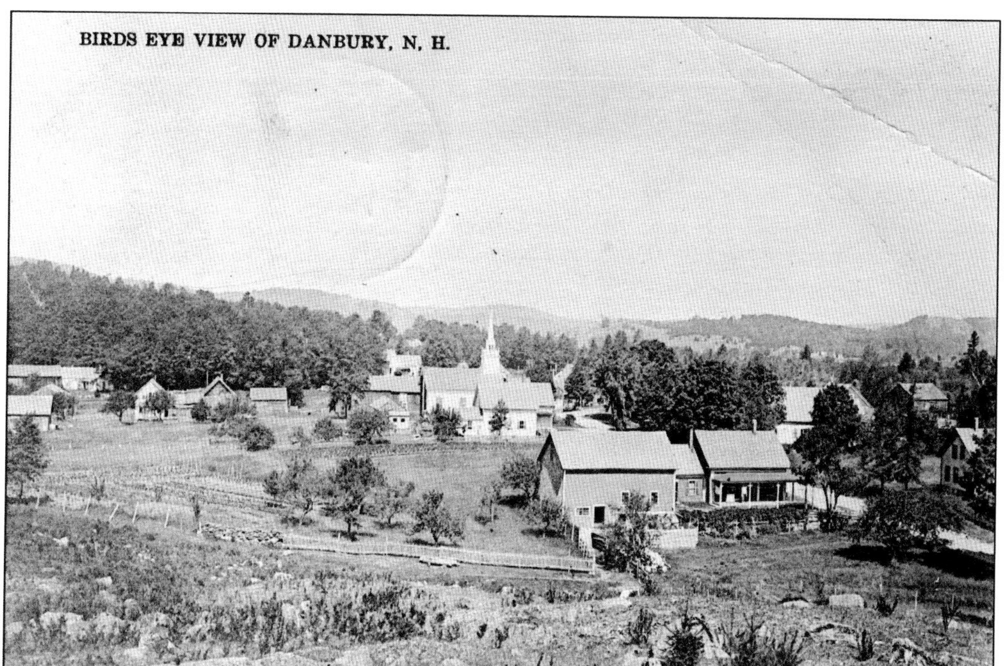

This pretty bird's-eye view of Danbury village showing several farms and the church steeple would be quite difficult to get today considering the forest growth since the date of this photograph in 1910. (MW.)

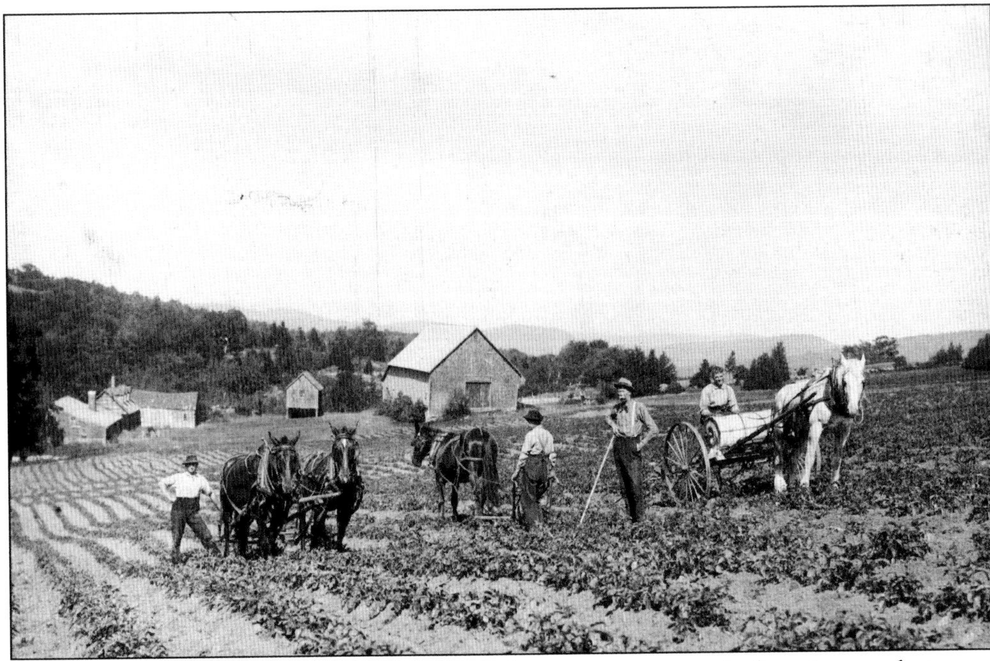

From 1850 to the early 1900s, New Hampshire towns saw a decline in population, as families moved west, young people traveled south to the mills, and the railroad pushed itself through the region to points north. However, the local farmer could still make a decent living. In this *c.* 1900 view at the David Atwood Farm in Bridgewater, workers tend large fields of produce. (WF.)

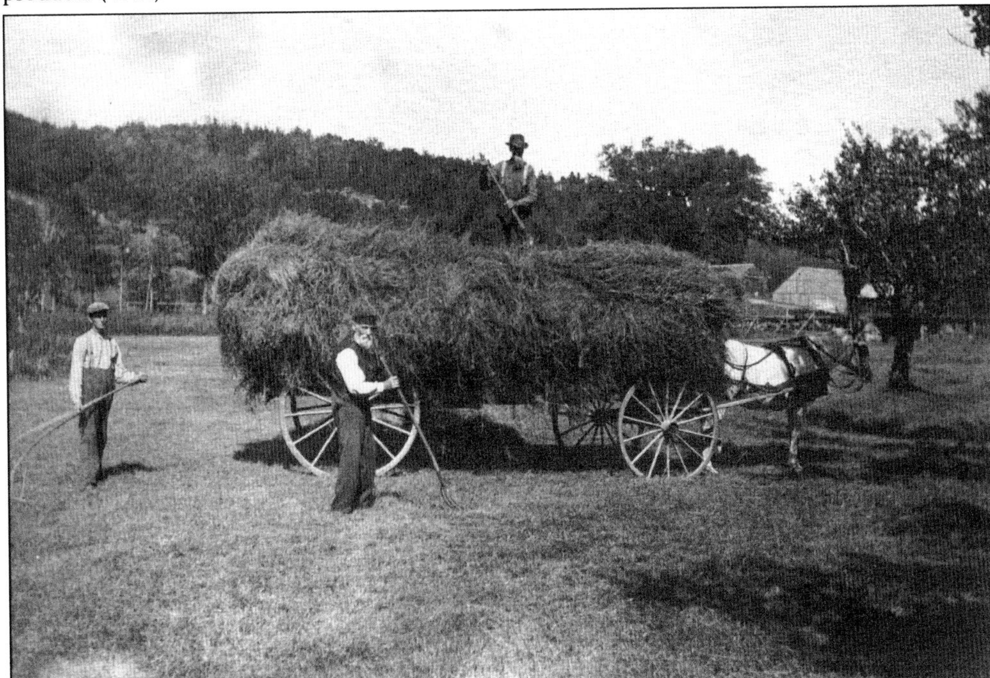

This image of Groton, taken sometime before 1910, shows young and old alike pitching-in to get the all-important crop of hay on its way to the barn. (HBHS.)

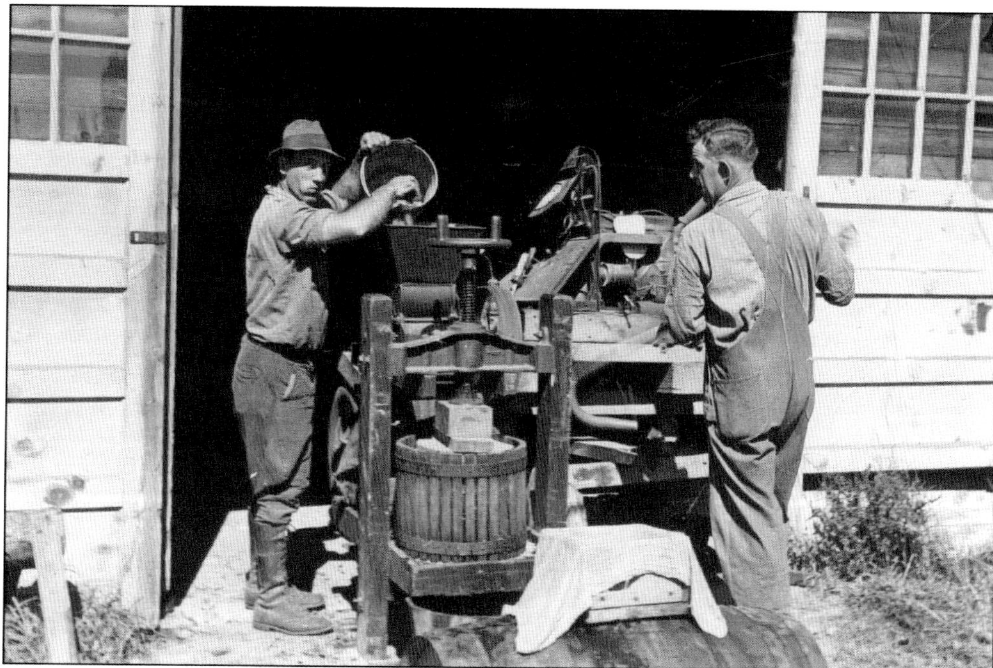

Through necessity, farmers have always been creative and practical in the supplementing of food and beverage. Here, Ozzie Morrill and Earl Gray of old Hill village crush apples for their larder of thirst-quenching cider. (HHS.)

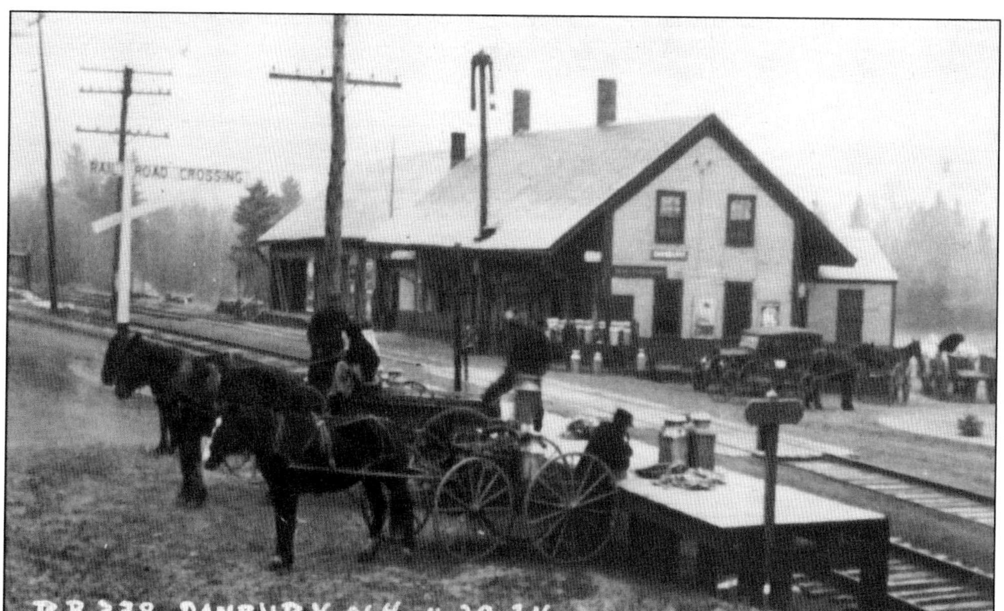

"Early to bed, early to rise" is an appropriate discipline for farmer A.J. Phelps Jr. Shown at Danbury station *c.* 1924, Phelps is picking up the milk jugs for the next delivery. (JP.)

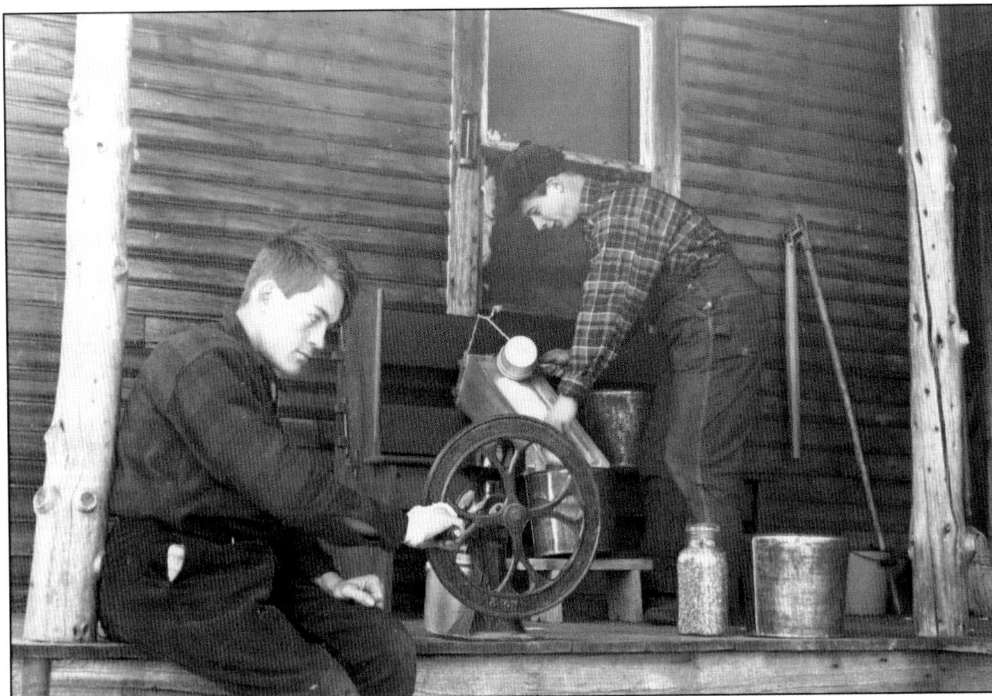

Nothing is more delectable than a slice of home-baked bread, warm from the oven. When flour was the yield of home-grown wheat and rye, milled to perfection by brothers Ernest and Sherman Wadhams of Alexandria, it must have been the best ever. This photograph was taken c. 1930. (AHS.)

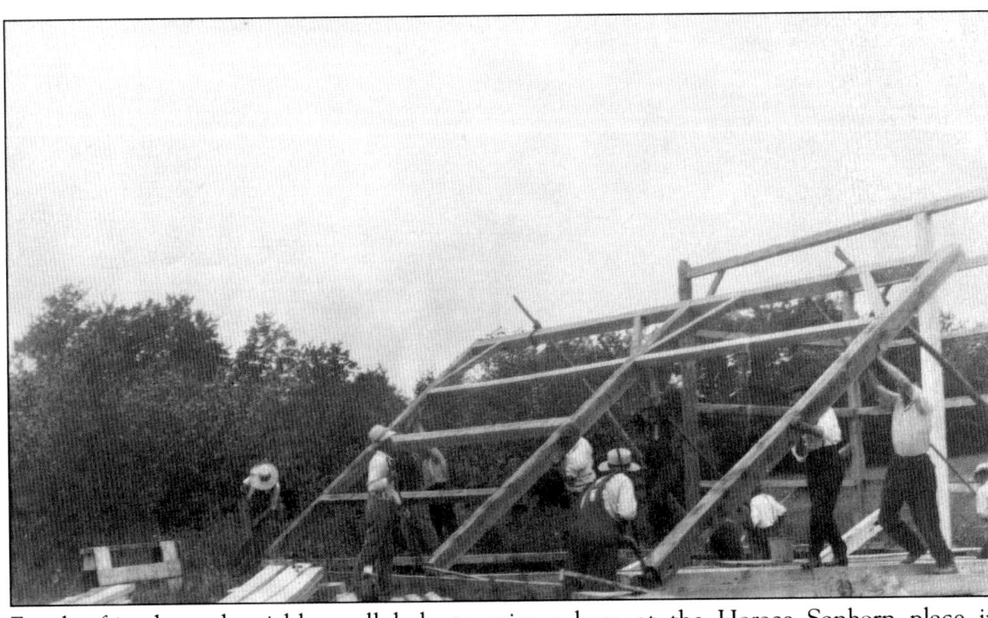

Family, friends, and neighbors all help to raise a barn at the Horace Sanborn place in Bridgewater. (BWHS.)

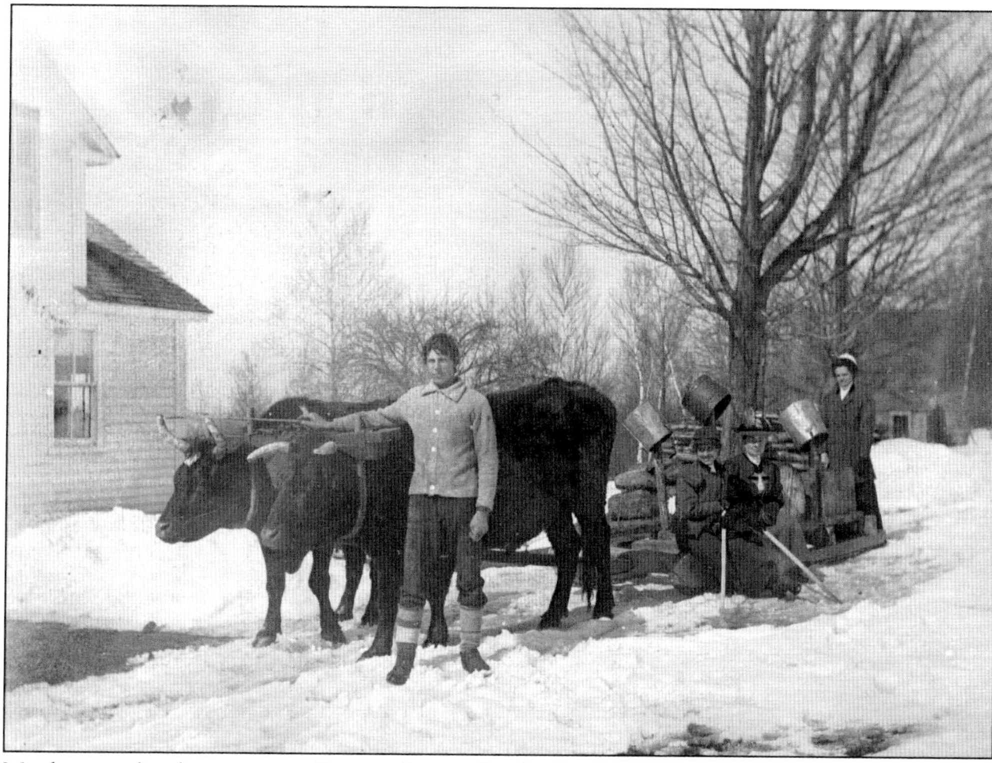

Maple syrup has been an excellent cash crop for the farmer with a substantial sugarbush on his acreage. In this *c.* 1912 photograph, taken at the Webster Farm in Bridgewater, sugaring was a family occasion led by a fine yoke of oxen. (WF.)

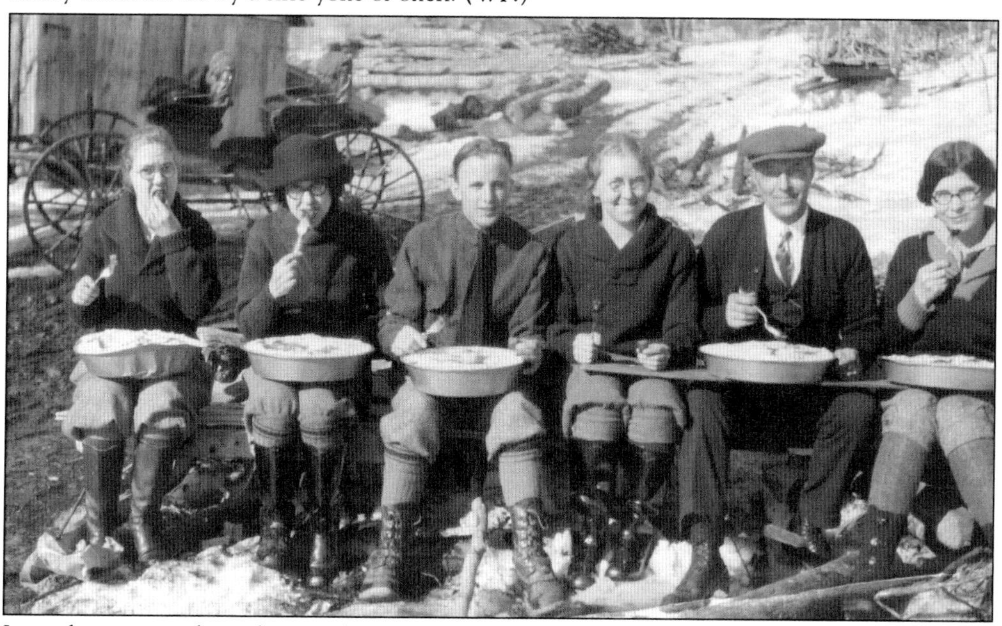

In early spring, when the maple sap is running and the snow is nearly gone, what better way to celebrate than with a sugaring-off party in Alexandria? This photograph was taken *c.* 1915. (AHS.)

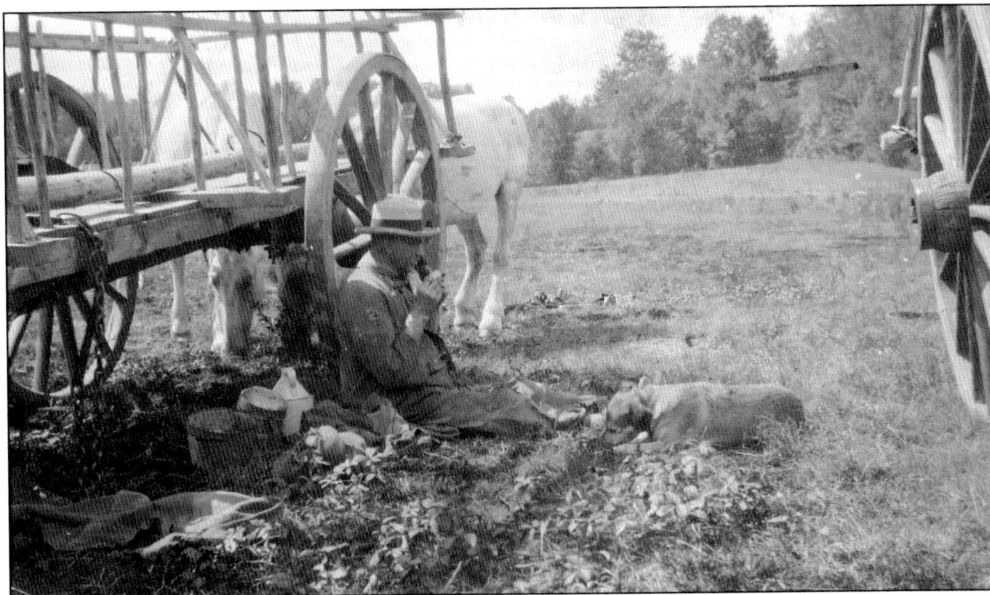

Long ago, somewhere in Danbury, a gentleman farmer took his noon meal alongside his faithful companions while hay wagons stood empty and idle. (JP.)

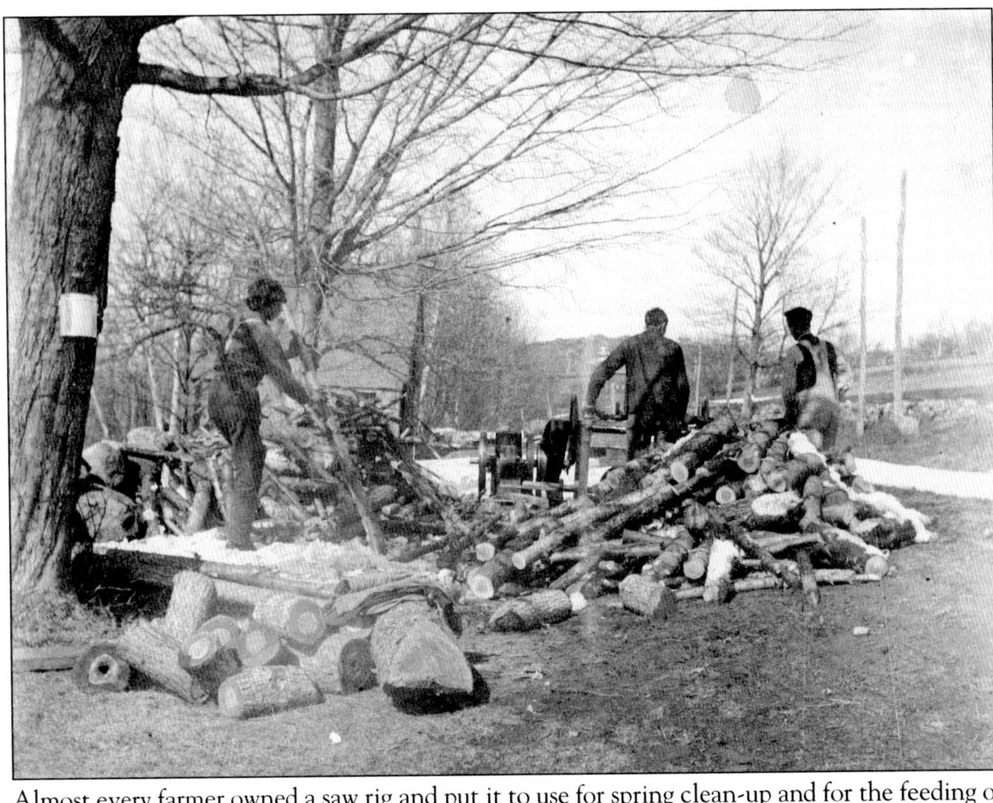

Almost every farmer owned a saw rig and put it to use for spring clean-up and for the feeding of numerous wood-burning stoves and fireplaces. In this *c.* 1903 photograph, the folks at Webster Farm in Bridgewater appear to be cleaning windfalls from winter's rage. (WF.)

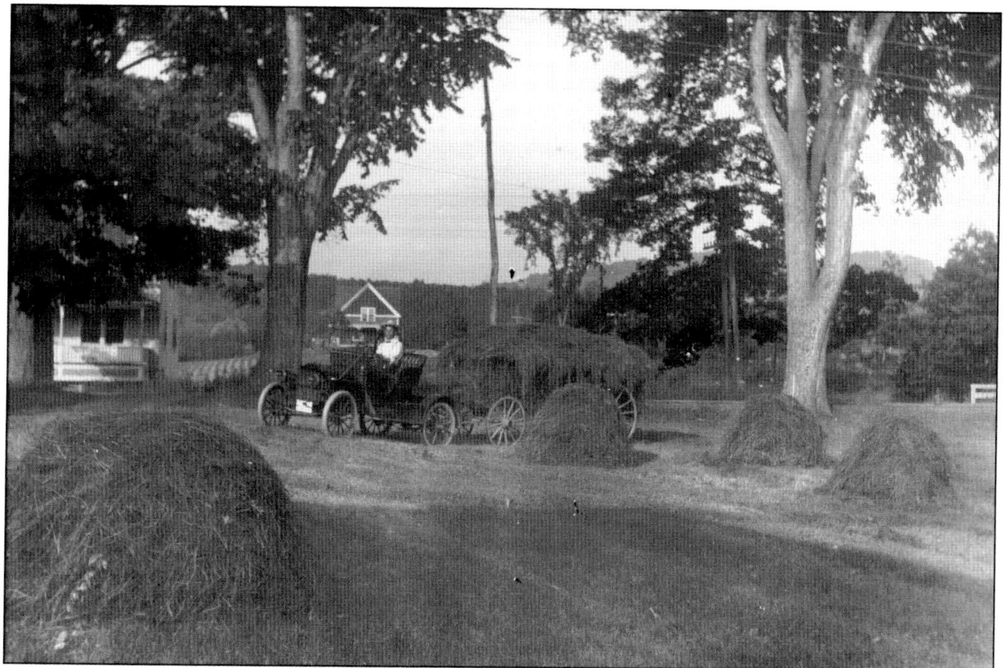

The character of the old-school farmer was just as honorably shown in his ingenuity as in his constant struggle with weather treacheries. It was crucial that the newly mown hay be taken to shelter—whether by horse, oxen, or Model T. This photograph was taken *c.* 1920. (HHS.)

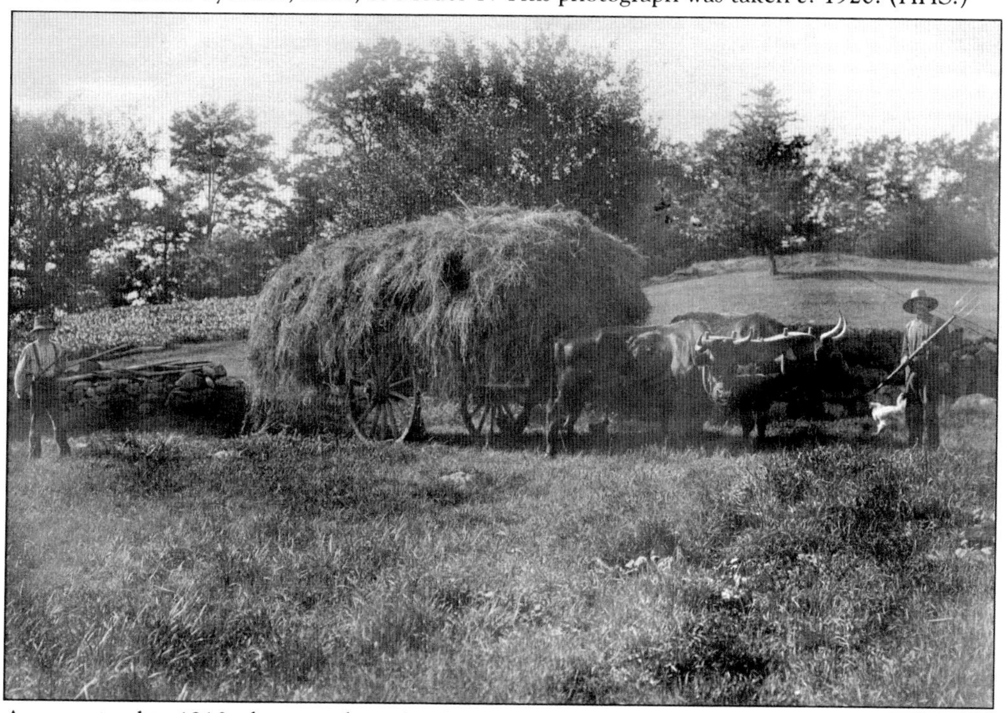

As seen in this 1910 photograph, a family farm in Hebron loads loose hay onto the wagon with pitchforks. It is strenuous work in hot weather, and uncertain clouds usually demanded expediency. (HBHS.)

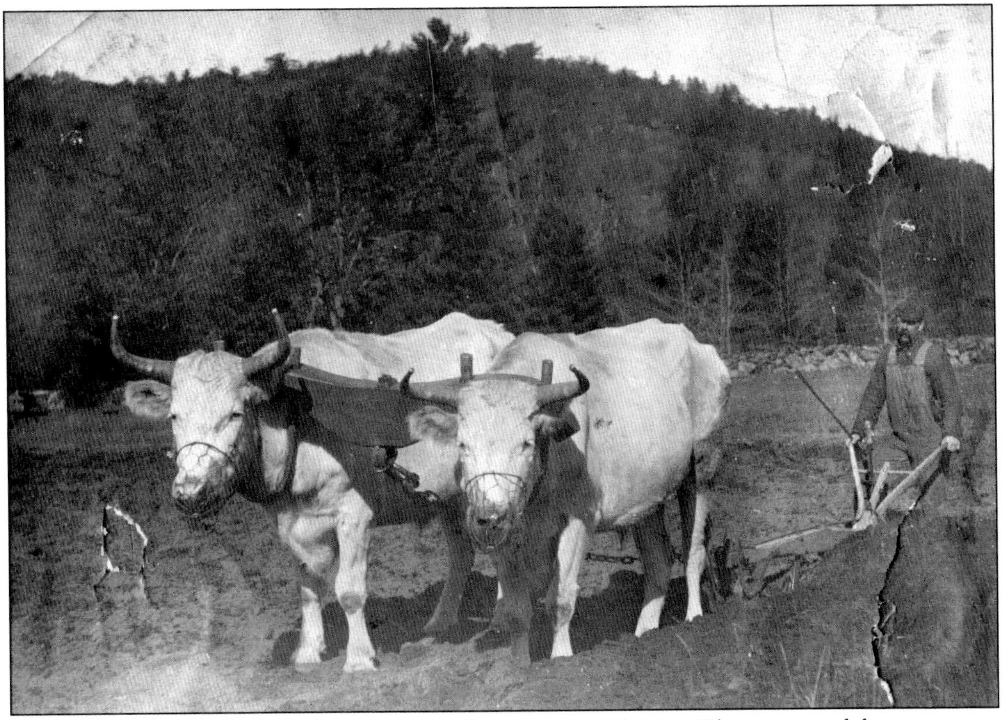

It is safe to say that no early farmer was without a team of oxen. The oxen and farmer were a unique unit with a special language between them. Here, J. Spaulding Morrison and his oxen are breaking ground at his Bridgewater farm in 1905. (BWHS.)

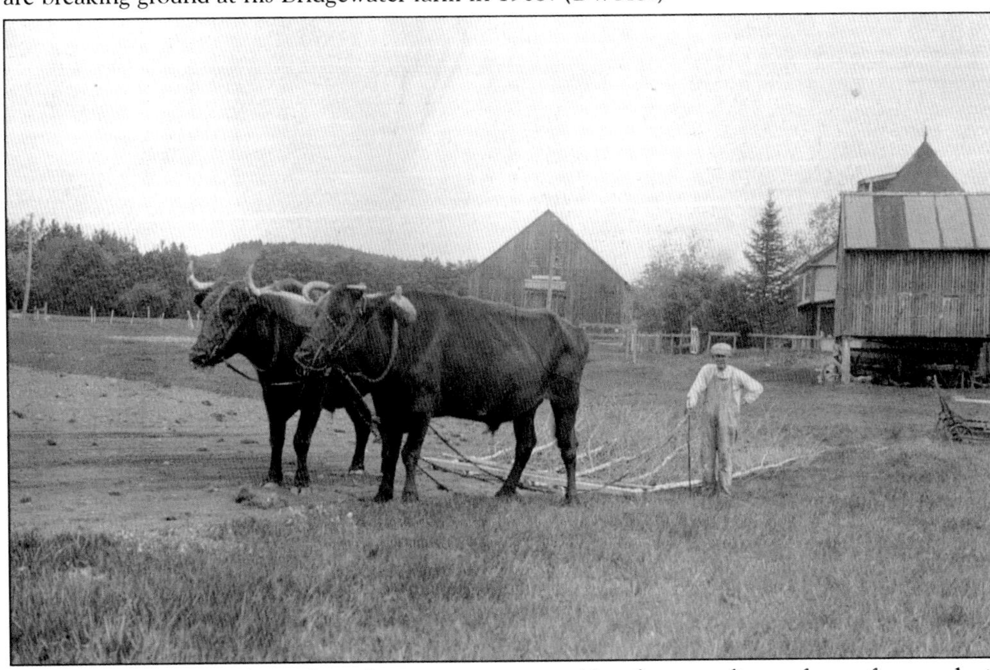

At the Fisk Farm in Alexandria, this oxen team, capable of extraordinary feats of strength, is led with the farmer's gentle word and hand to proceed with precision for this rather delicate chore. This photograph was taken *c.* 1920. (AHS.)

This c. 1915 winter scene shows three friends, from left to right, Paul Day, E. Gordon Parker, and Walter Dickerson, with Parker's oxen at Murray Hill in Hill. It is quite probable that the sleigh is carrying a load of firewood. (HHS.)

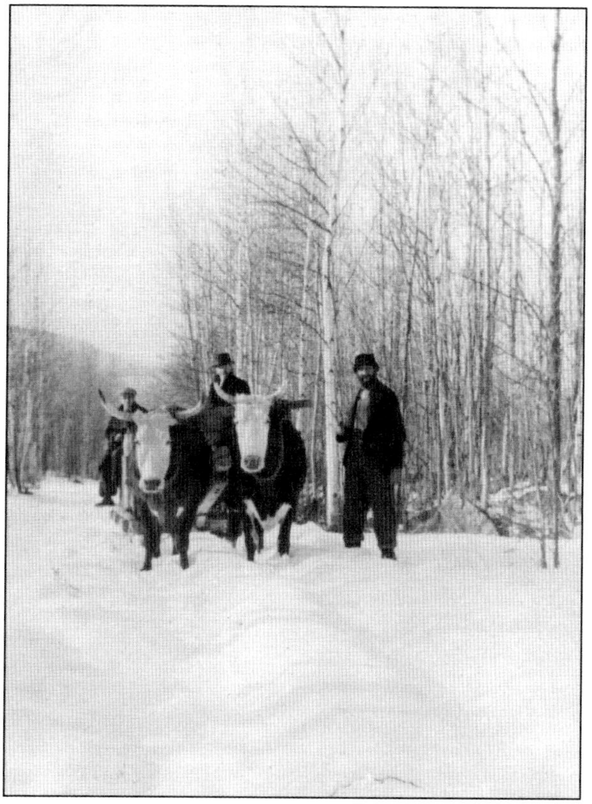

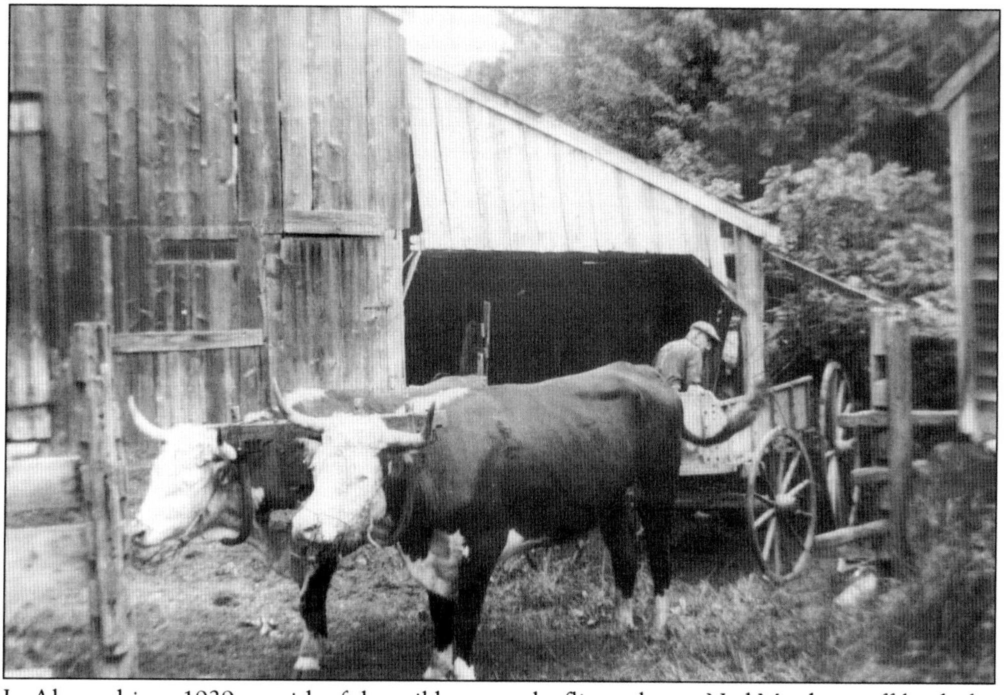

In Alexandria c. 1939, a swish of the tail keeps pesky flies at bay as Ned Matthews off-loads the cart being hauled by oxen that belong to Archie Bucklin. (AHS.)

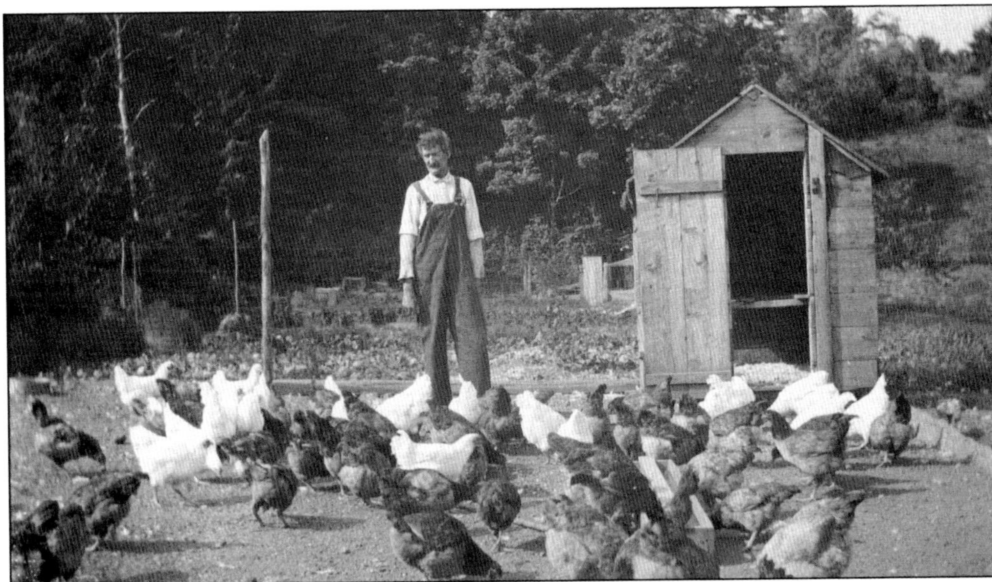

At one time every farm had chickens, which provided meat and eggs for the table. Those eggs not needed in the kitchen were taken to town and sold. Traditionally, the farmer's wife would care for the chickens, and the egg money would be hers for something special. Chickens require only modest housing and a minimal amount of feed. They are fun to observe as they dance about in search of bugs, worms, and tiny pebbles. In this *c.* 1920 view, Joel A. Dufur, of old Hill shows off his beautiful flock of chickens. (HHS.)

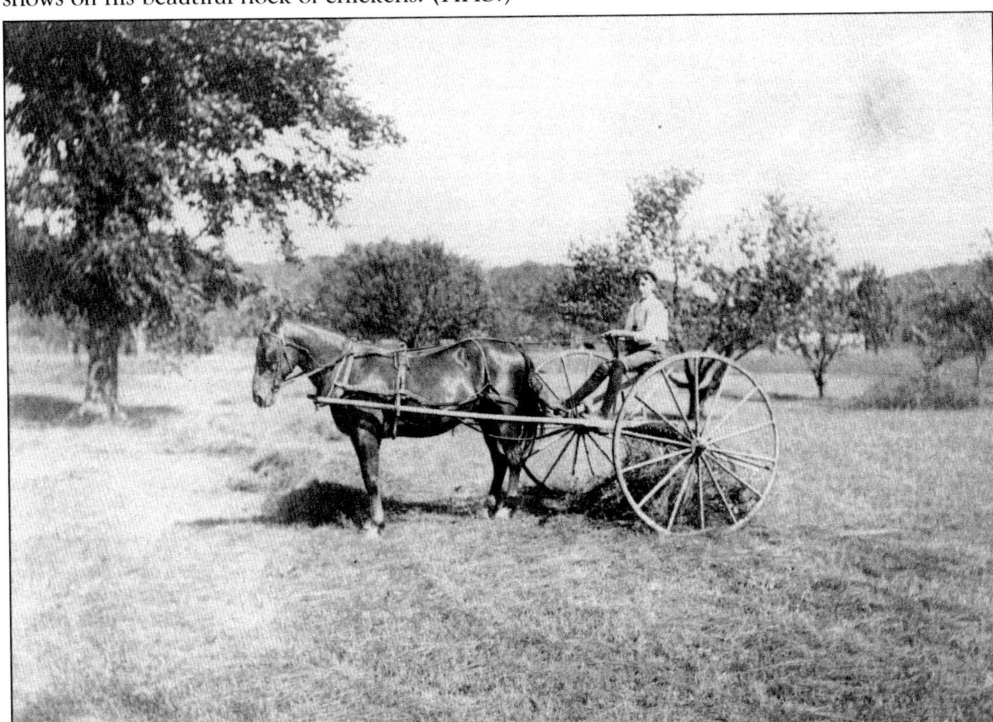

Henry Blodgett of Groton rakes his orchard with horse and modern ride-in rake. This photograph was taken before 1910. (HBHS.)

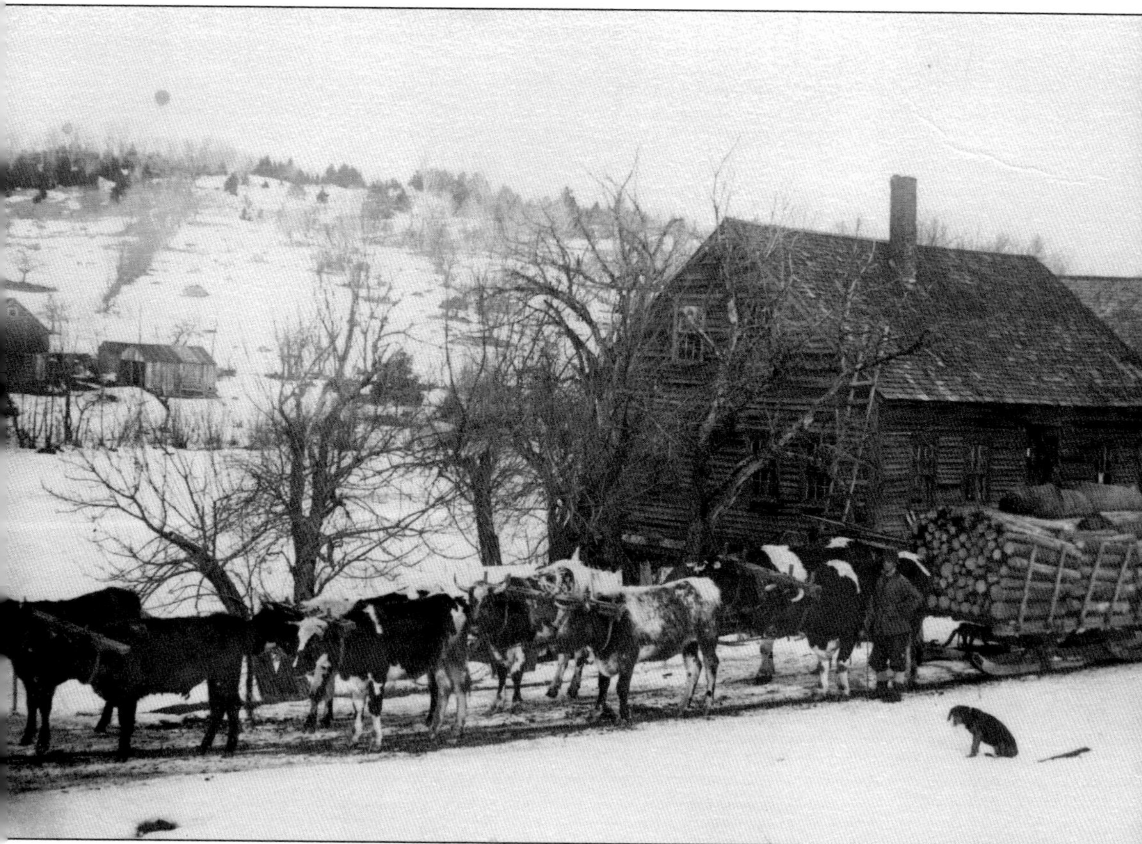

In the winter, logs were hauled by a logging sled, or skidway, led by oxen or horses. Some of the cordwood was taken to a local sawmill, and some was cut into "chimney-place" lengths with a farmer's saw rig. The trees were felled one by one with an axe or crosscut saw. The trees were then rolled onto the sled. In this *c.* 1920 view, Lyle Gale of Alexandria has just brought in cordwood with four teams of oxen. (AHS.)

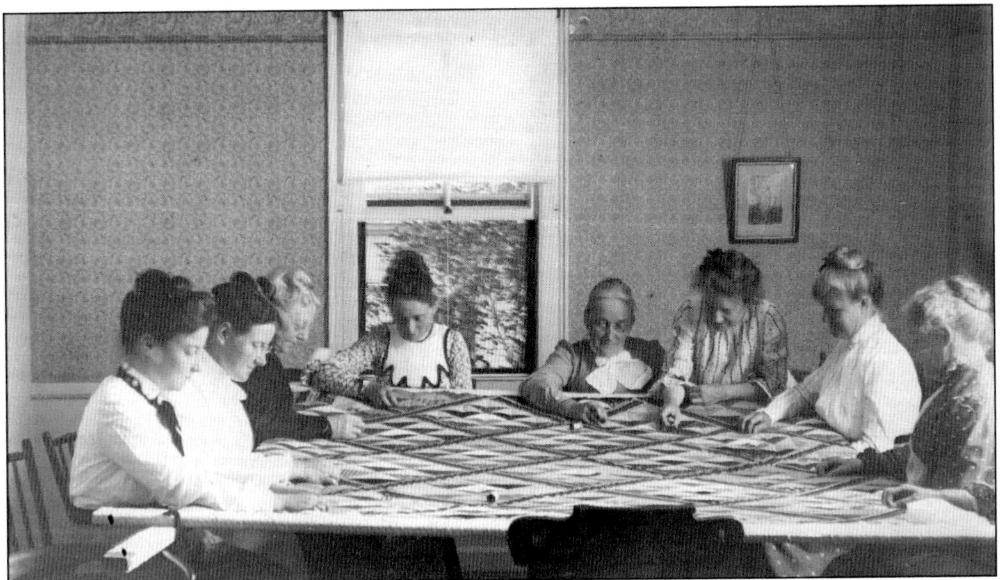

Quilt making in America was at its height between 1830 and 1870. However, women of the prairies had been utilizing fabric from old calico dresses for patchwork quilts since as early as 1750. Fabrics were brought from Europe and were costly, making it imperative that every scrap be used by the woman of the household to make bedding. Soon, quilt making evolved into a social event known as a quilting bee, where neighbors, both men and women, would attend daylong parties that included a supper, dancing, and singing. In this *c.* 1904 view, women at Webster Farm join for the festive occasion. (WF.)

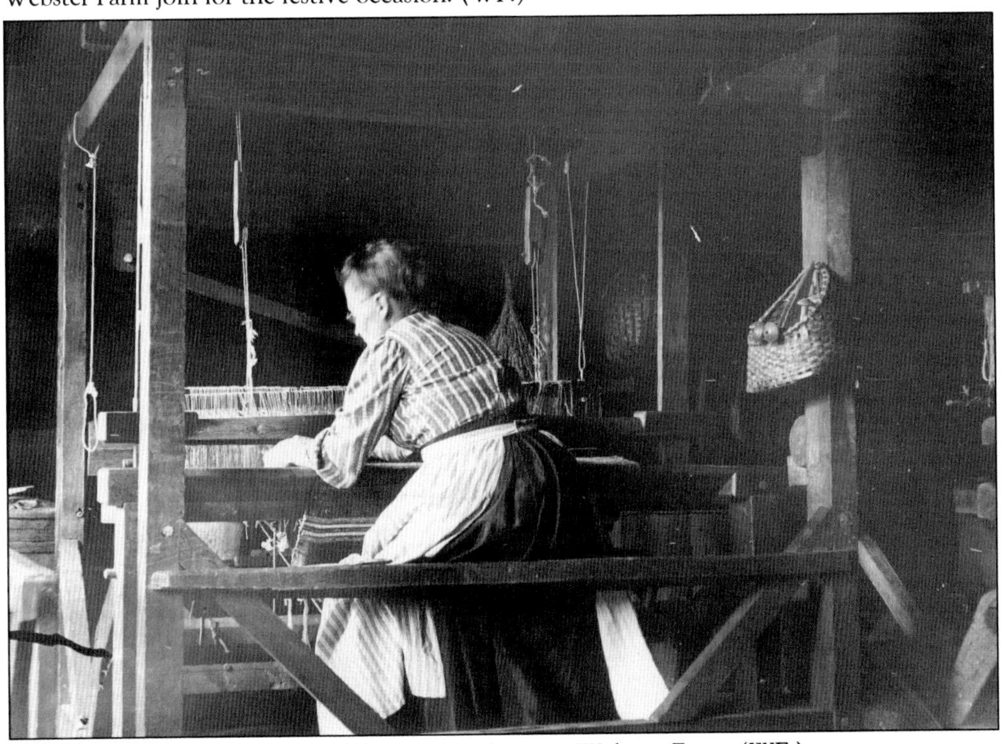

Here, a woman weaves a beautiful rug on the loom at Webster Farm. (WF.)

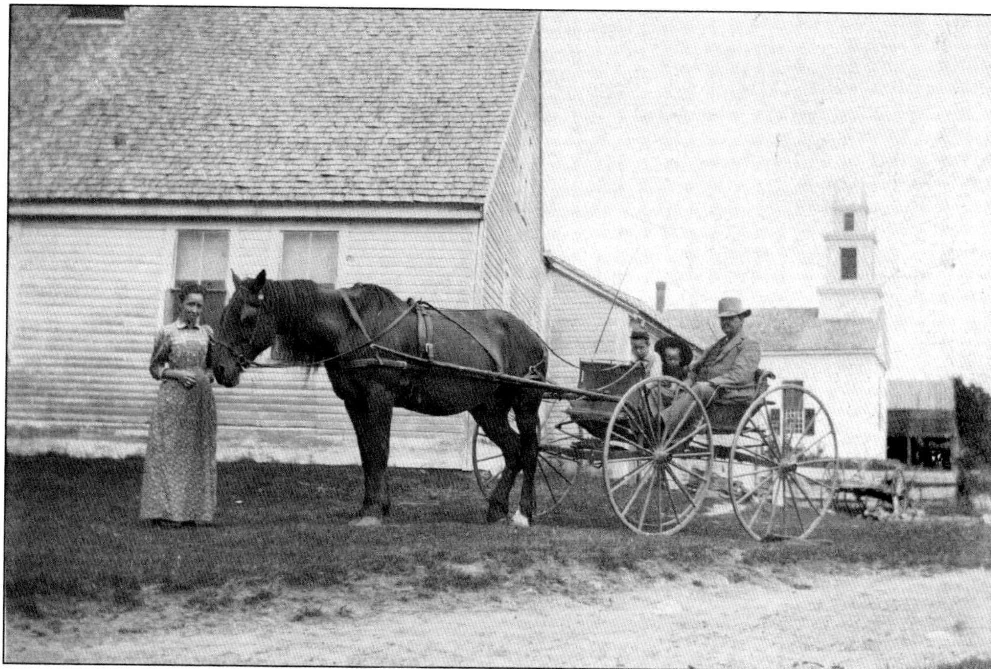

Inscribed in simple fashion upon this early photograph are the names of this family in North Groton. From left to right, they are, Amy, Old Pete the horse, Albert, Roscoe, and Perly Duncklee. The house behind them is one of Groton's oldest homesteads. (GHS.)

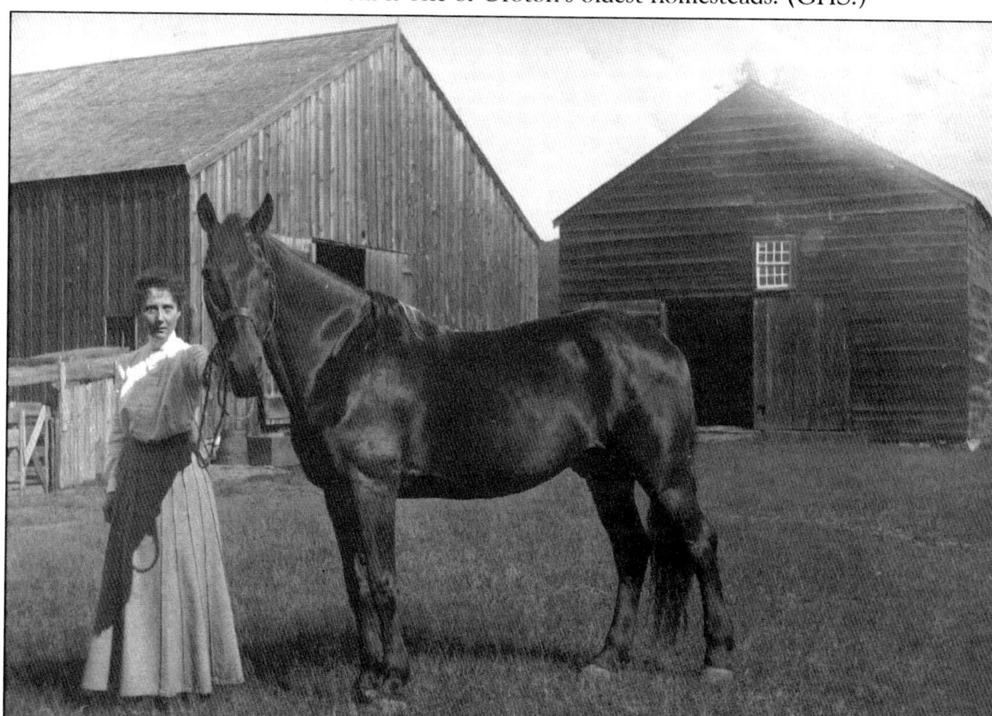

A splendid horse and an admiring young woman pose for this c. 1890 photograph at Webster Farm in Bridgewater. (WF.)

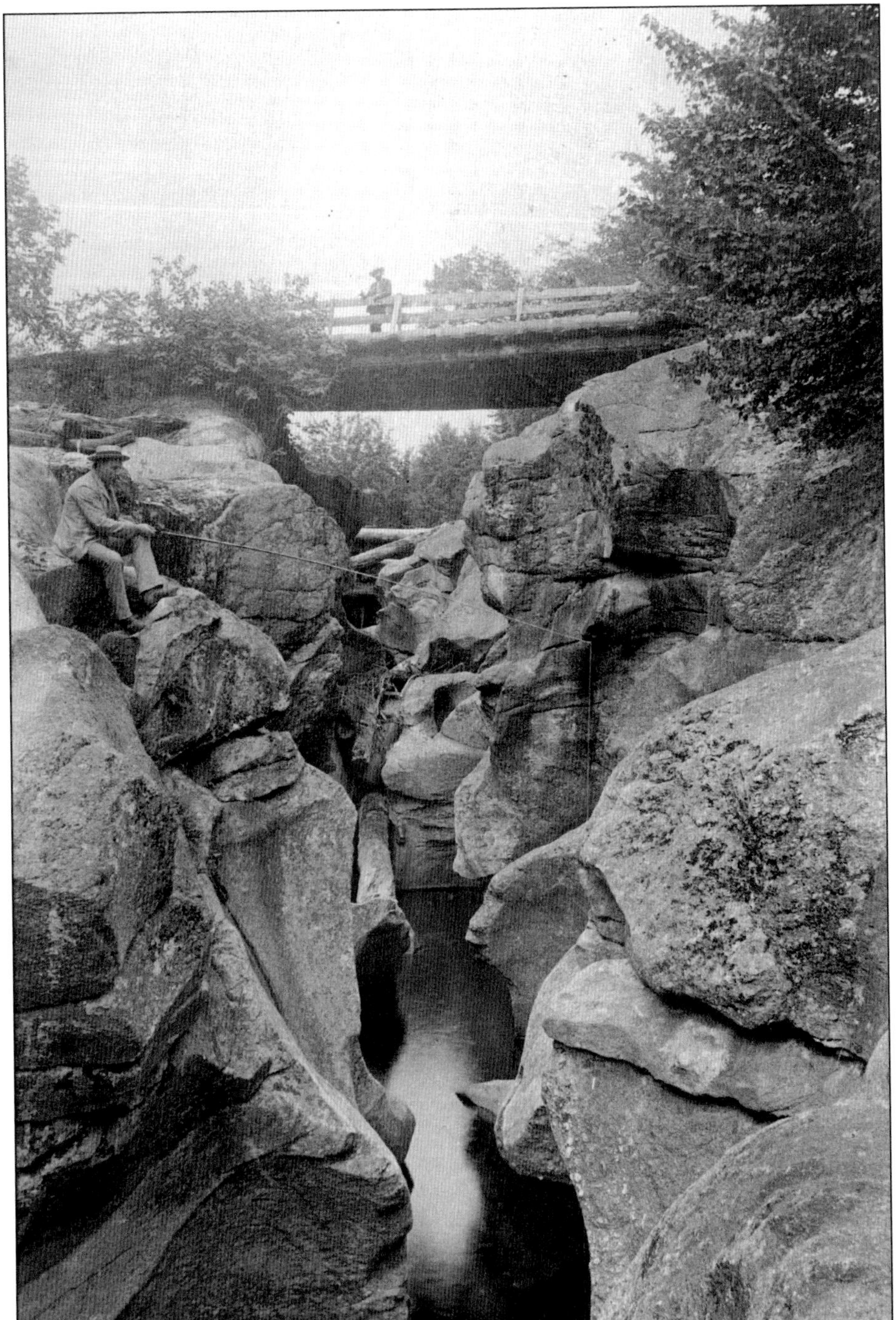

Sculptured Rocks, located in Groton, is an unusual area of graceful, curious potholes that have been carved and shaped by waterborne stones and sediment over several millennia. The Cockermouth River is the water source over which a wooden bridge was constructed. There, excellent views of the romantic pools, falls, and rock formations can be enjoyed. The Cockermouth is said to be a splendid source for catching fish. Apparently, the fellow perched atop a rock at the left agrees. (GHS.)

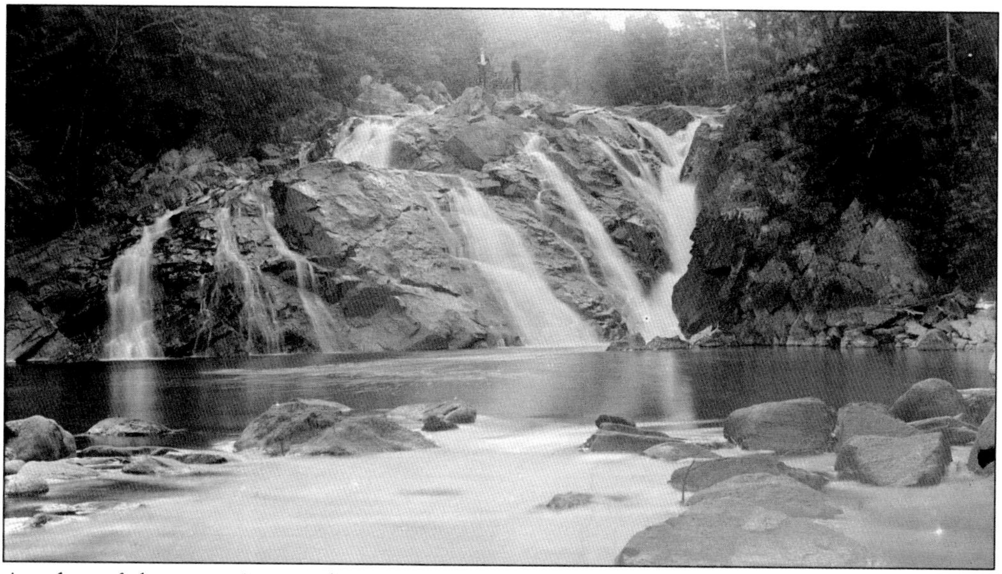

Another of the region's special sites is Profile Falls, located about two miles south of Bristol village in Hill, where the clear waters of Smith's River cascade over the ledges. In the early 1890s, a hamlet simply referred to as "the foot of the mountain" was located here. It had a store, post office, school, excelsior mill, and a dozen dwellings. Byron B. Tobie discovered the excellent profile on a rock outcropping and named the falls and the village Profile Falls. (HHS.)

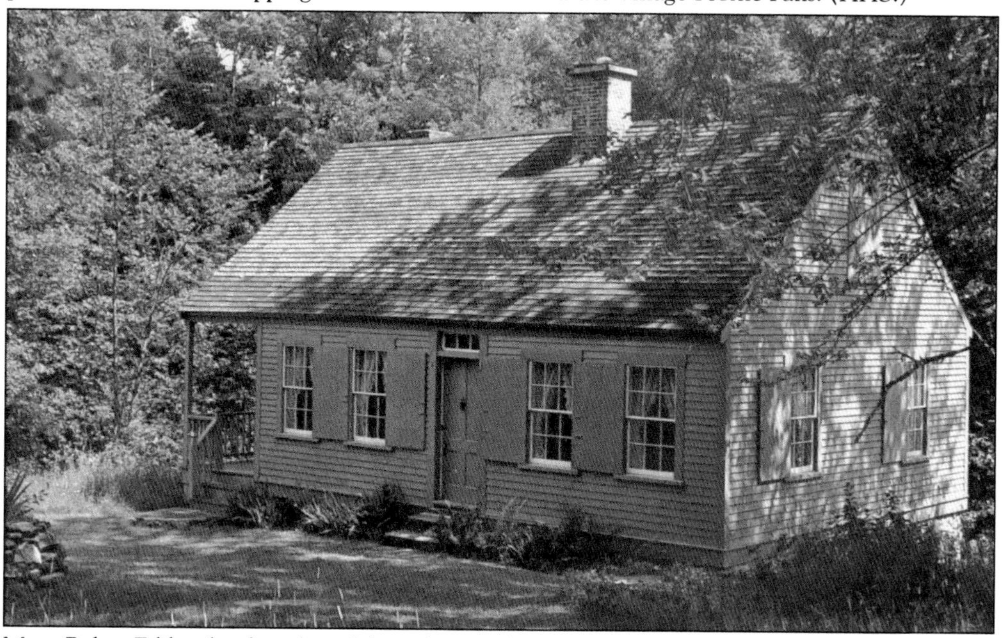

Mary Baker Eddy, the founder of the religious denomination the Church of Christ, Scientist, or more commonly, Christian Science, was born in 1821. She was an invalid until an inspiring experience transformed her life. Compelled to share her views, she wrote *Science and Health with Key to the Scriptures*, which was published in 1875. She also established the newspaper the *Christian Science Monitor* in 1908. The historic house pictured here is where she lived in the late 1850s. Located in North Groton, it is now owned by the Longyear Historical Society, and is open for public tours. (GHS.)

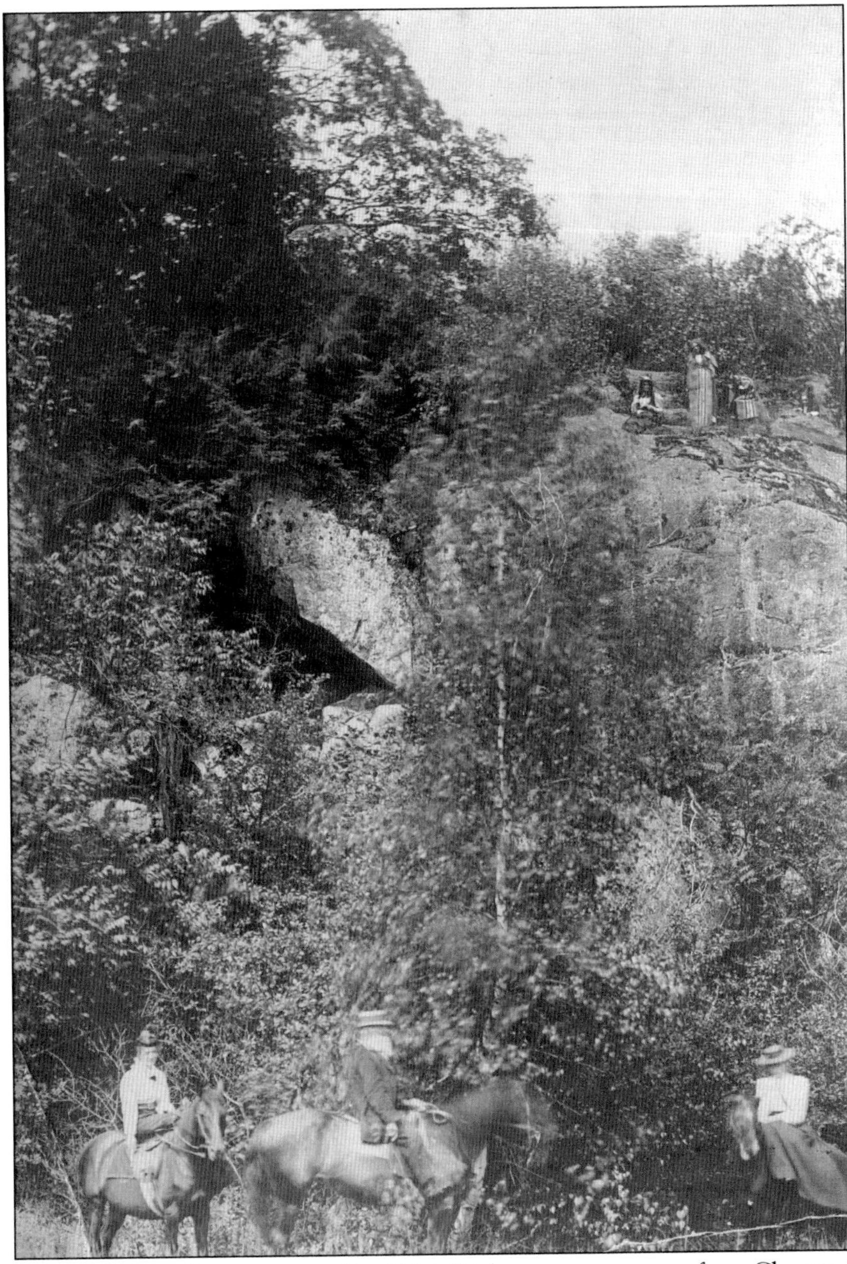

In October of 1764, as the story goes, David M. Webster, a young man from Chester, built his new cabin on a plot of land located at the confluence of the Pemigewasset and Baker Rivers in Plymouth. He then sent word for his wife, Elizabeth, to join him in the wilderness. Along the river near New Hampton, the horse stumbled and threw Elizabeth Webster and her baby into the river. Drying their clothing had caused a long delay, and they were still a long way from Plymouth when darkness made it difficult to see the trail. They then discovered a cave and took refuge there. During the night, Indians held a pow-wow on the top of the cave and Elizabeth "had to choke the baby almost to death to keep him from crying." The next day, they safely reached Plymouth. The Websters and their descendants came to play an important role in the settling and history of Bridgewater. (WF.)

Six

Getting Around

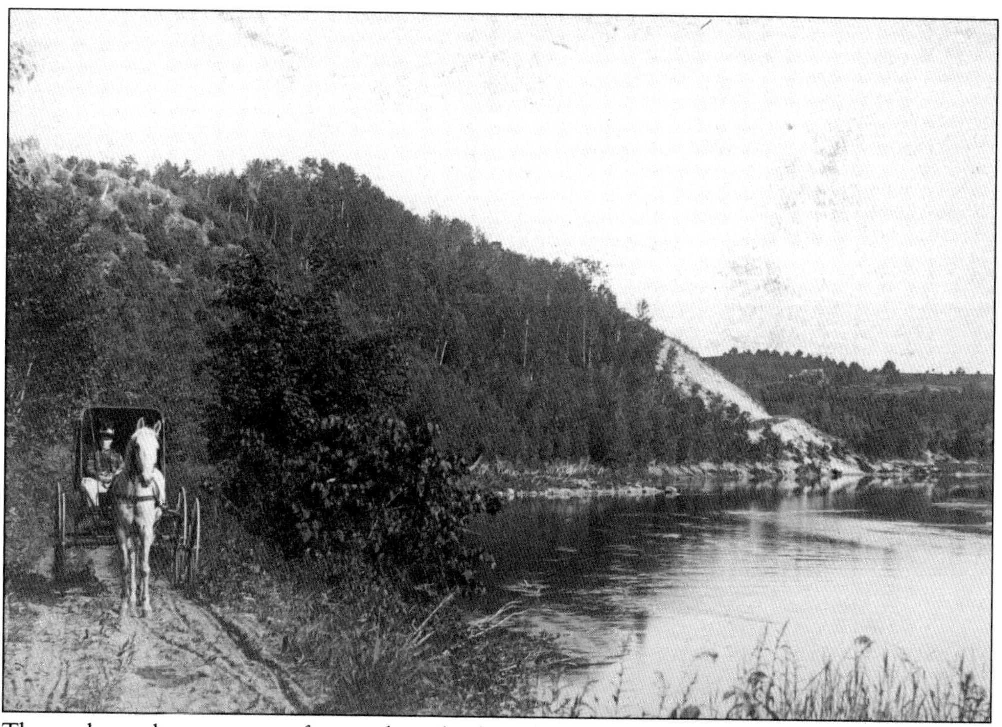

The early settlers came on foot or horseback or bumped along cart trails to the Newfound Lake region. Most carried only an axe for clearing land on which to build a crude shelter, a meager allotment of food, a flint for striking a fire, a bedtick, and a firearm for protection. Little consideration was given at that time to building and maintaining roads that would later carry vehicles, the likes of which could not have been imagined. Once settled, however, the rough trails of the 1700s developed into clear, wide turnpikes. The building of the railroads offered greater opportunities for industry and tourist trade, and the contrivance of the automobile dramatically changed the lives of all Americans. In this c. 1890s image, a traveler with horse and buggy makes his way along the Pemigewasset River in Hill . (HHS.)

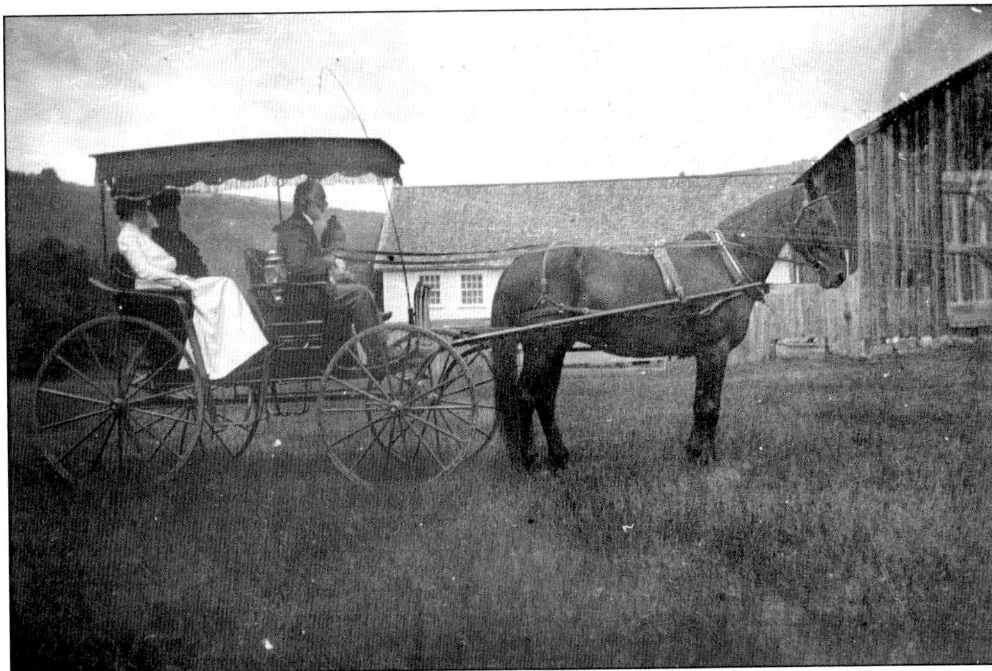

Going out in the "surrey with the fringe on top," these women of Webster Farm await the driver's command to the willing horse. (WF.)

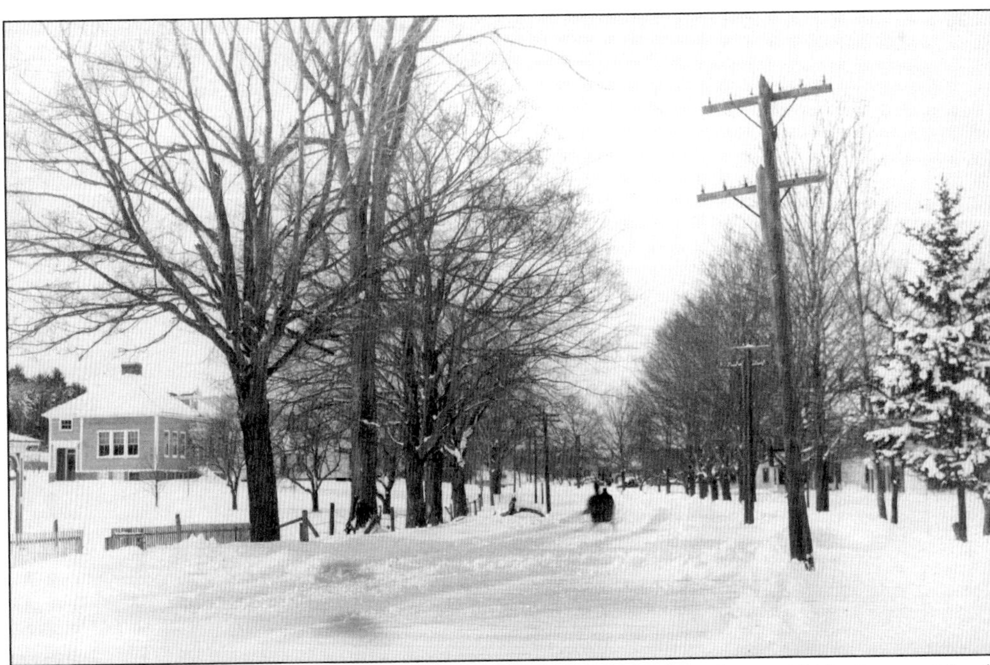

Winter snows often decreed the use of the sleigh for outings, as in this *c.* 1910 view on North Main Street in old Hill village. (HHS.)

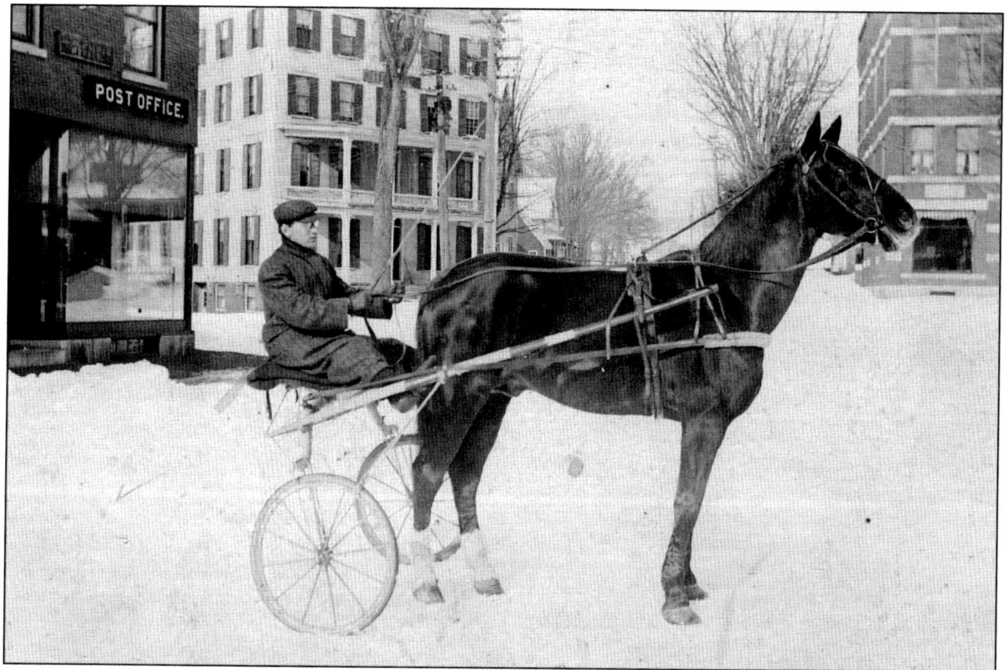

A sturdy horse and skilled sulky driver seem to have discovered a fine mode of transportation for the snow-covered streets of Bristol's Central Square. The old Hotel Bristol is pictured in the left center. (BHS.)

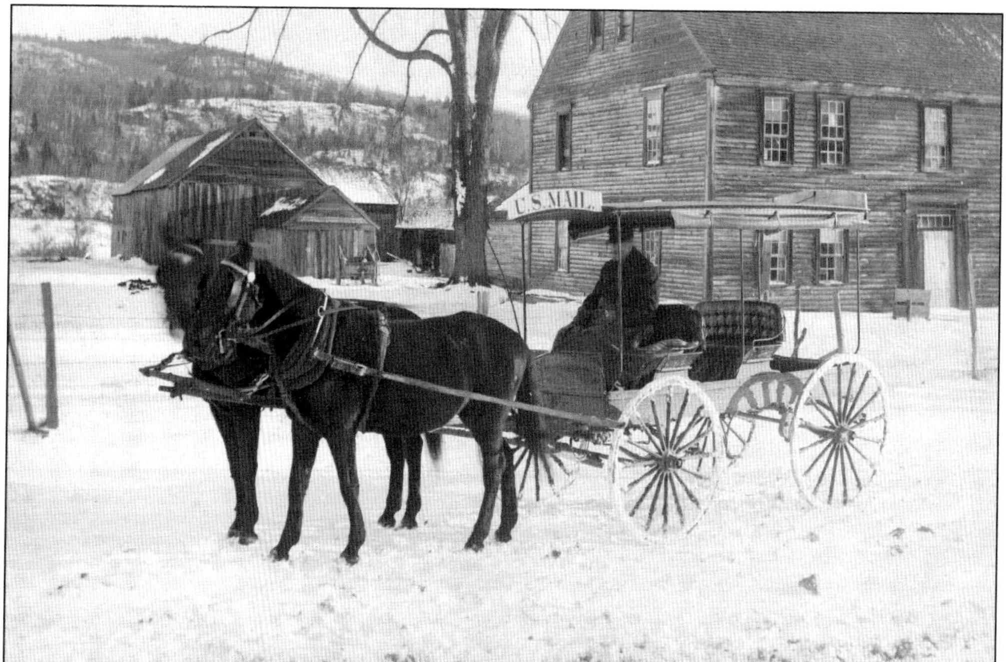

The U.S. mail was carried by stage from Bristol to Hebron and Groton on alternating days of the week. The stages that carried the mail all the way to Haverhill from Concord were four-horse coaches. Seen at the old Wheeler place in this *c.* 1909 photograph is driver Harry Ferrin. (HBHS.)

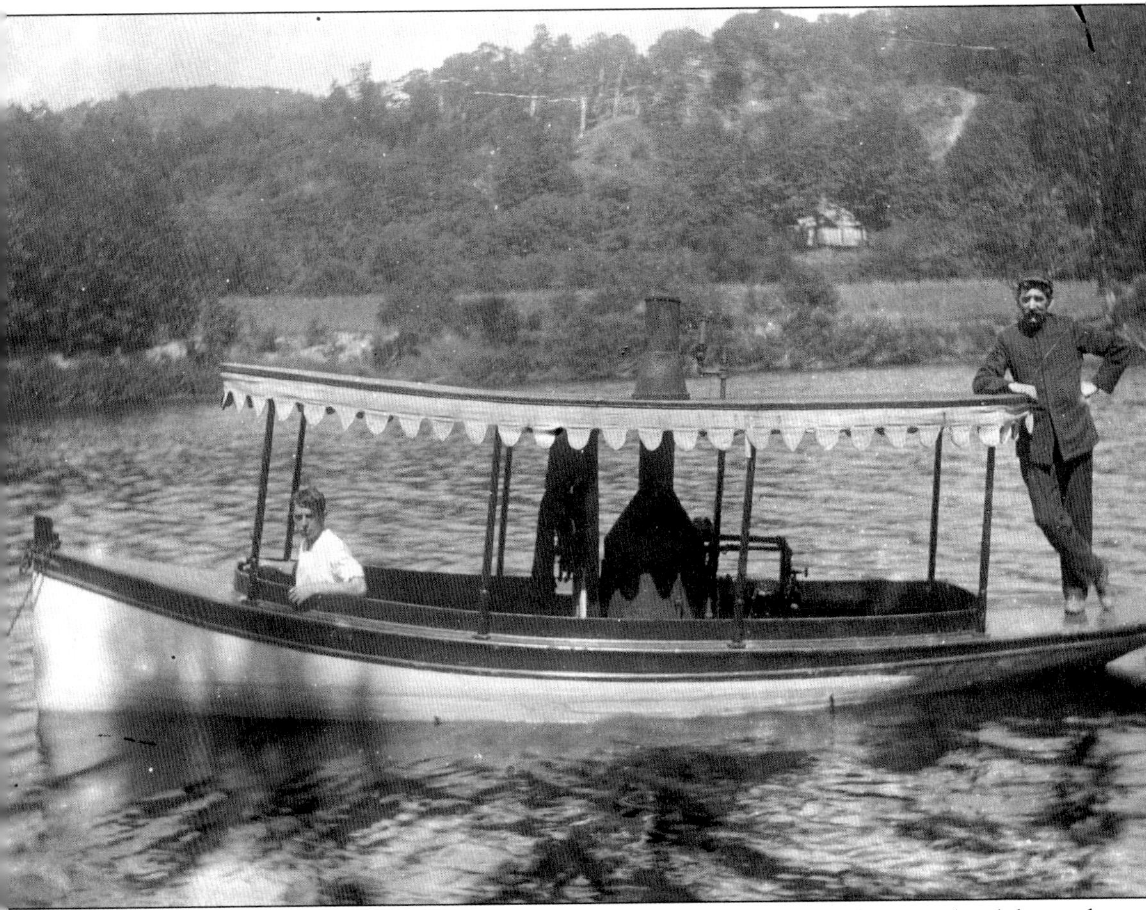

Crossing the Pemigewasset River by boat was a great challenge because the water level dropped about 10 feet every mile, making it rapid and dangerous. Cutting Favor, the first settler, ran a ferry across because he had land and sons on both sides of the river. By 1794, a Sanbornton man began running a public ferry, charging a fee for man and animal. Seen here is the public ferry, *c.* 1910. (HHS.)

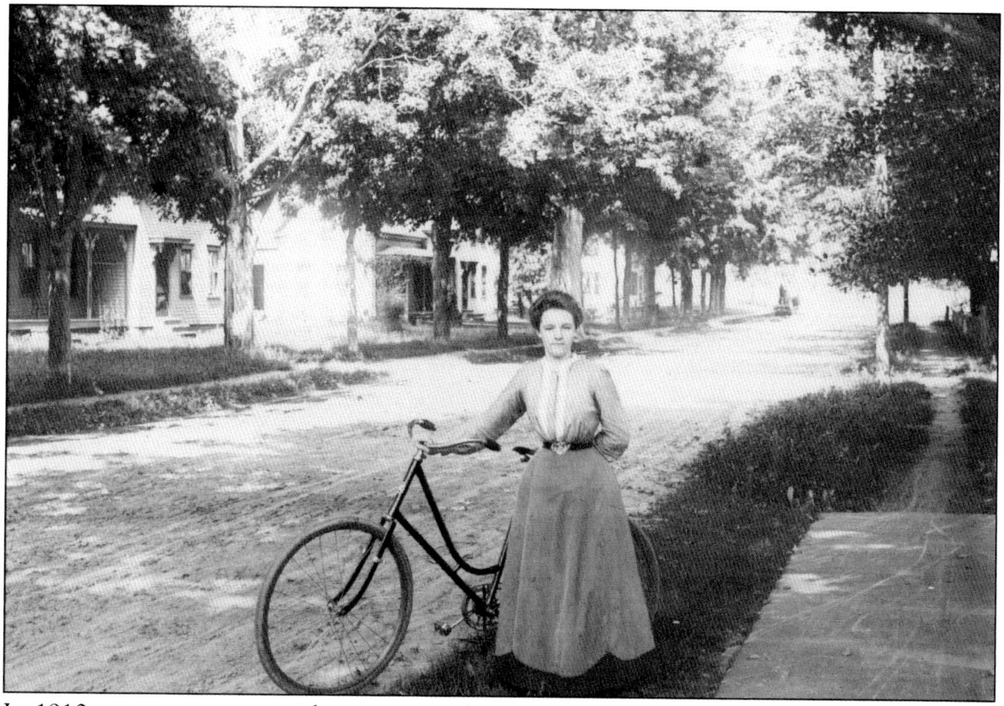

In 1910, a young woman with access to a fine bicycle was indeed fortunate. Here, on South Main Street in old Hill village, is one such person. (HHS.)

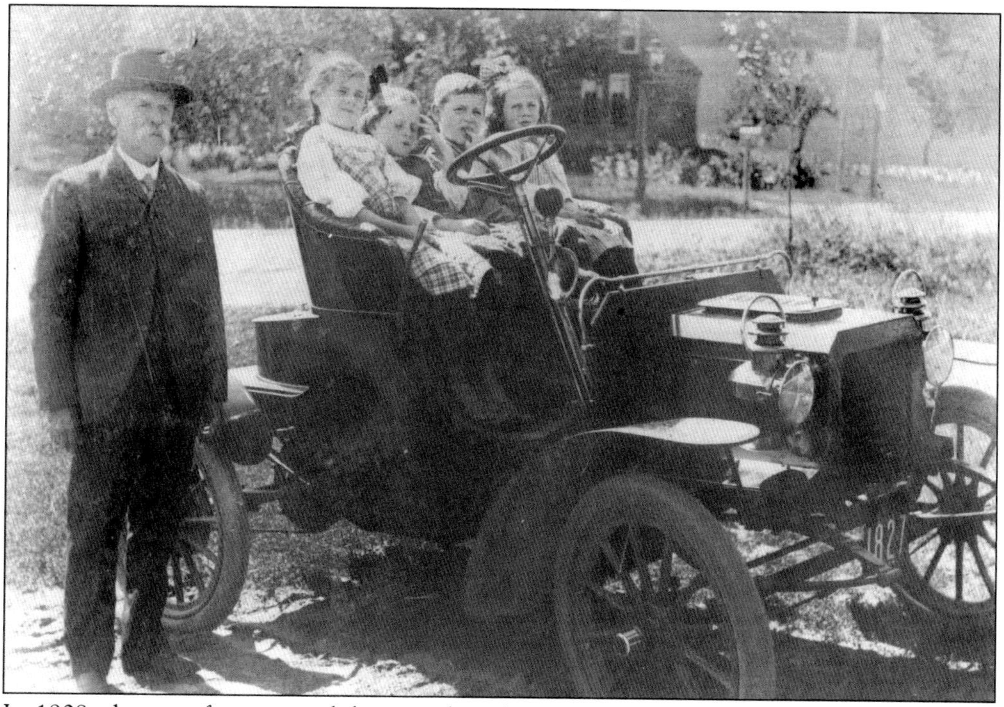

In 1908, the very first automobile arrived in the town of Hill. It was owned by William C. Kelley. His delighted passengers, from left to right, are Marion Mason, Margaret Kelley, Dana Kelley, and Myla Mason. (HHS.)

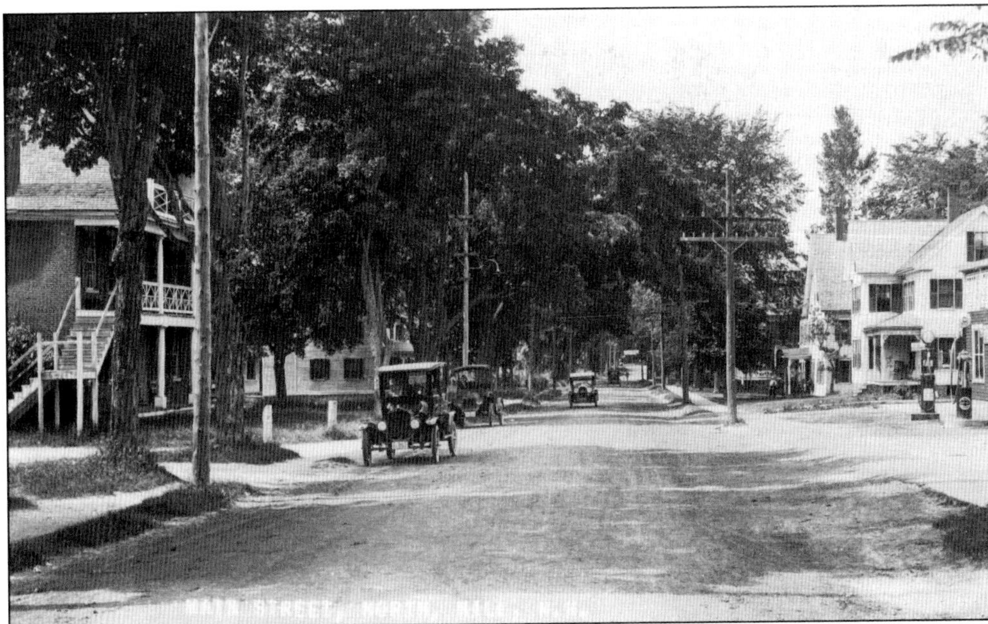

The drivers of these classic automobiles did not have to worry about rush-hour traffic or congestion on Main Street in Hill. On the left, the old hotel appears as it looked after it was converted to an apartment building. This photograph was taken *c.* 1930. (HHS.)

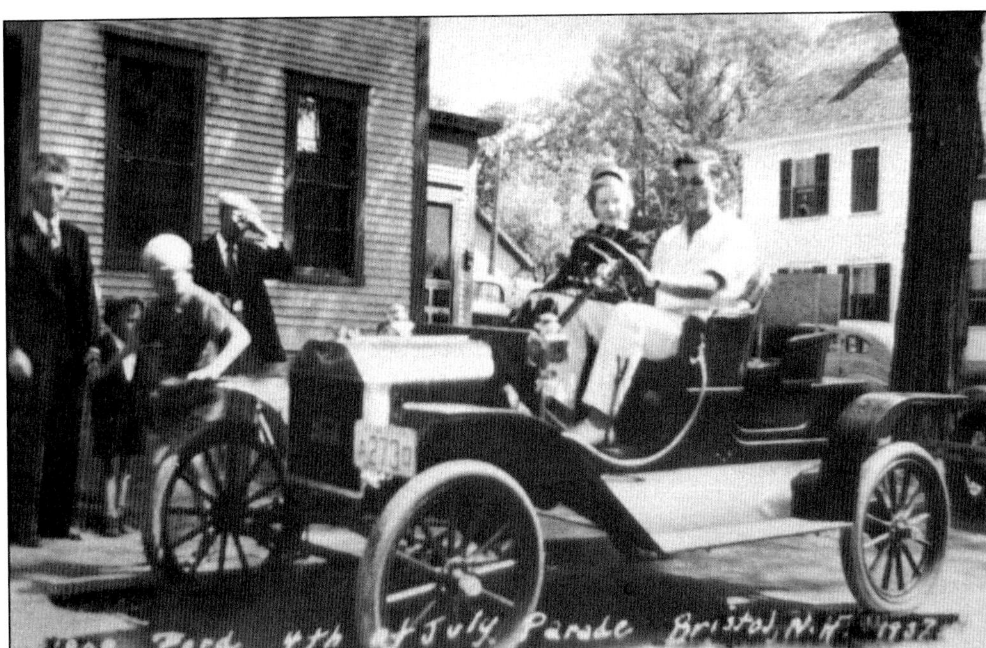

This photograph shows Seth Patten's 1909 Ford automobile in the 1937 Independence Day parade in Bristol. (AHS.)

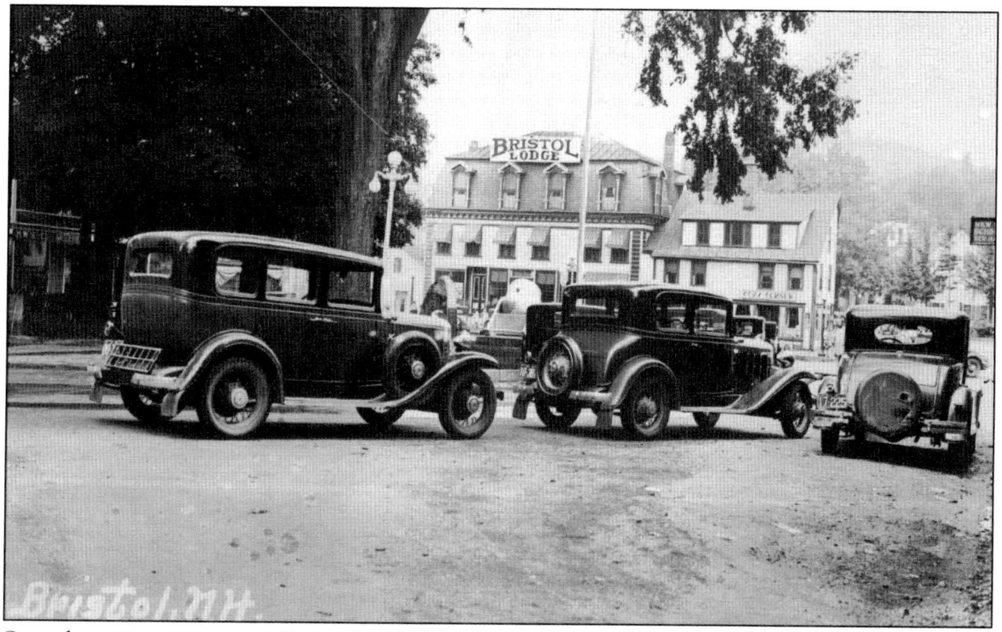

Seen here is a nice sampling of c. 1930s automobiles in Central Square, Bristol. Perhaps Saturdays then, as now, were busy with shopping and banking; or perhaps these people were jockeying for a good parking place from which to view a parade. The Bristol Lodge is pictured in the background. (BHS.)

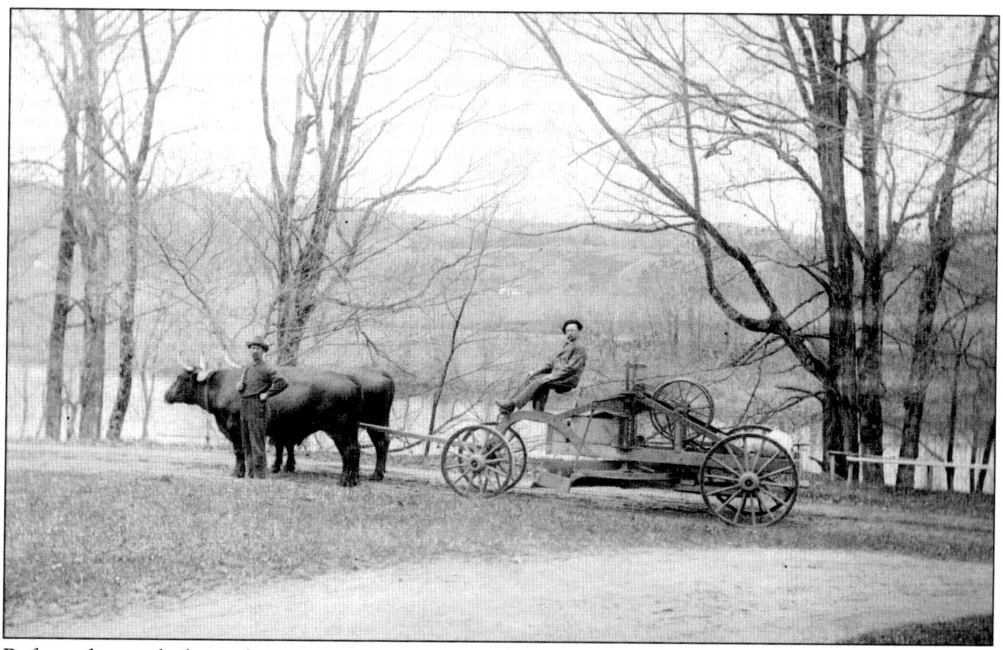

Before the asphalt surface came into use, road maintenance was accomplished with a road grader pulled by oxen. The road agent and assistant seen here are grading along the river in old Hill village. (HHS.)

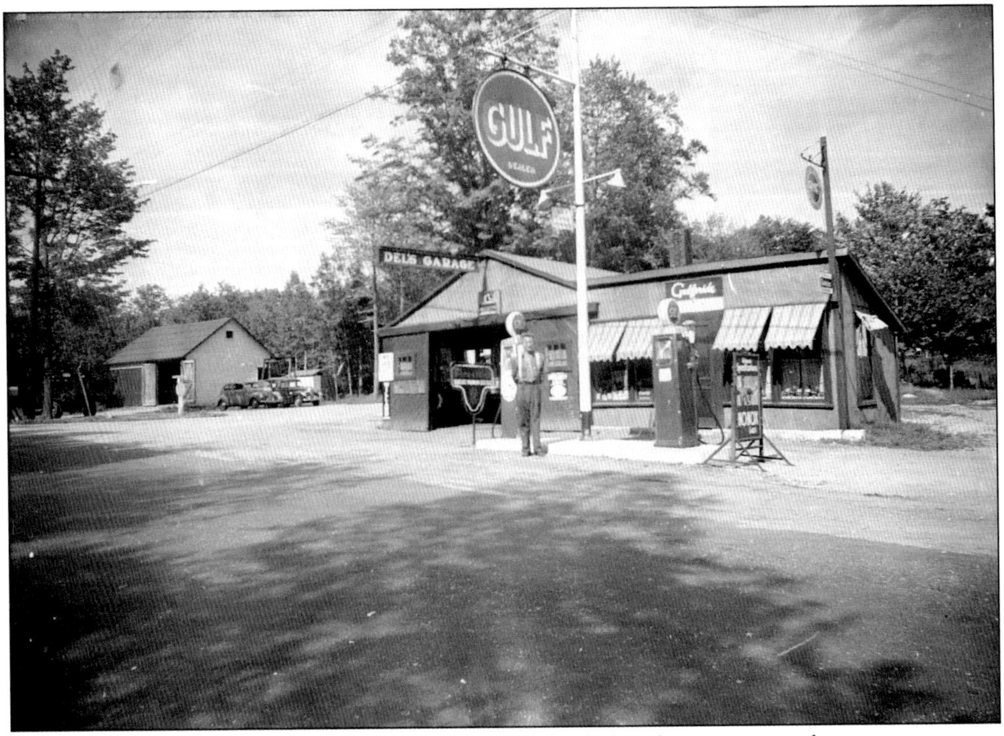

With the development of the automobile, facilities for fuel and maintenance became necessary. These facilities were usually called filling stations. Del's Garage, pictured here, was located at the intersection of Route 3A and Dick Brown Road in Bridgewater. (BWHS.)

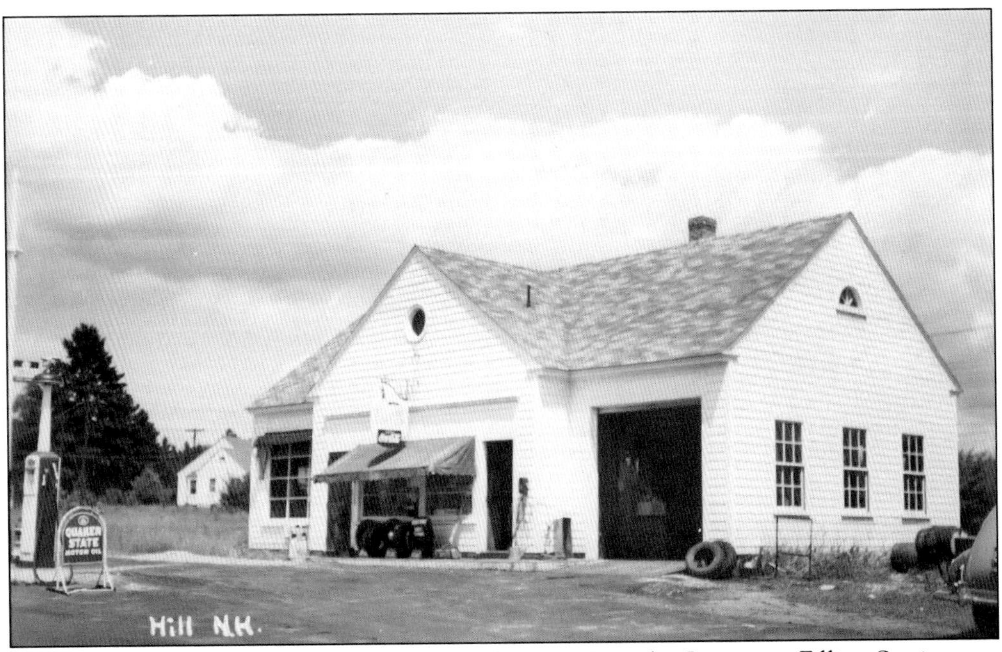

When the residents of Hill built their new village in 1941, the Severance Filling Station was built on Commerce Street. (HHS)

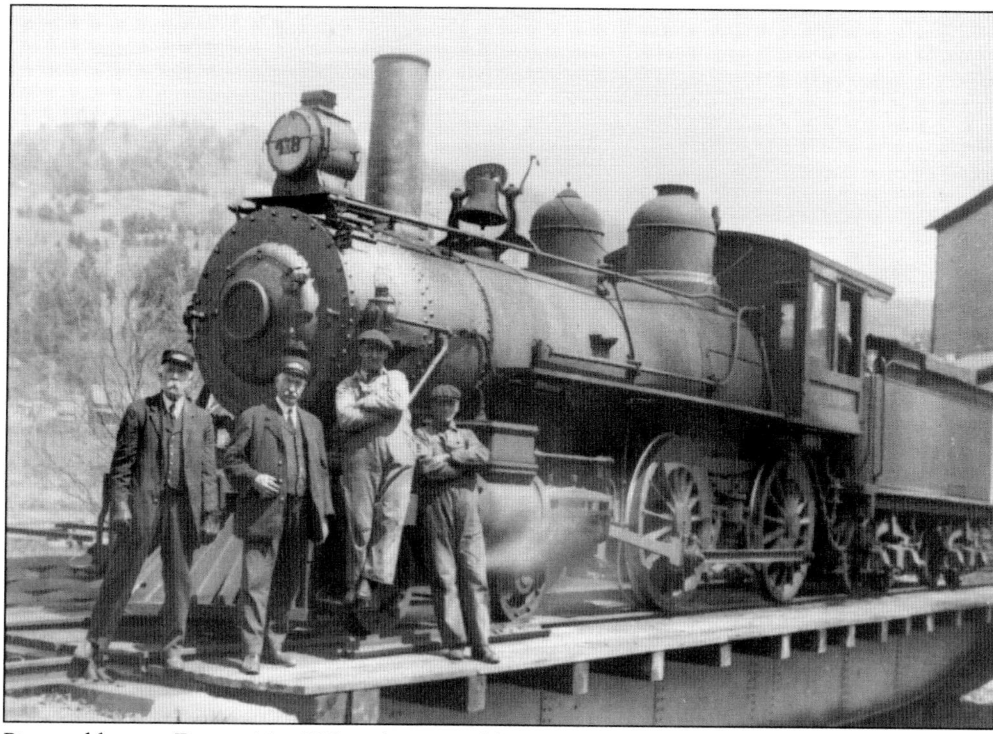

Pictured here is Engine No. 787 at the turntable in Bristol in 1915. The members of the crew, from left to right are, Mr. Robinson, Mr. Brown, Ed Chase, and Mr. Favor. (HHS.)

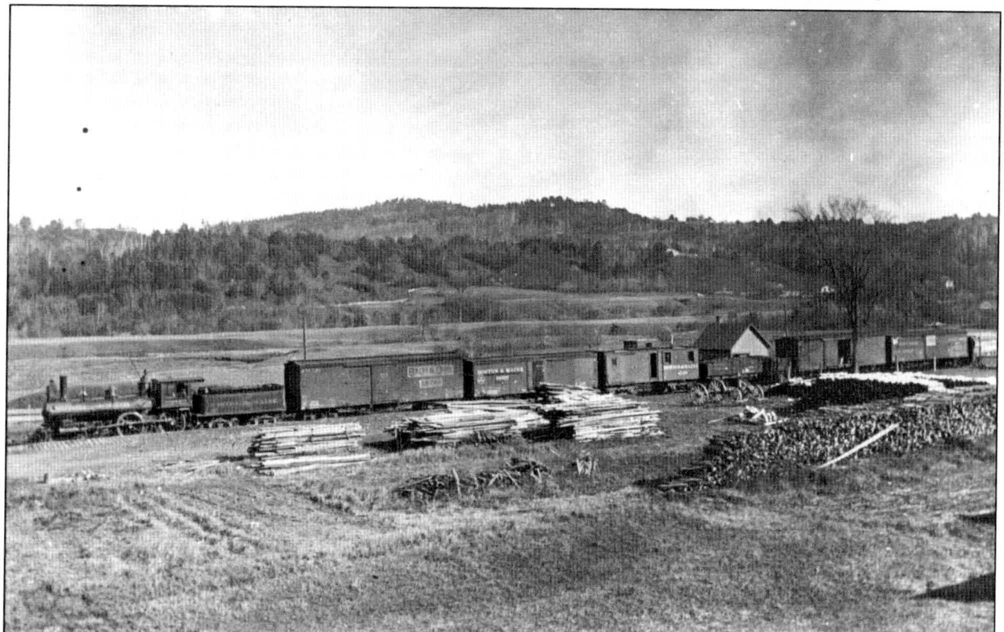

The Boston & Maine Railroad played an integral part in the transport of goods between Concord and Bristol in the early 1900s. In this view, the train appears to be stopped briefly for a delivery in Hill. This photograph was taken c. 1904. (HHS.)

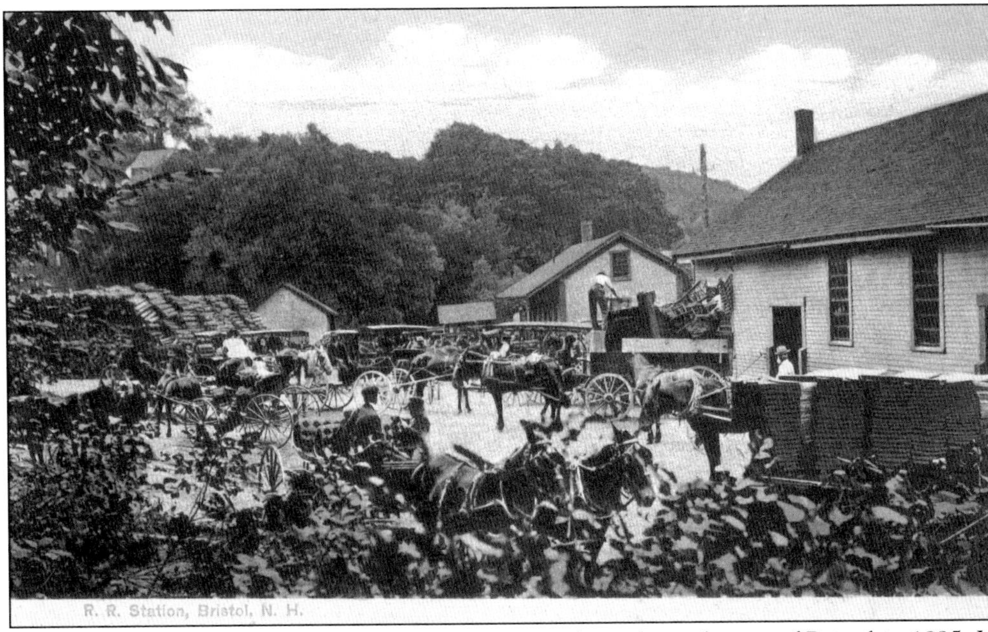

This image shows the importance of rail transport in the industrial town of Bristol in 1895. In viewing this scene, one can easily sense the excitement. (MW.)

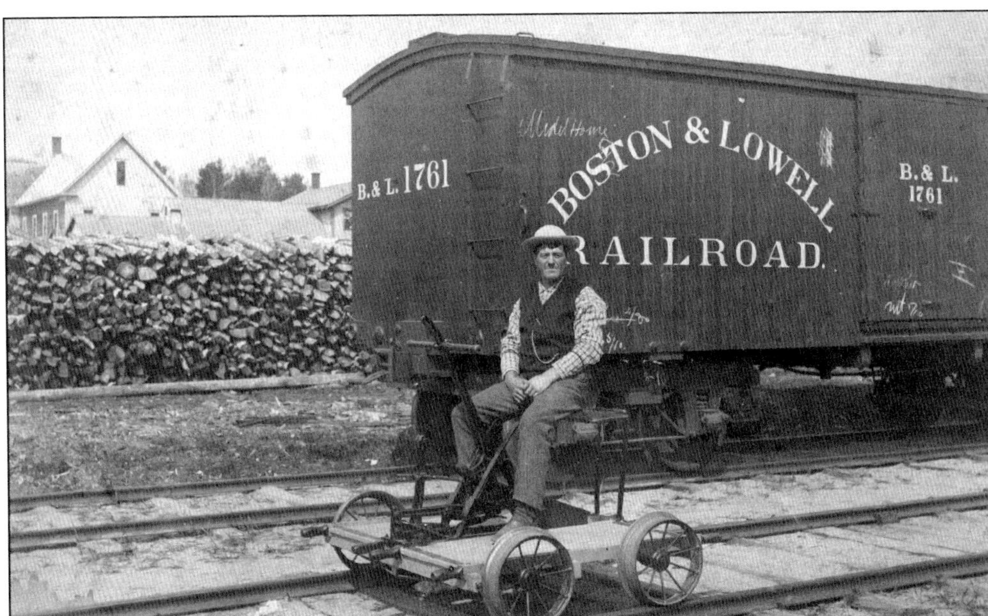

This pert gentleman poses on a handcar belonging to the Boston & Lowell Railroad. The handcar was a means of transportation for railroad workers, who were known as gandy dancers because of movements made while using tools from the Gandy Manufacturing Company. (BHS.)

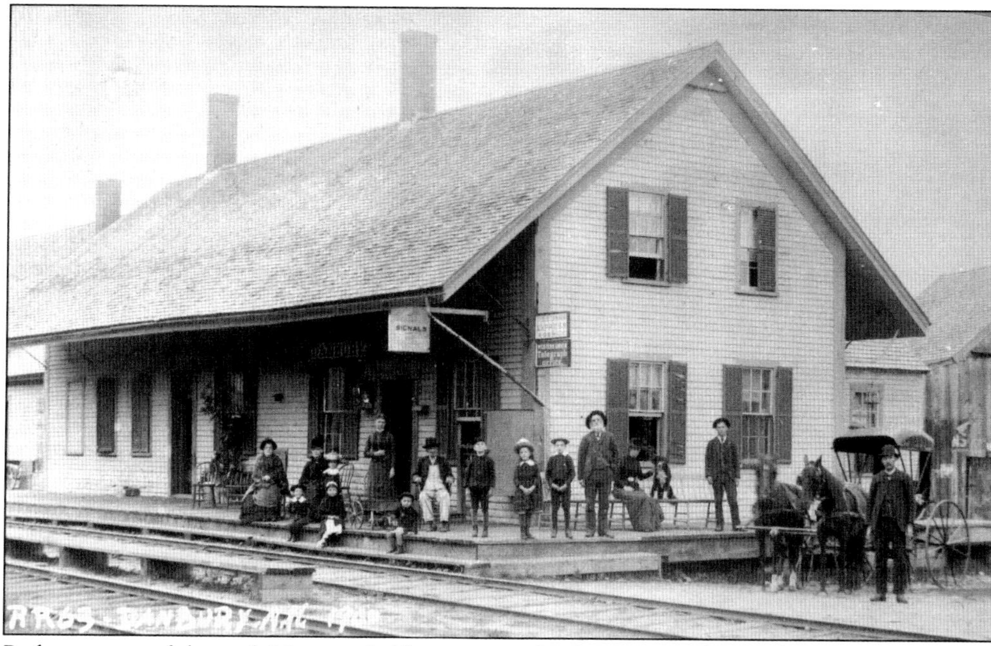

Perhaps some of these children and elders waiting for the train at the Danbury Station in 1900 may have been anticipating their very first rail excursion. (MW.)

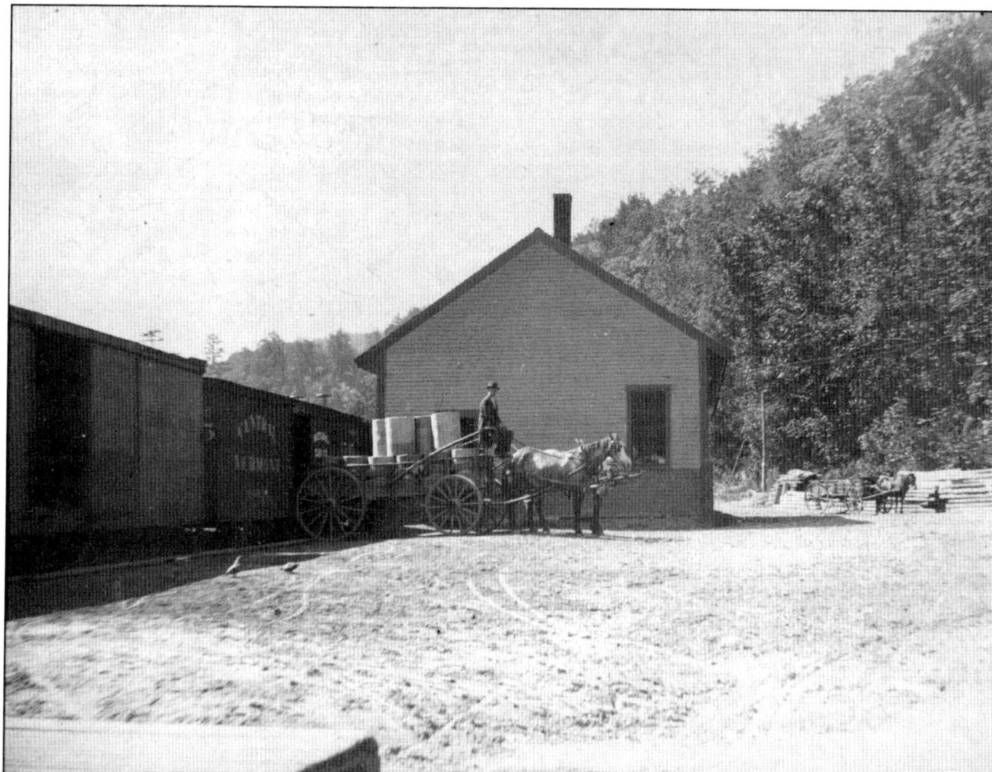

This farmer may be delivering grain or flour for shipment to a city on a day in the 1890s. The Bristol Freight Station seems not as busy as usual. (BHS.)

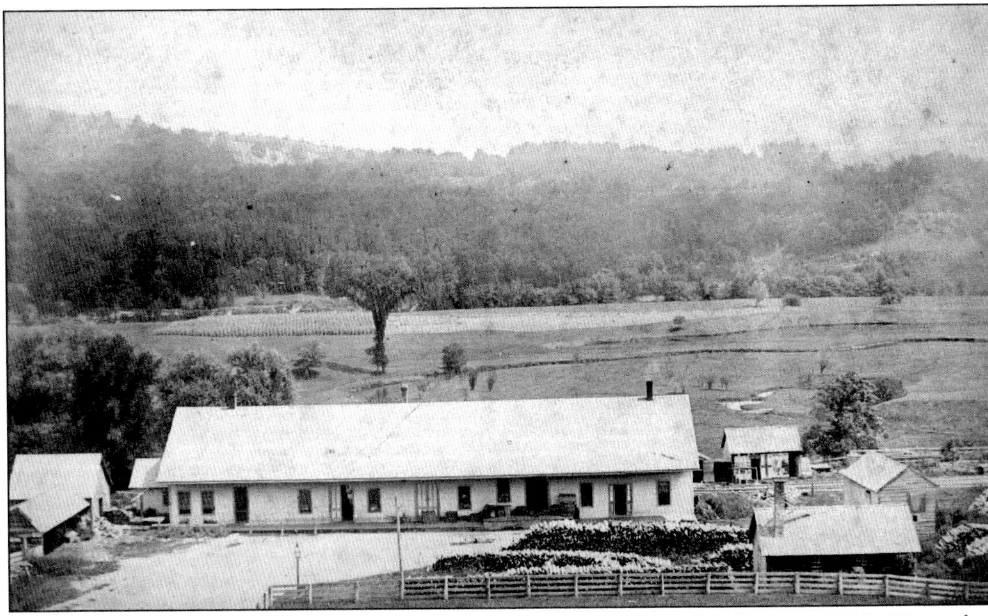

This excellent view was taken from the church belfry in old Hill village in 1900. Housed in the railroad station, from left to right, are the depot office, post office, Severance store, express office, and an apartment. (HHS.)

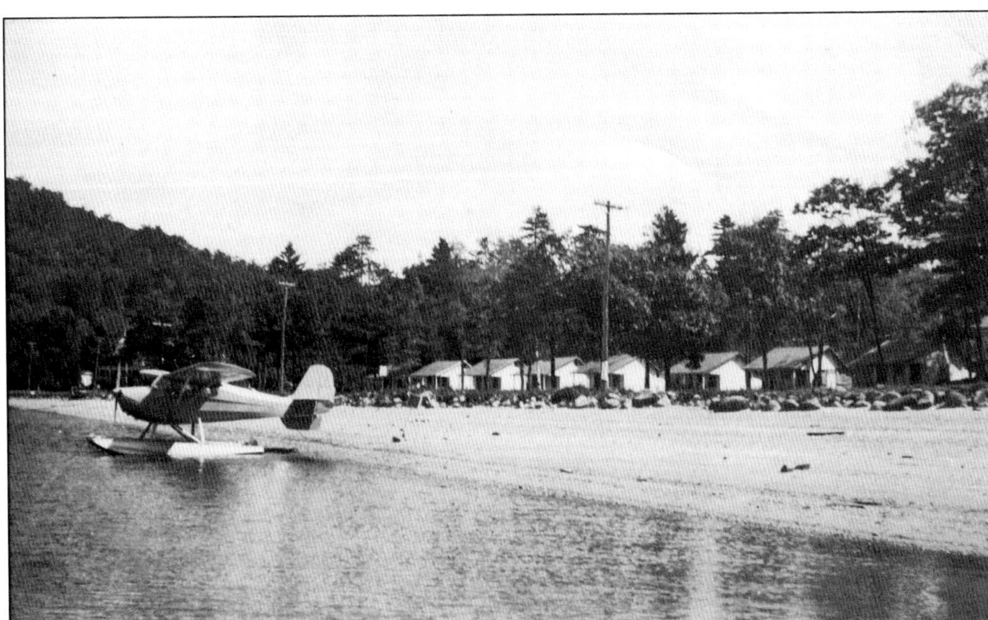

On the historic date of August 9, 1929, the first hydroplane landed on the waters of Newfound Lake. The plane was piloted by Capt. G.K. Berry and carried several passengers. Upon leaving the lake, Berry "gave a fine exhibition of diving and circling." (MW.)

Seven

CATASTROPHE AND RECOVERY

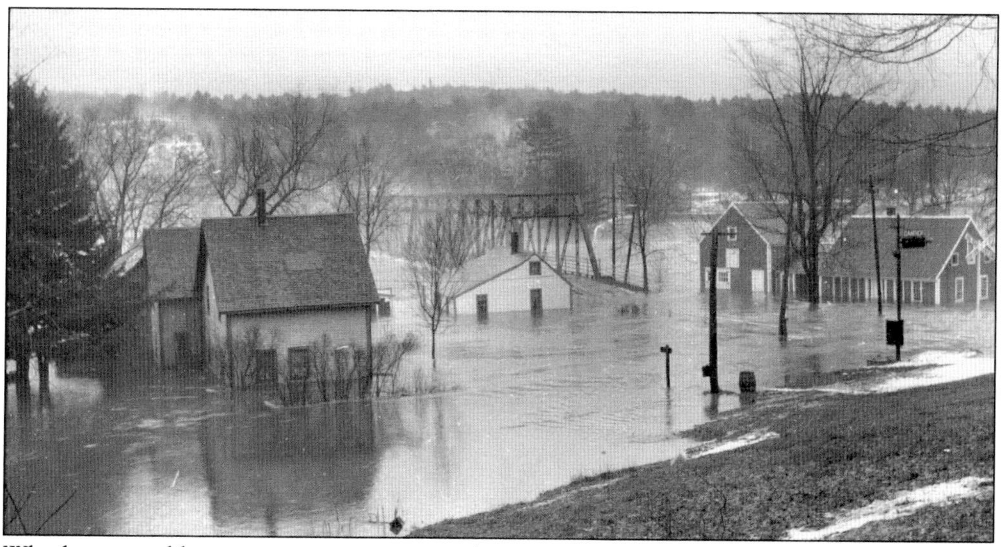

Whether caused by man or nature, catastrophe wears many faces. Fires have destroyed forests, villages, factories, homes, families, and lives. The marriage of spring rains and melting snow has borne floodwaters of immense proportions, sweeping away all in their path. Roofs of buildings and whole bridges have surrendered to deep snow and ice jams. These events are forever locked into the memories of the men, women, and children who were witness to their mischief. One of the most memorable natural disasters in New England was the hurricane of September 1938, which caused monumental destruction of property and loss of life. Nearly 700 lives were lost, and flooding on the major rivers destroyed 12 dams and damaged 60 others. Settlements along the waterways were particularly vulnerable and in the Newfound Region, the village of Hill went to combat against natural disasters more often than would seem tolerable. This view shows the Hill-Sanbornton Bridge and the surrounding area under floodwater in March 1936—a result of two floods that occurred just six days apart. (HHS.)

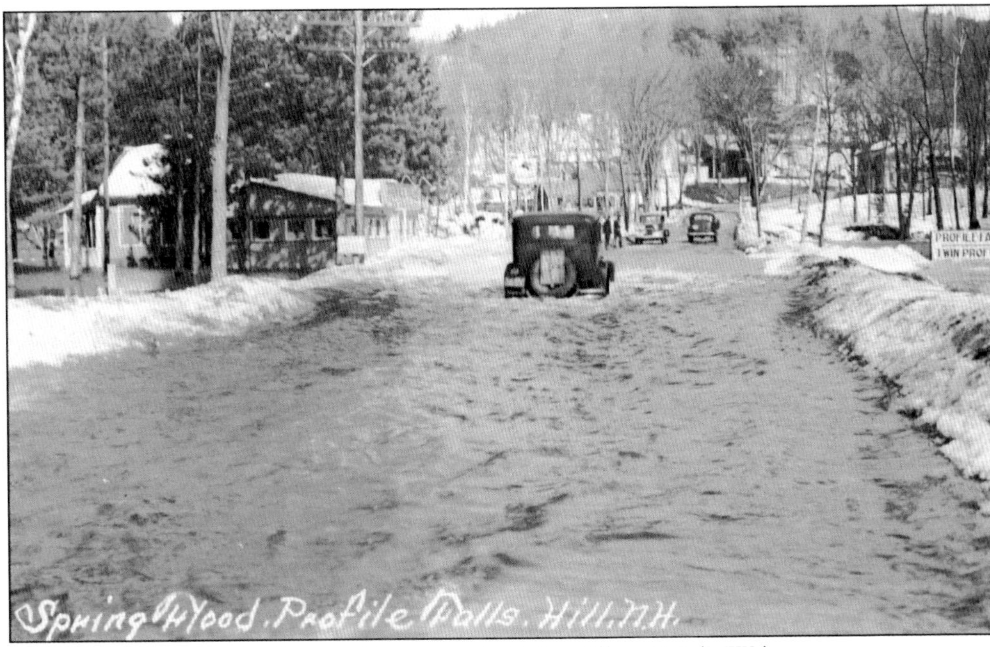

Simply stated, this is the "Spring Flood. Profile Falls, Hill, N.H." (MW.)

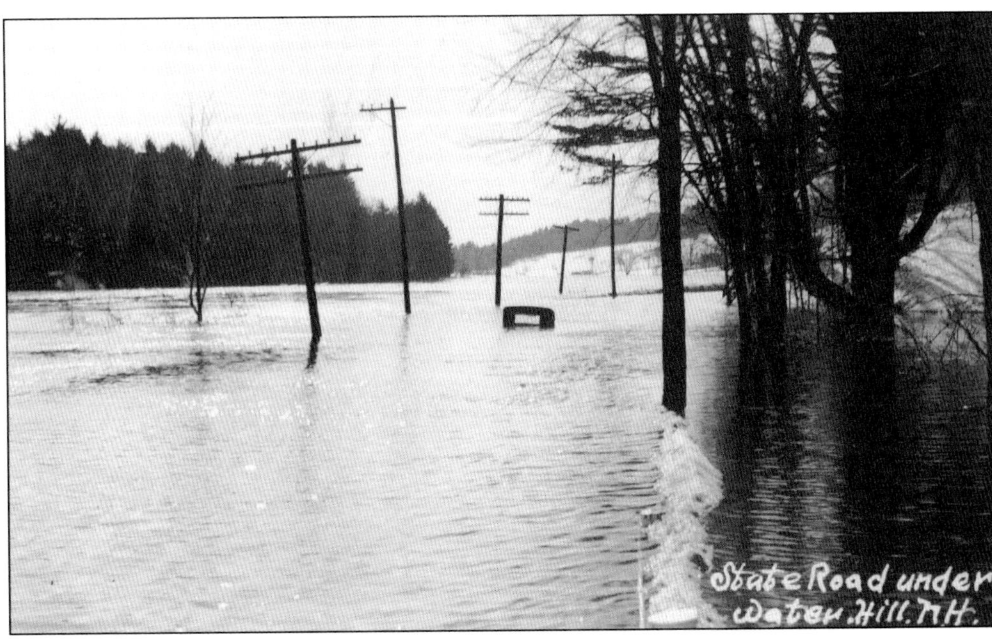

Seen here is the state road under water in Hill. (DP.)

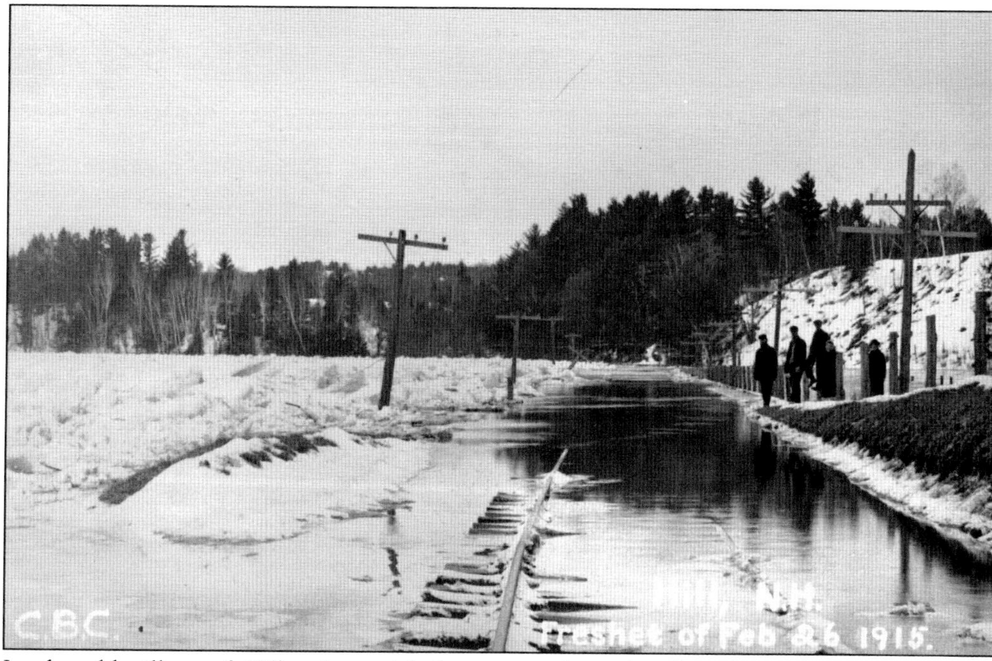

In the old village of Hill, substantial damage to the railroad tracks and power poles was sustained during the freshet of February 26, 1915. (HHS.)

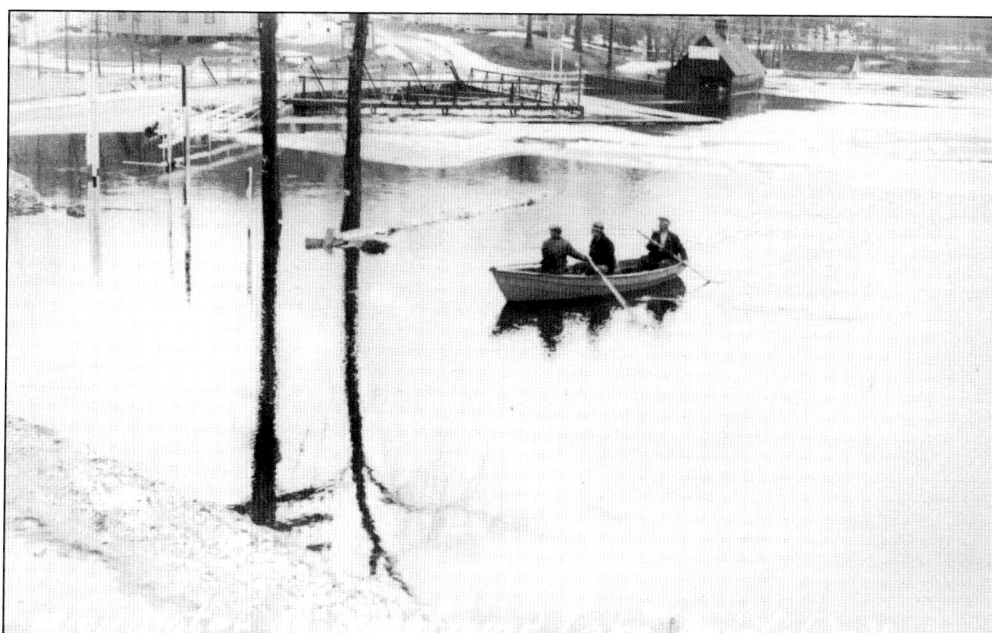

Men navigate a rowboat on the west shore of Newfound Lake in Bristol at the crest of floodwaters. The fish screens and a small mill building are visible. (MW.)

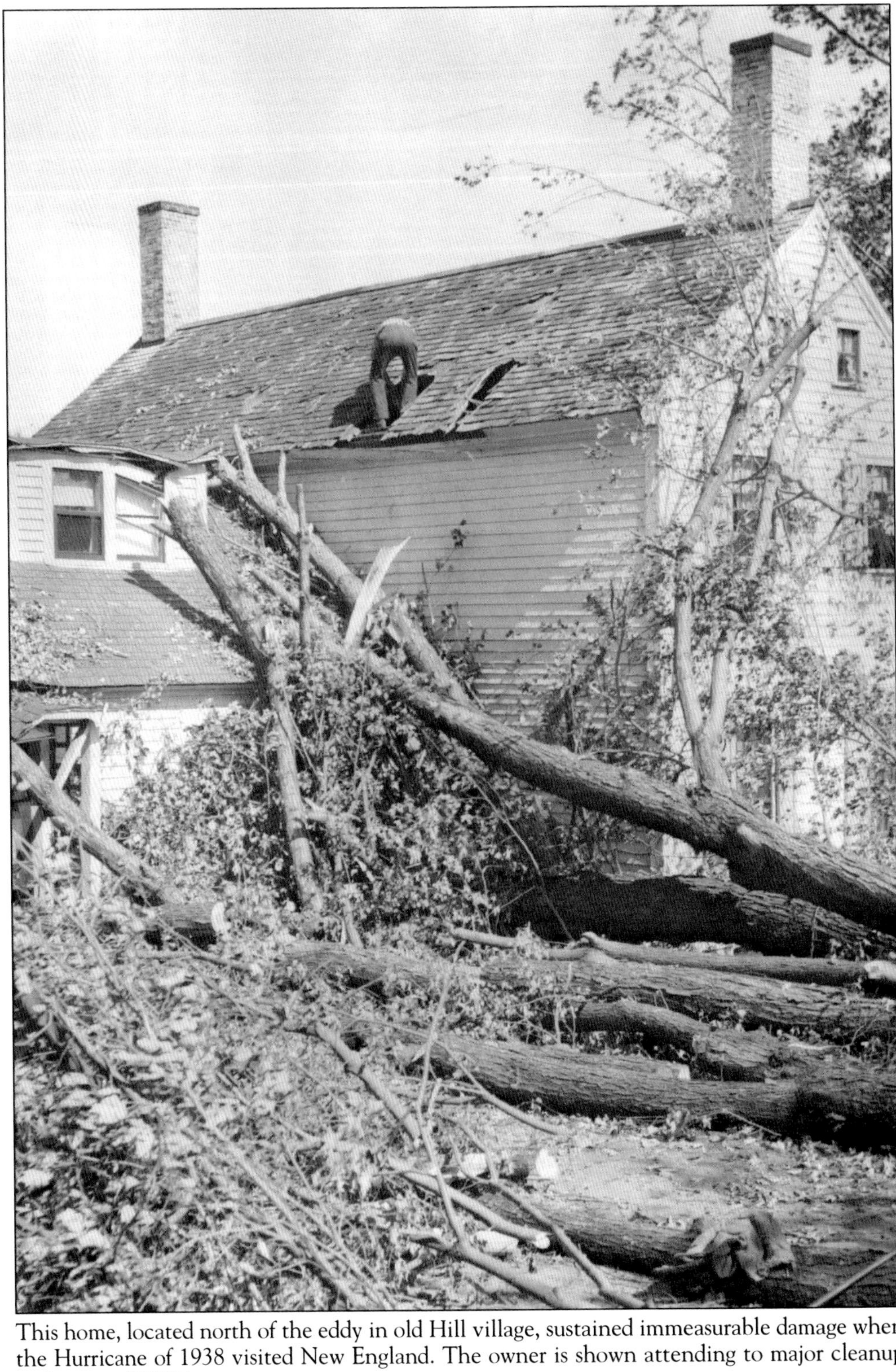

This home, located north of the eddy in old Hill village, sustained immeasurable damage when the Hurricane of 1938 visited New England. The owner is shown attending to major cleanup and repair. (HHS.)

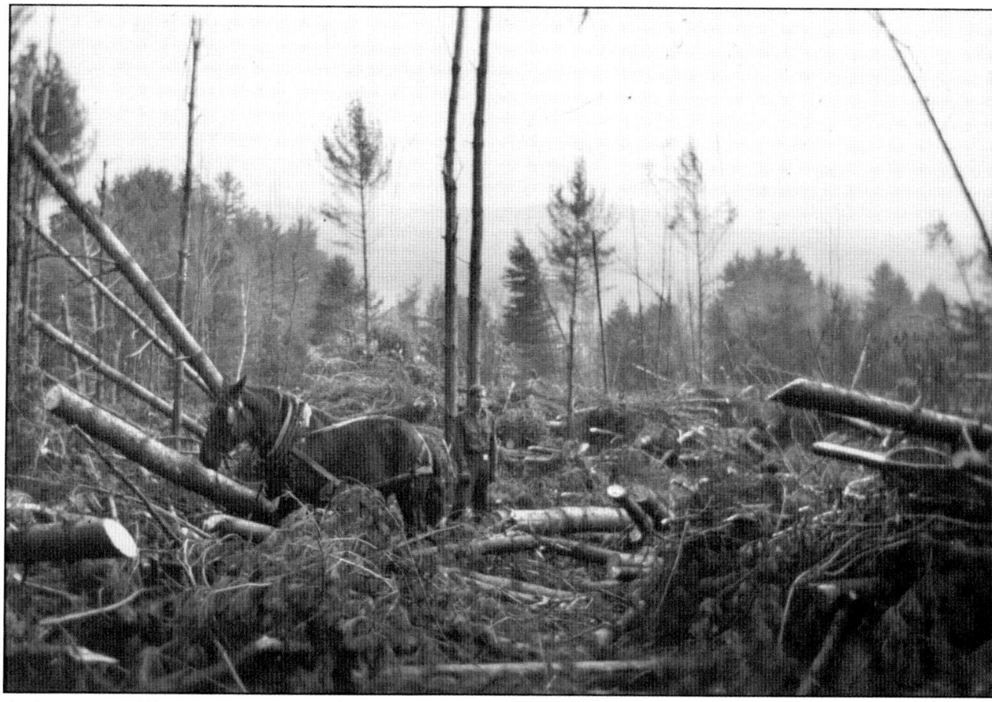
A farmer and his team contemplate a strategy for clearing the hurricane timber at the Webster Farm in Bridgewater in the spring of 1939. (WF.)

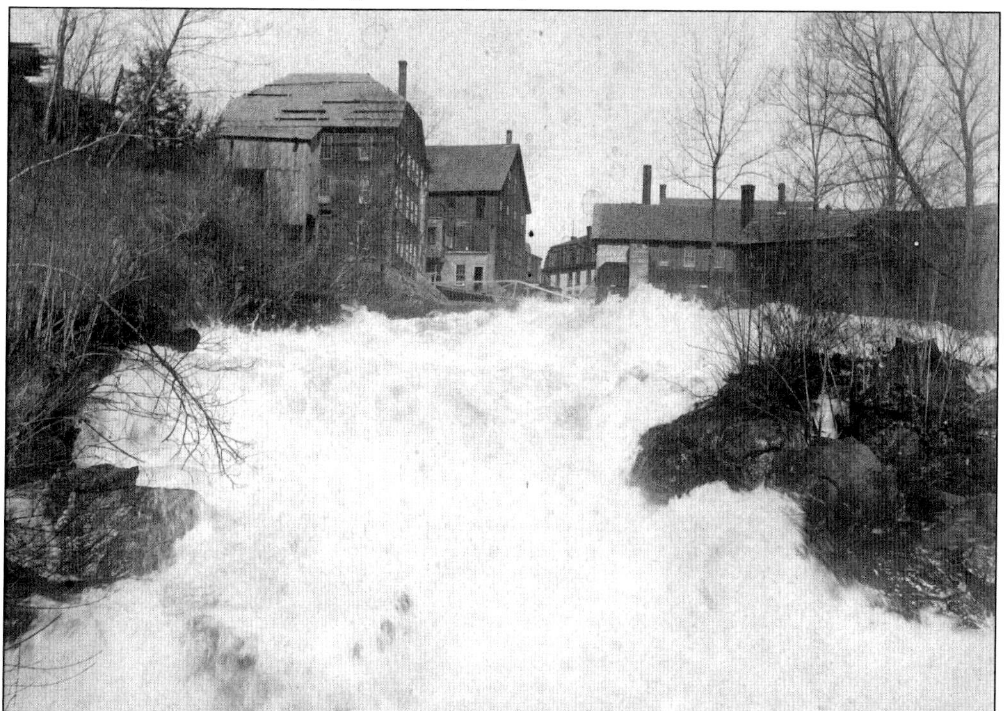
A typical spring freshet in the Newfound River, below the bridge at Central square in Bristol, shows its fury. (BHS.)

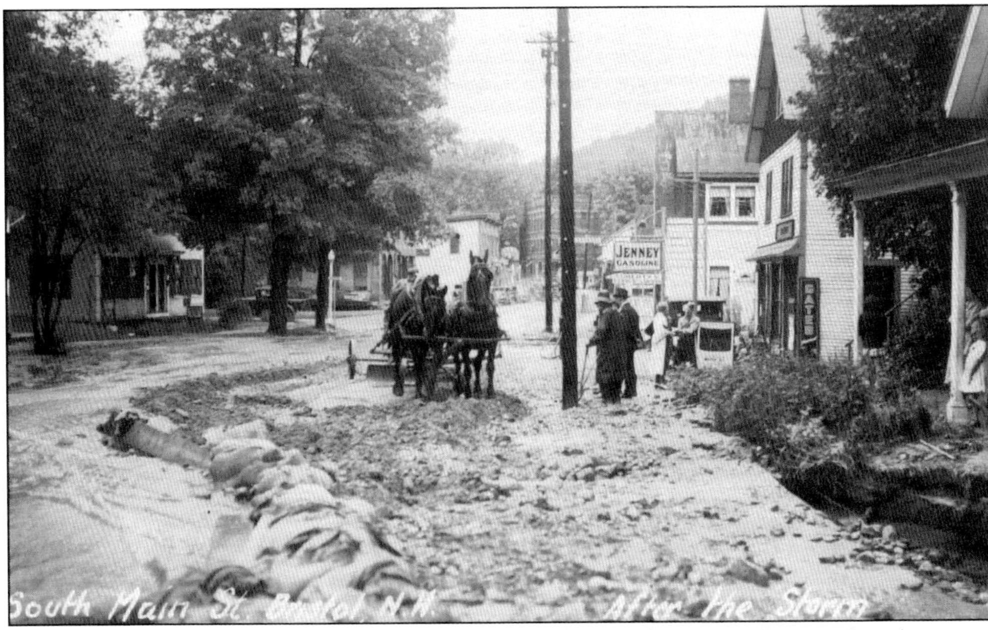

The Bristol road-grader crew attempts to clean up and repair hurricane damage that the row of sandbags could not contain on Main Street. (MW.)

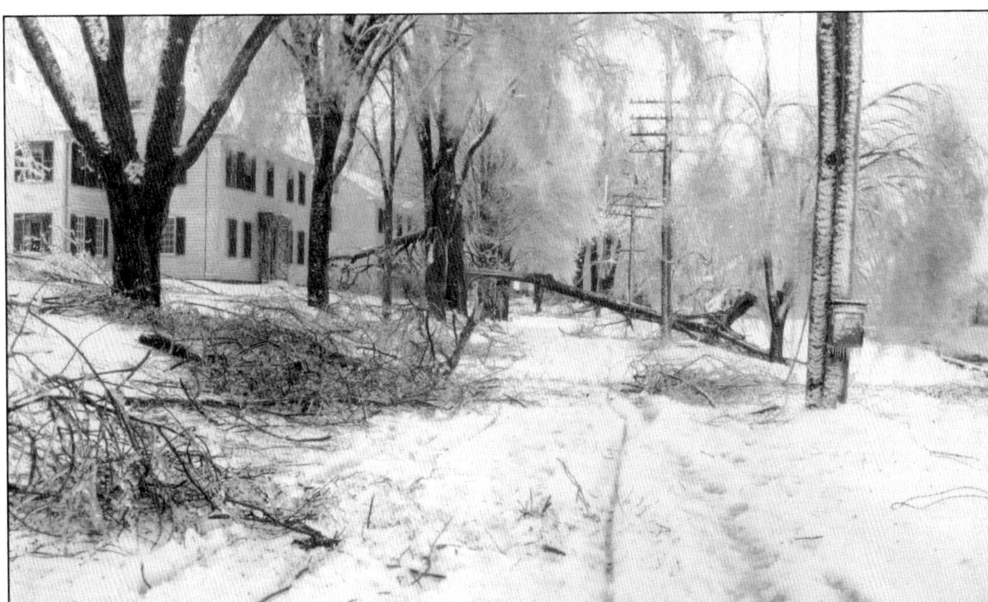

After an ice storm, tree limbs hang heavy with ice above debris on the unplowed streets of Danbury. (JP.)

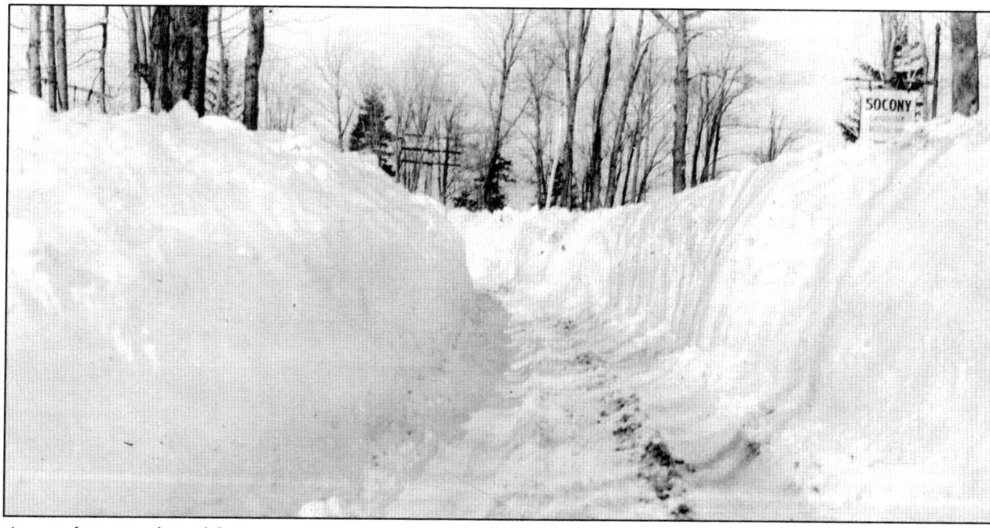

According to the old-timers, the real snowstorms were the snowstorms of their day. This view, taken on February 28, 1934, approaching Bungalow Village south of Newfound Lake, lends merit to their testimony. (DP.)

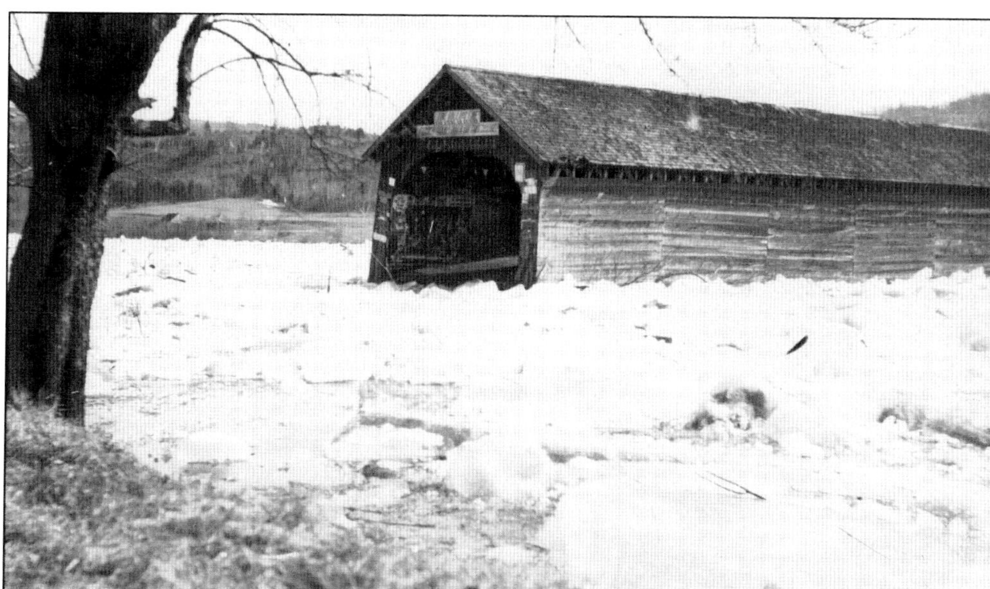

The Hill-Sanbornton double-span covered bridge is carried downriver in an ice jam on March 22, 1913. (DP.)

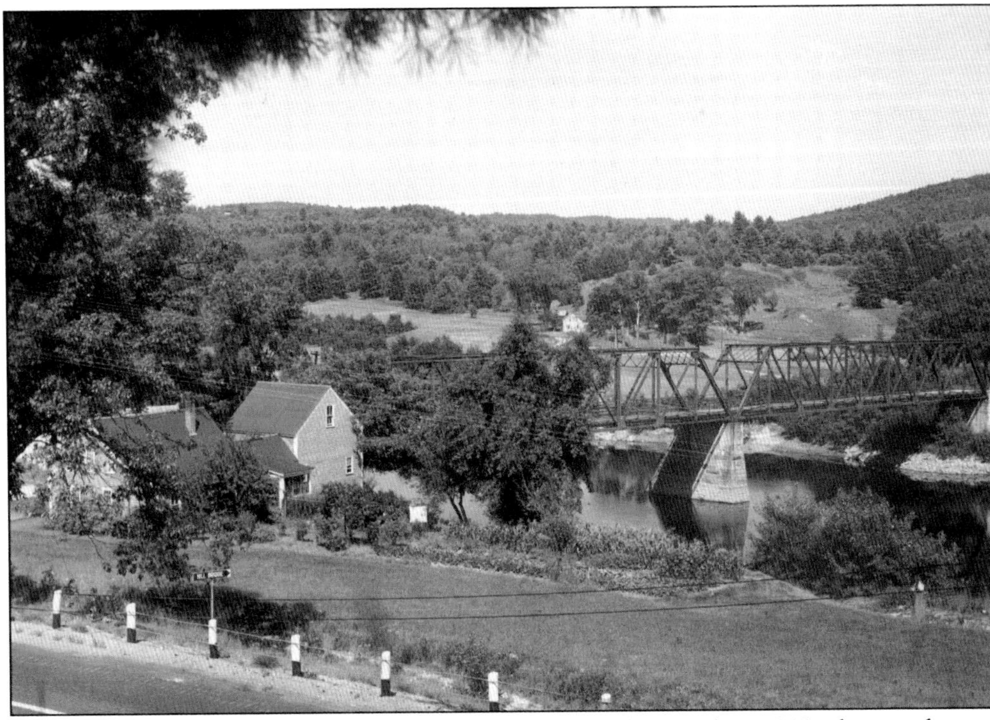

Soon after the old Hill-Sanbornton covered bridge was destroyed in 1913, this sturdy steel bridge was constructed over the Pemigewasset River. The valley is beautiful in this 1939 scene. (HHS.)

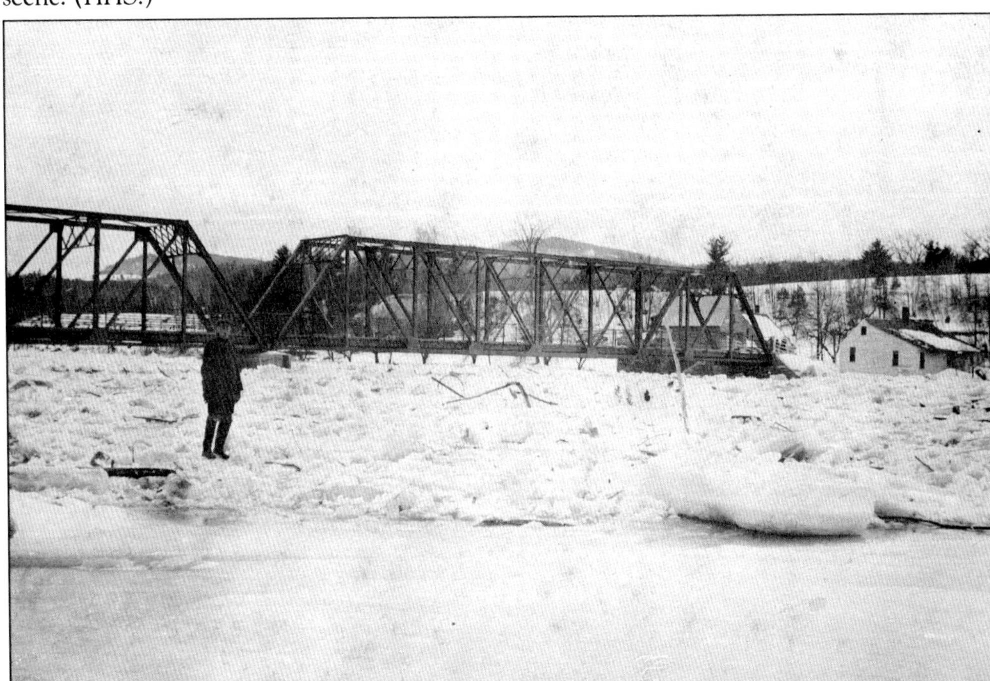

Later, however, the steel bridge was demolished. Never again would there be a bridge spanning the river at this place. (HHS.)

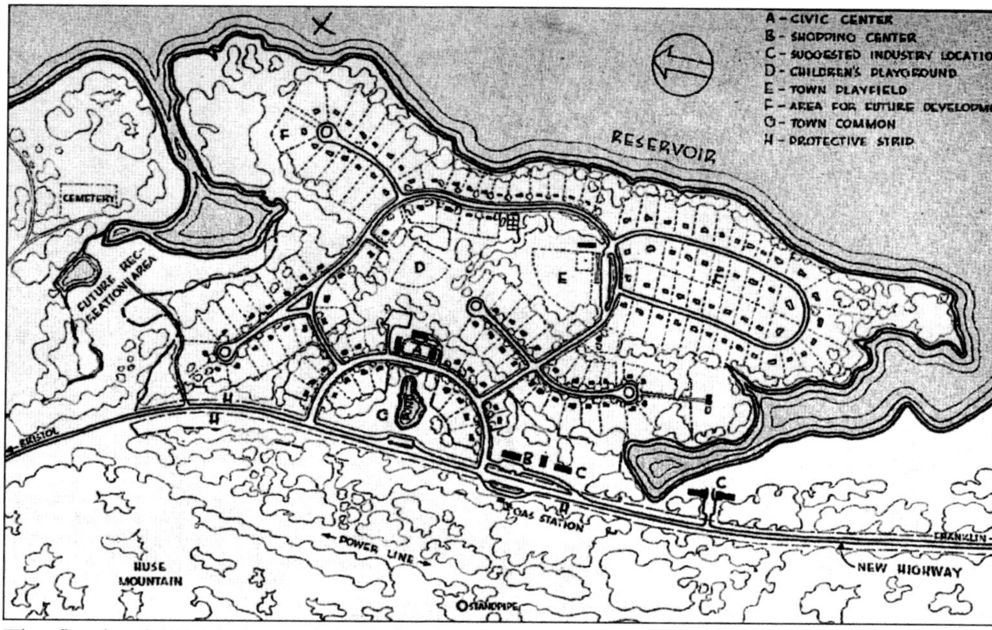

The floods of 1936 led to a federal flood-control program, which greatly impacted the town of Hill. In 1938, a dam to control the Pemigewasset River at Franklin Falls was authorized. A reservoir to protect downstream cities would engulf this upstream village, and the residents of Hill, through long negotiations with the State Planning and Development Commission, chose to relocate to a soundly planned new community on higher ground. By March 1940, work on the new site had begun and by midsummer one year later, many of the new houses were occupied. The community underwent profound sociological, economic, and physical changes. The criteria for this planned community were economy in layout and construction, modern convenience, attractiveness, safety, and insurance for the future of the town. As a result of this program, Hill became a precedent for planned communities. (HHS.)

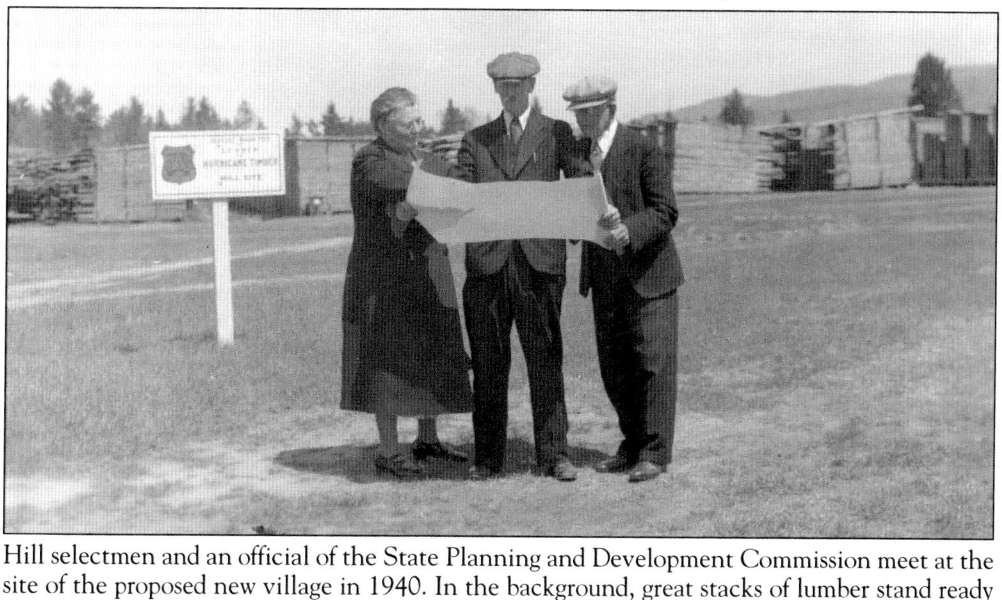

Hill selectmen and an official of the State Planning and Development Commission meet at the site of the proposed new village in 1940. In the background, great stacks of lumber stand ready for construction to begin. (HHS.)

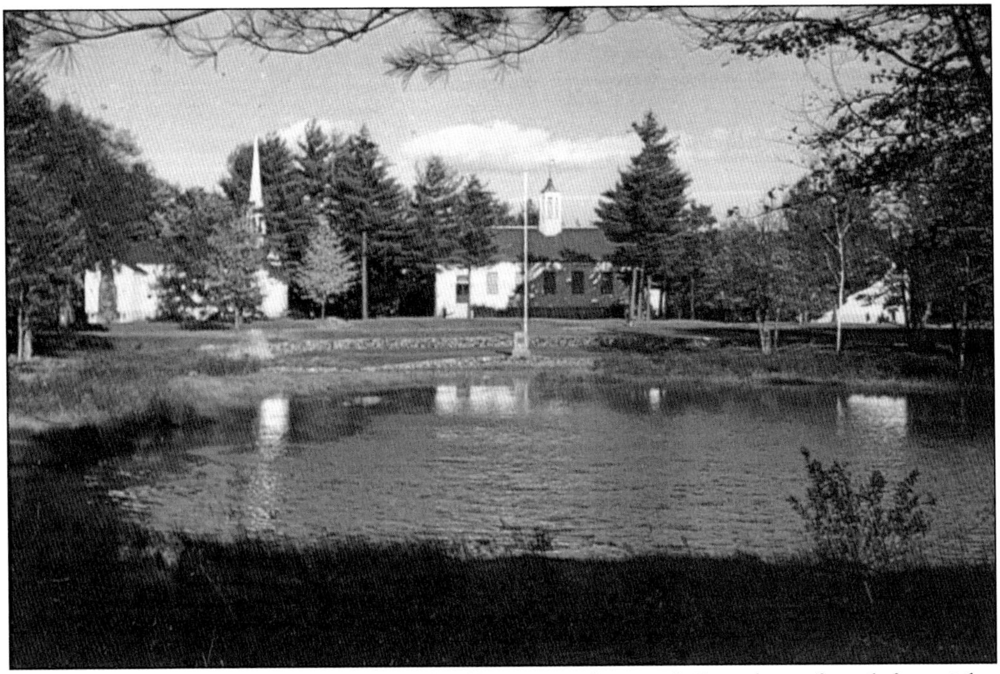

This beautiful view of the new village of Hill captures the pond. Seen here, from left to right, are the church, the civic center that houses a library, an auditorium, a dining room, and town offices. The Jenny D. Blake School is seen at the far right. (MW.)

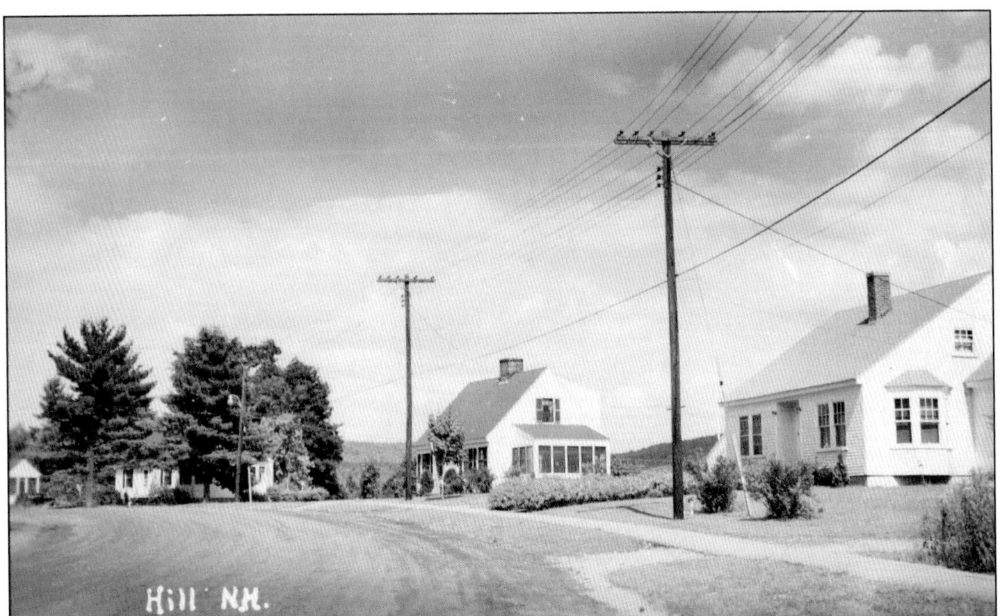

This view of a residential street shows the modern homes built in the new Hill village in 1941. (HHS.)

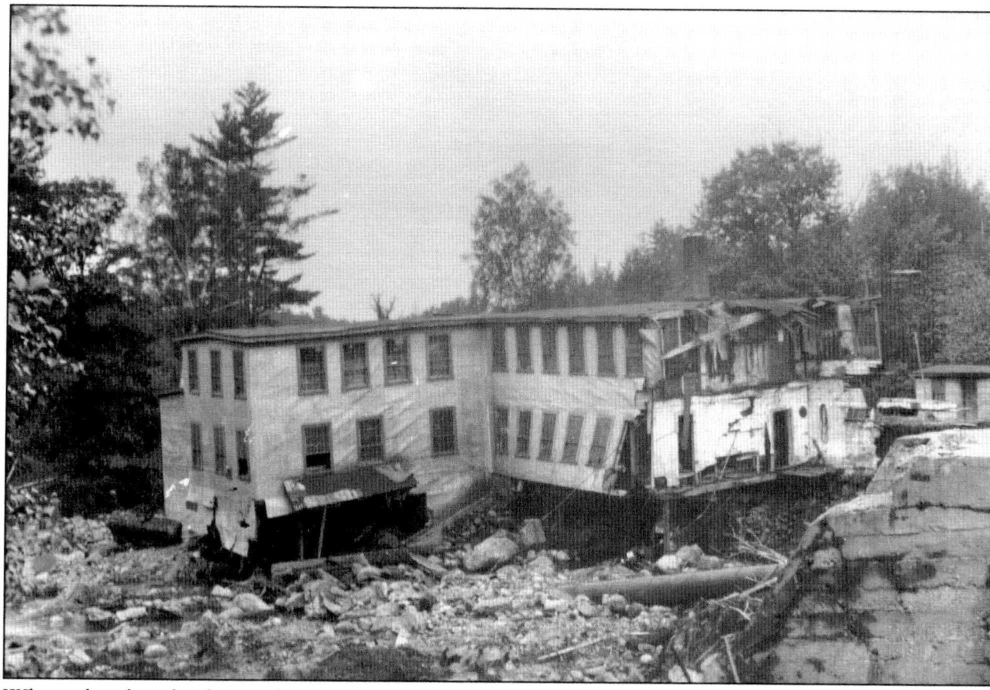

When the dam broke at the New England Novelty Works of old Hill village (above) in May 1918, the powerful surge of the water destroyed the building, along with the mill's tenement house (below). One life was lost due to drowning in this mishap as well. (HHS.)

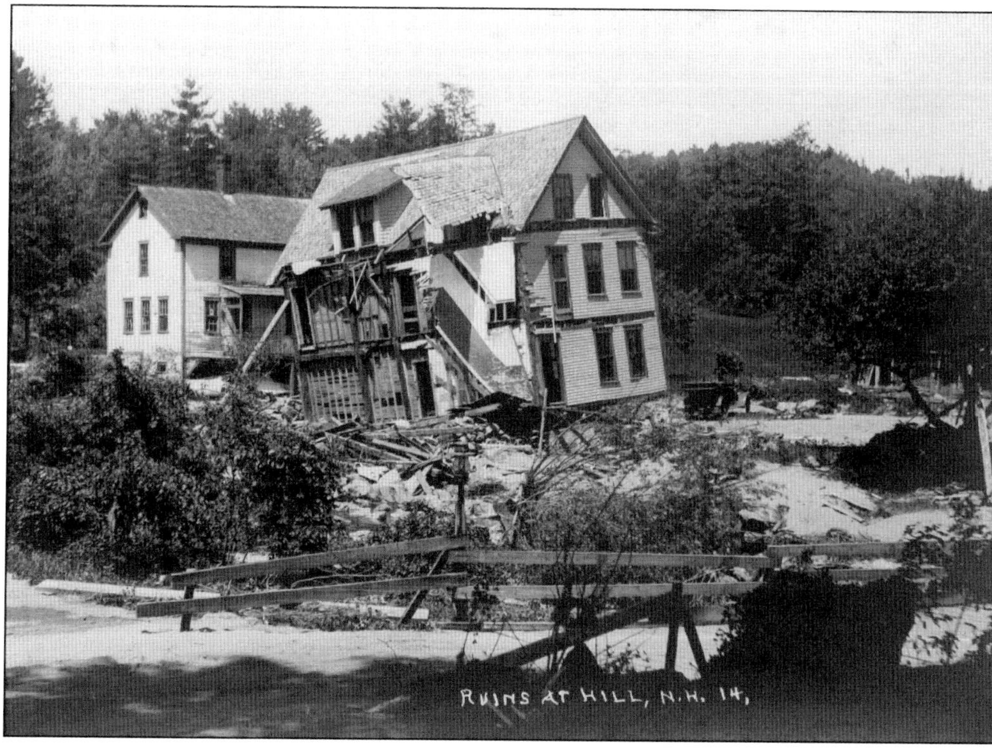

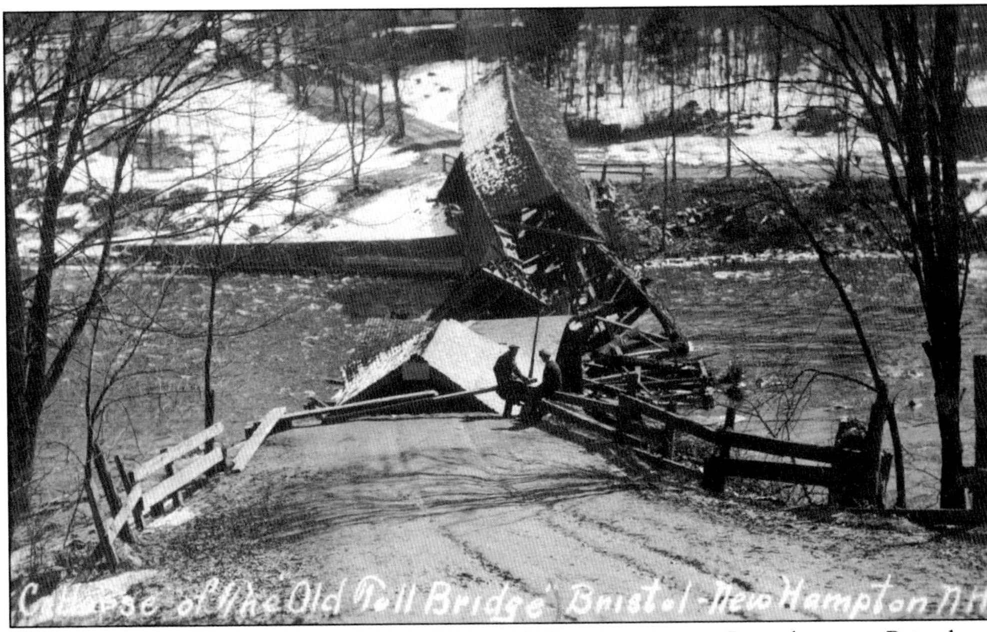

Central Bridge, or the old Toll Bridge that crossed the Pemigewasset River between Bristol and New Hampton, was built in 1823 and was rebuilt in 1836. When the floods of 1927 and 1928 weakened the covered bridge, it collapsed and was carried downriver with the high water. A new steel bridge was built the next year. (NHHS.)

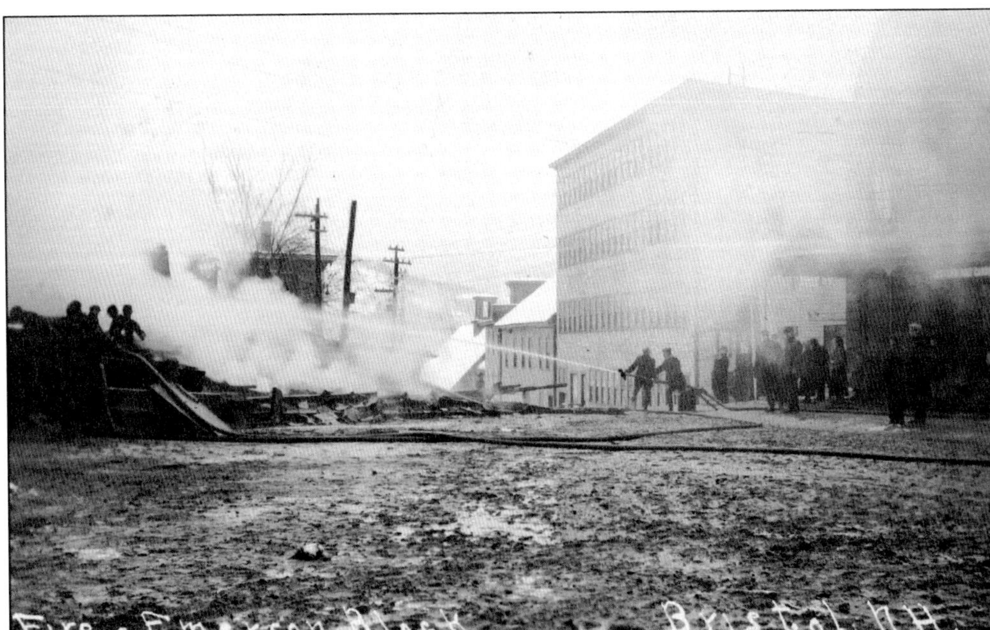

The Emerson block on Central Square in Bristol was the oldest mercantile house built there. In 1797, it was built as a residence that consisted of only two floors and remained so until 1869, when a shoe store was operated from one side of the first floor. The building changed hands many times in the following several decades. Sadly, as seen in this photograph, the block was destroyed by fire in 1911. (DP.)

Eight

LEISURE

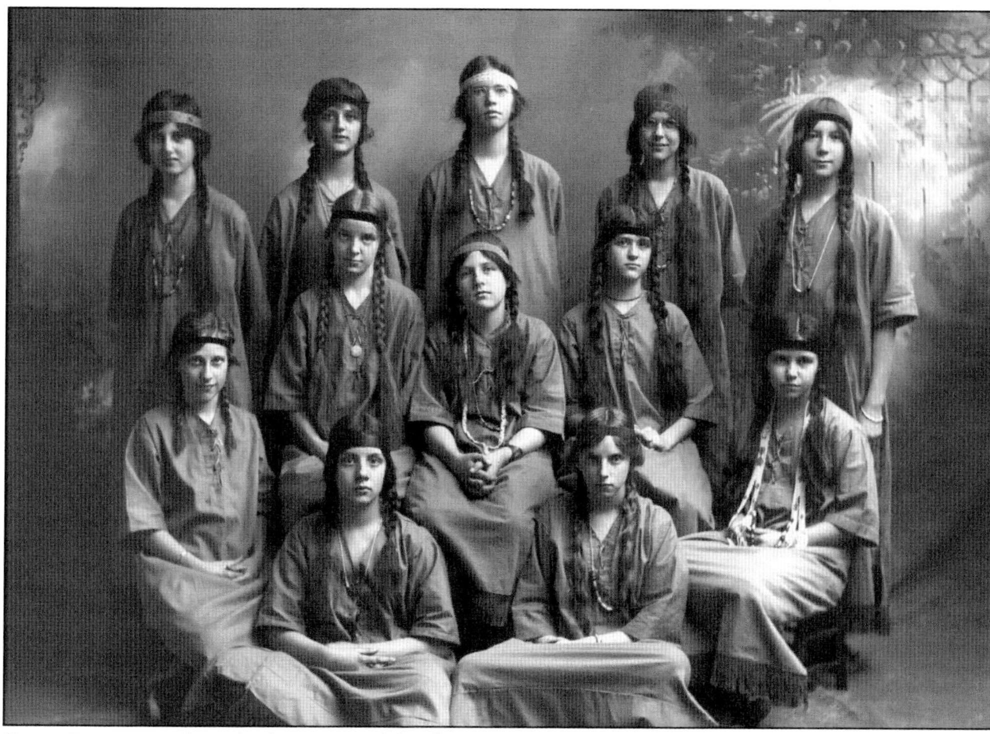

Over the years, when the business of the farm or factory had been satisfied, at least temporarily, men and women would seek out forms of social interaction. Becoming part of an association or society brought with it a sense of community, an avenue to new friendships, and a vehicle with which to express one's talent or giftedness. Folks joined the Grange, which was an extension of their life on the farm, or drama, singing, or literary groups or a town band that played in parades and summer concerts on the common. Team sports and recreation at the lake were also popular leisure activities. In 1910, Dr. and Mrs. Luther Gulick founded Campfire Girls, the first nonsectarian organization for girls in the United States. Shown here, in ceremonial dress, are the Bristol Campfire Girls of 1914. (BM.)

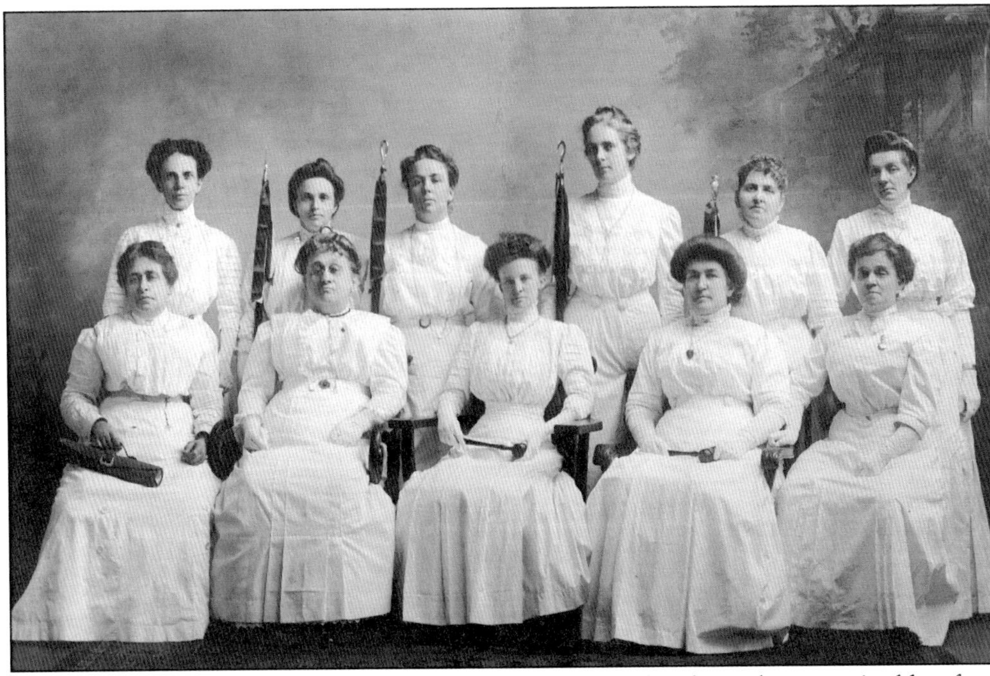

Founded in 1867, the Grange of the order of Patrons of Husbandry is the nation's oldest farm organization. These Grange women served this family fraternity in Bristol in 1890. (BHS.)

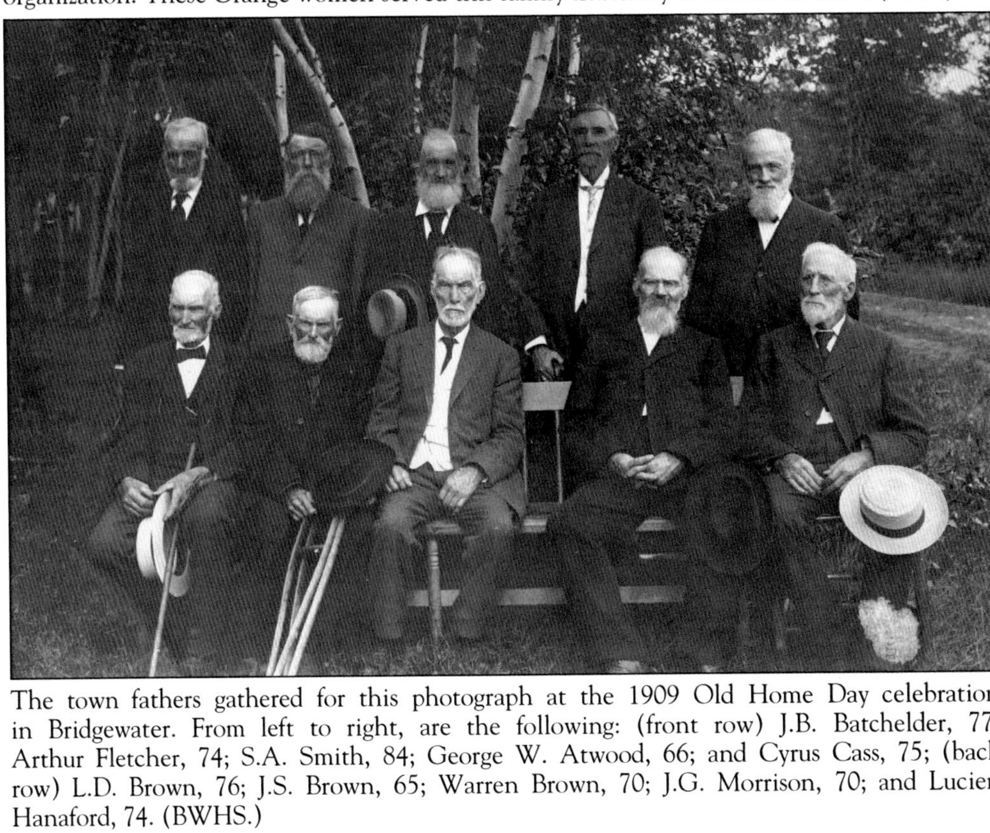

The town fathers gathered for this photograph at the 1909 Old Home Day celebration in Bridgewater. From left to right, are the following: (front row) J.B. Batchelder, 77; Arthur Fletcher, 74; S.A. Smith, 84; George W. Atwood, 66; and Cyrus Cass, 75; (back row) L.D. Brown, 76; J.S. Brown, 65; Warren Brown, 70; J.G. Morrison, 70; and Lucien Hanaford, 74. (BWHS.)

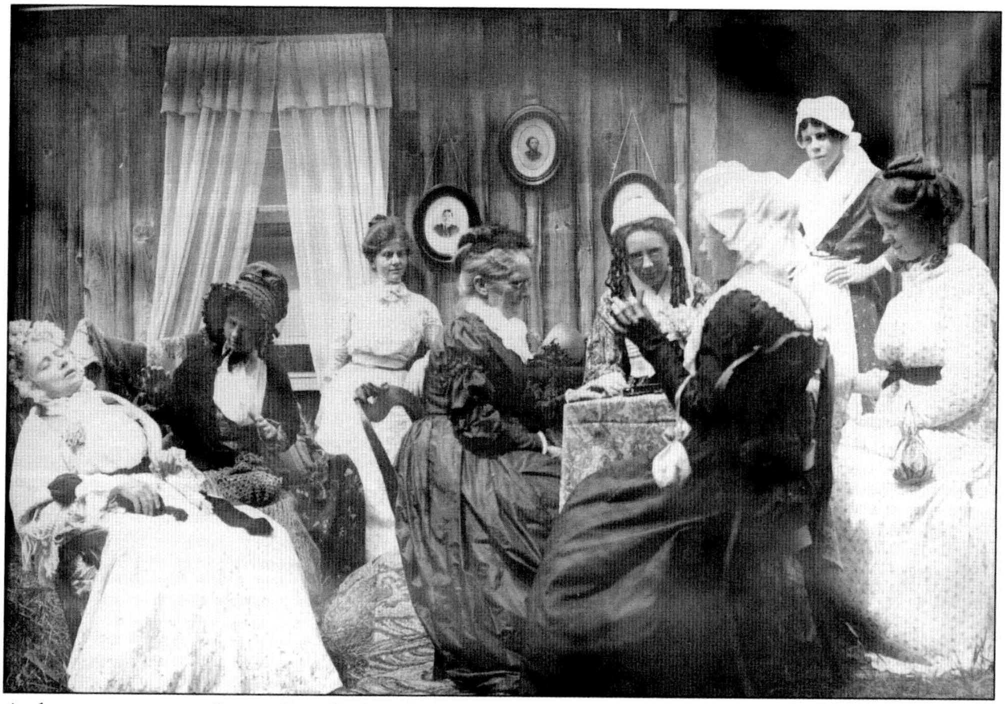

A theater group performs *Cranford* at Cummings Cottage in Groton *c.* 1902. (HBHS.)

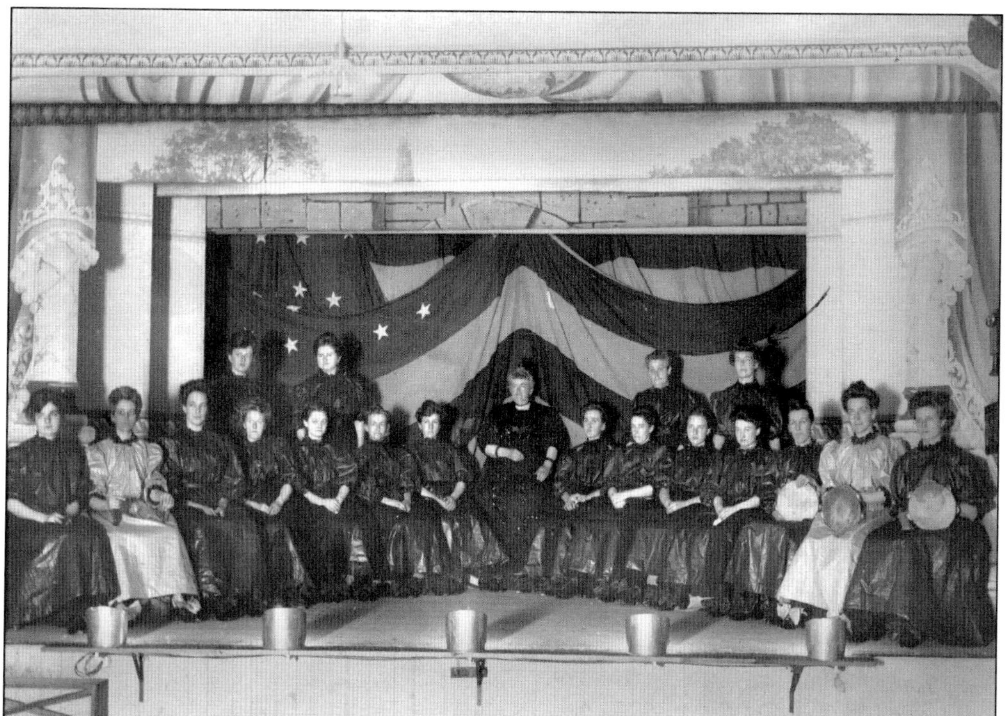

The Ladies Minstrels performed for large audiences at the Bristol Town Hall during the early 1900s. (BHS.)

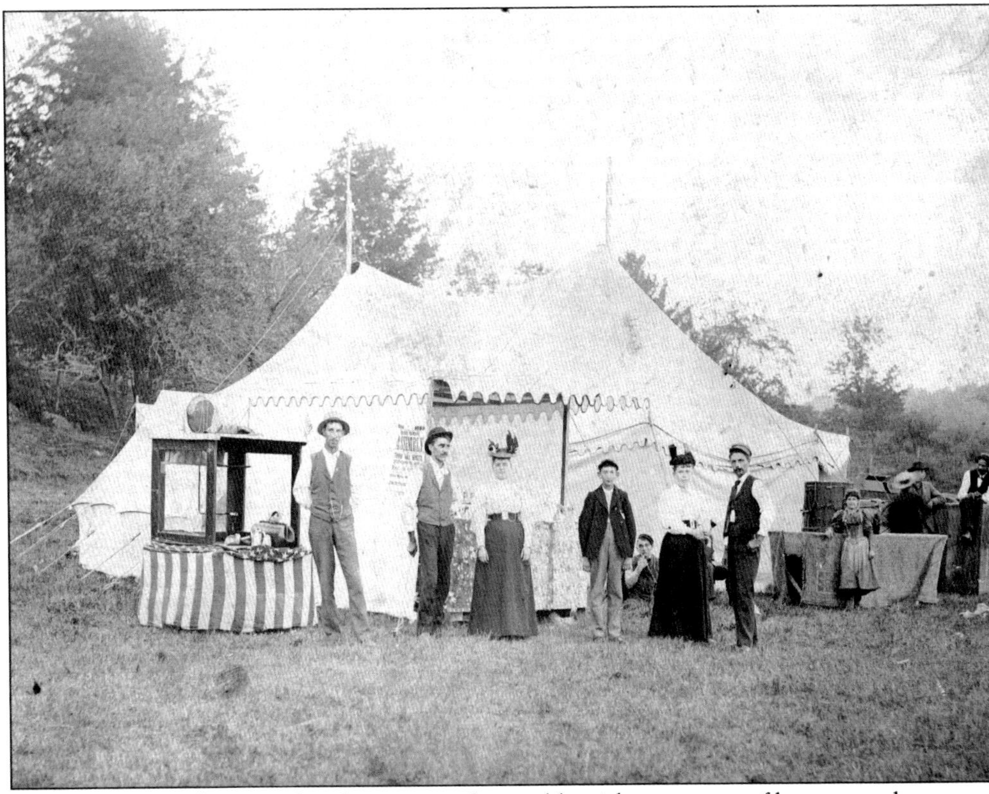

Chautauqua, an educational and recreational assembly with a program of lectures and concerts, was held at Shaw's Field in Bristol. (BHS.)

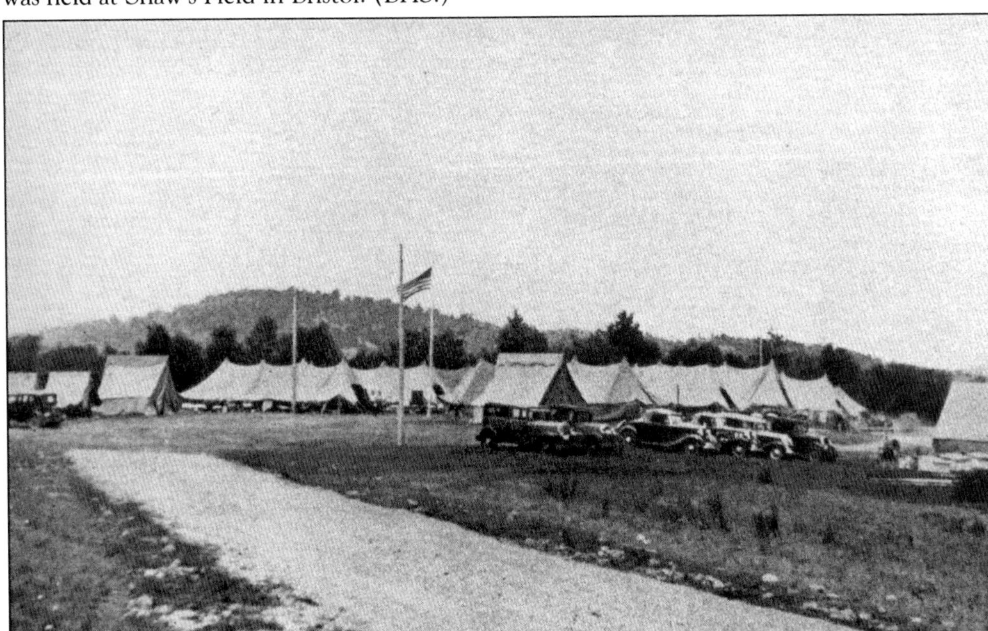

In the late 1930s, the Cardigan Forest Camp, 126th Company of the Civilian Conservation Corps, settled a camp community in Danbury. (JP.)

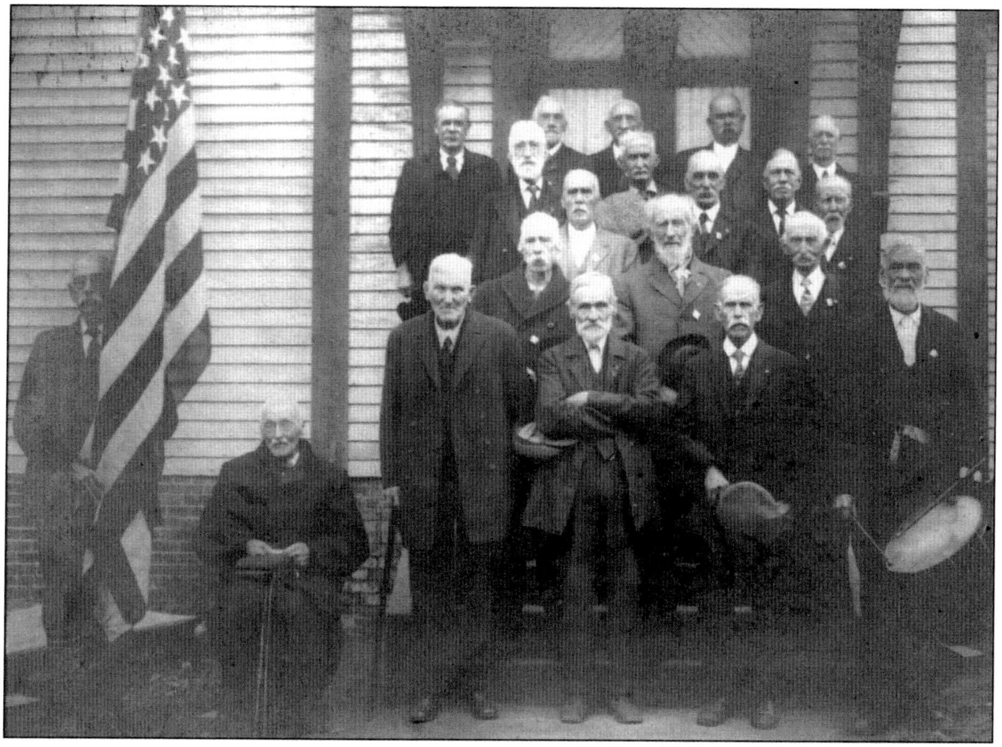

On September 20, 1922, this group of survivors of the 12th Regiment, New Hampshire Veterans, met for a reunion in Hill. This regiment left the state on September 27, 1862, with 1,040 officers and men. (BHS.)

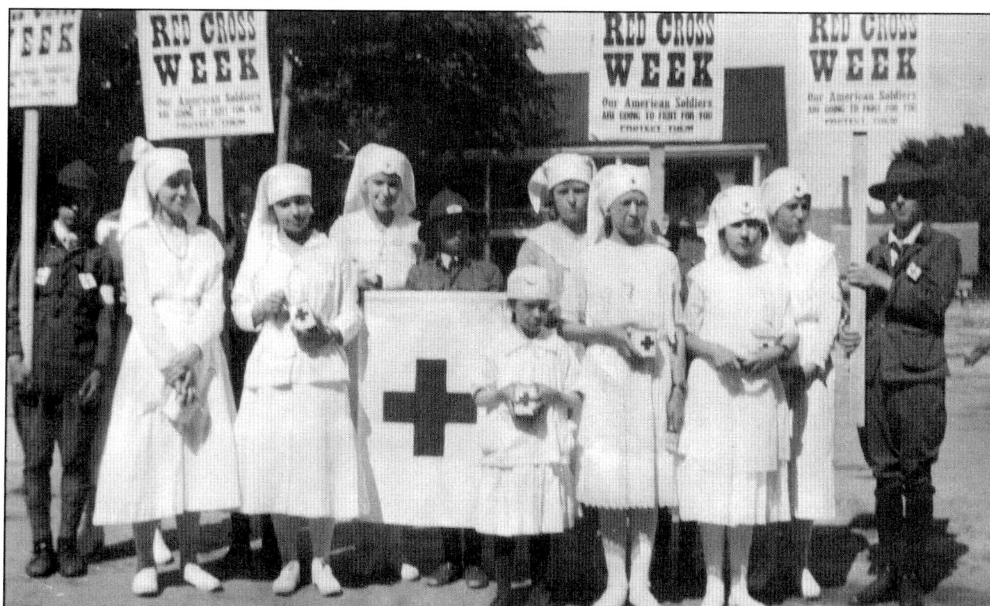

Dedicated American Red Cross volunteers raise funds during Red Cross Week in Bristol. Their placards predicate that "Our American Soldiers Are Going to Fight for You—Protect Them." (MW.)

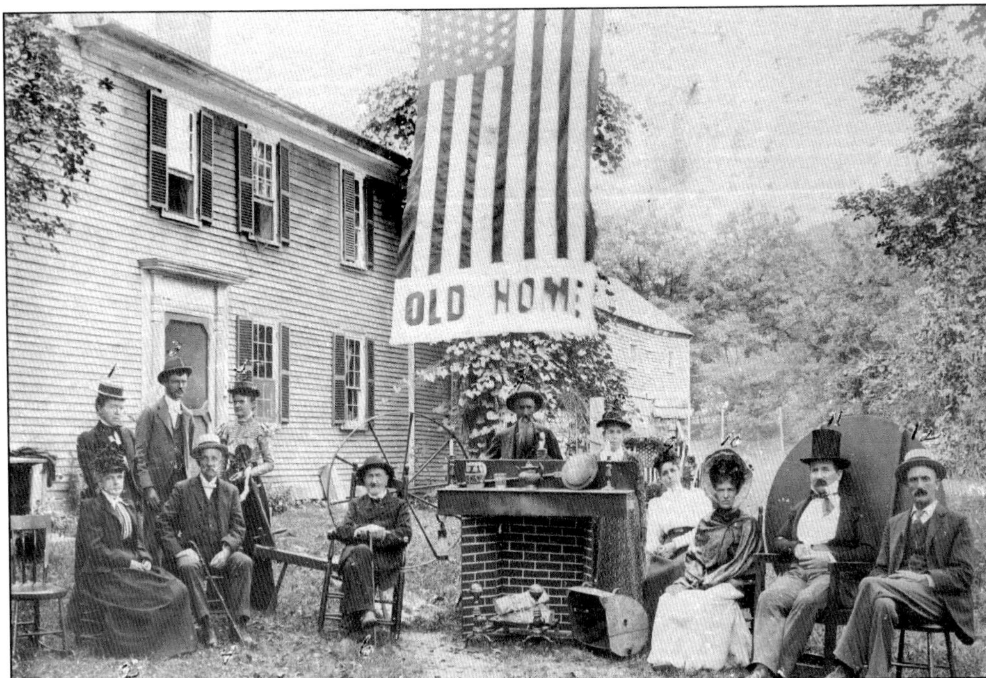

On August 29, 1899, the first Old Home Day celebration took place in Bristol at the Bartlett Homestead, on Pleasant Street. Frank West Rollins, New Hampshire's governor from 1899 to 1901, proposed the creation of annual Old Home Day celebrations in order to help the state in "providing good roads, restored forests and the development of economic and scenic resources of the state." (BHS.)

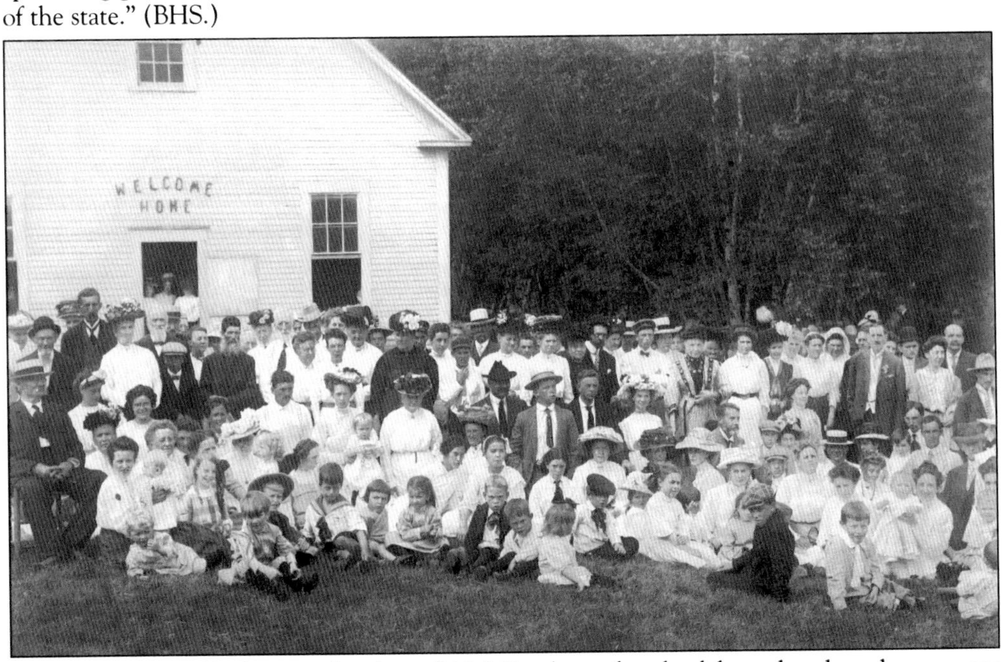

Old Home Day in Bridgewater has been faithfully planned and celebrated each and every year since the occasion was first proposed in 1899. To this day, a group photograph is taken in front of the old meetinghouse with a vintage camera, just as it was for this 1910 image. (BWHS.)

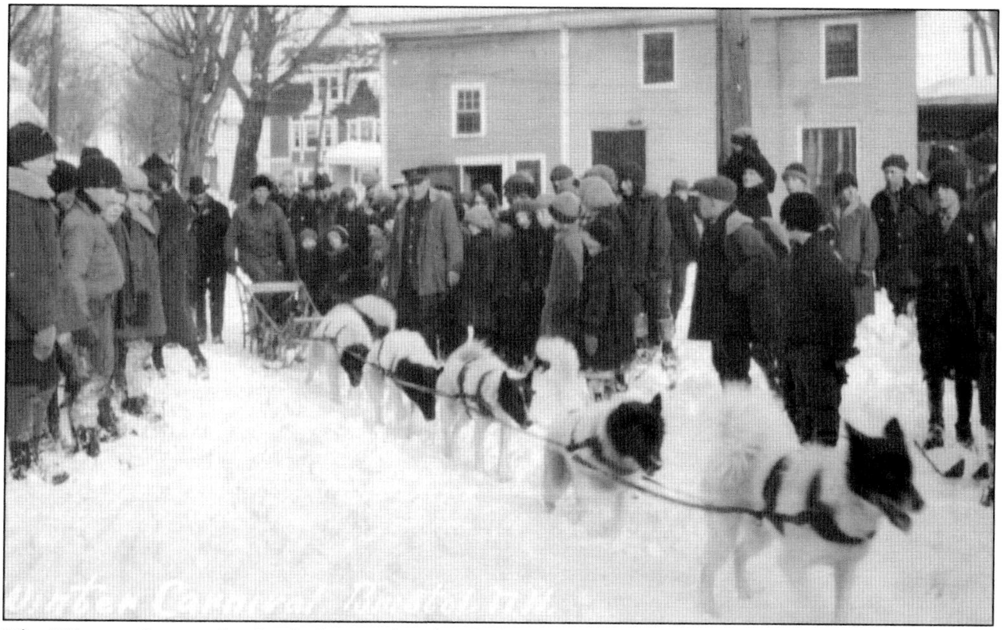

The Winter Carnival, which featured a dogsled event, was always a joyous occasion in Bristol. The one in 1925 was no exception. A friendly goat gives the "carnival queen"(below) a tour of the festivities. (DP and MW.)

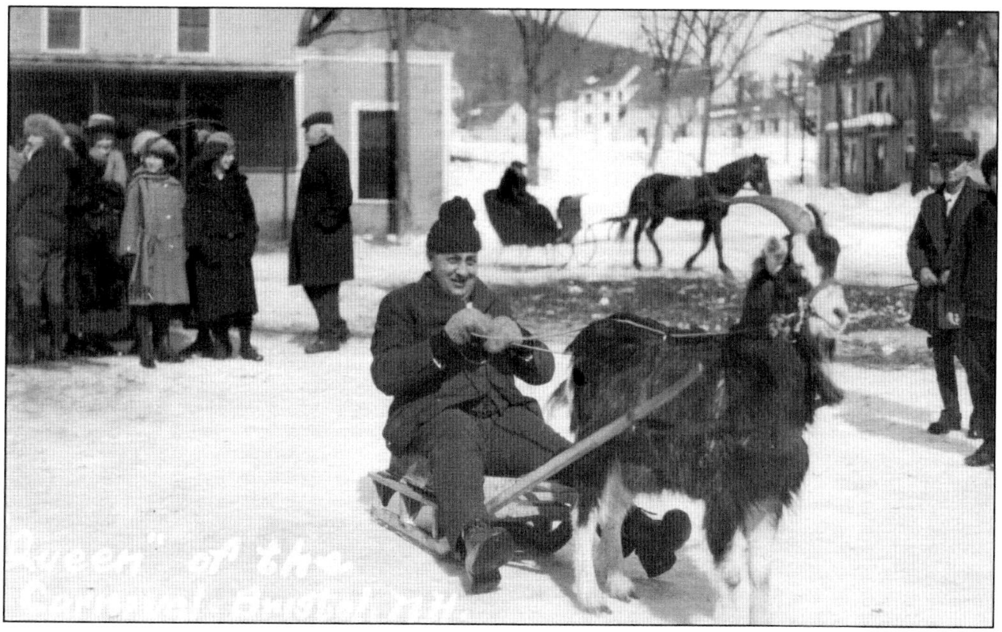

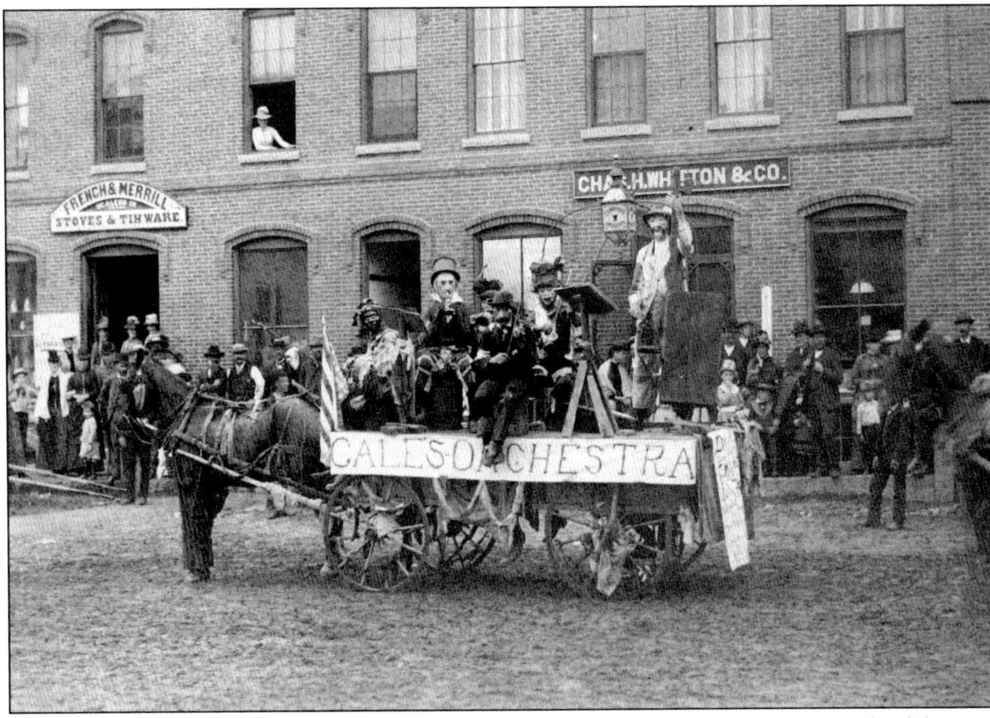

Made-up and ready for fun, members of Gales Orchestra join the parade at a Bristol celebration in the 1890s. (BHS.)

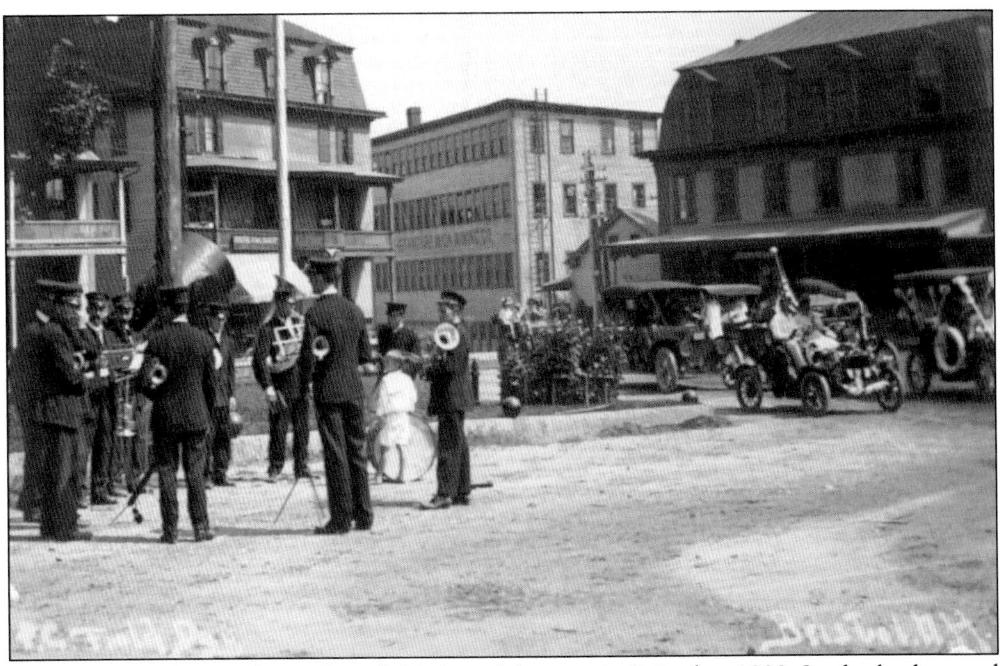

The parade is about to begin for a field day celebration in Bristol *c.* 1890. In the background are the four-story Emerson block, which was later destroyed by fire, the Standard Mica Mining Company mill, and the old Bristol Lodge. (BHS.)

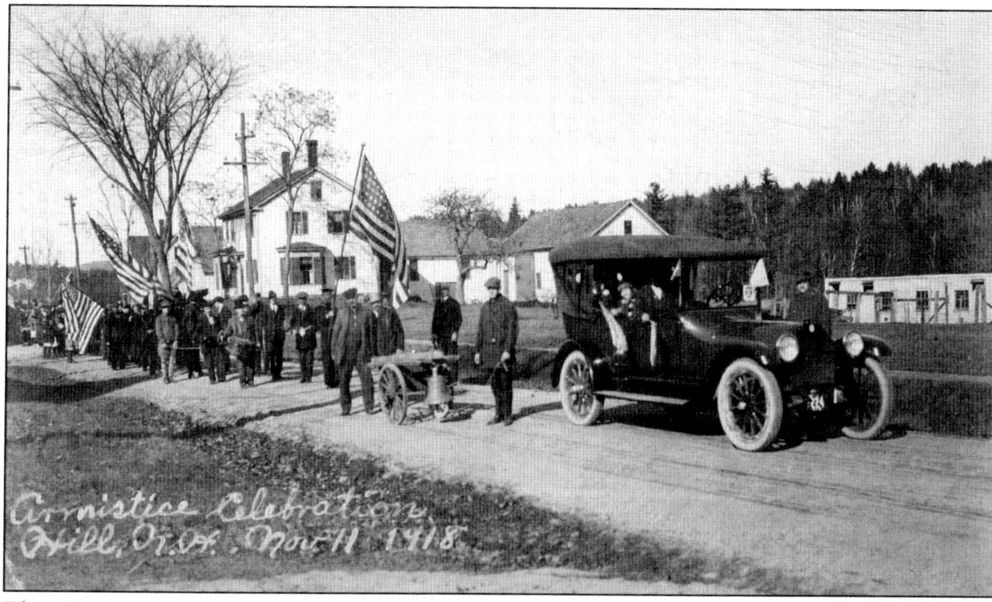

The Armistice Day celebration begins with a parade in old Hill village. The date was November 11, 1918. (CR.)

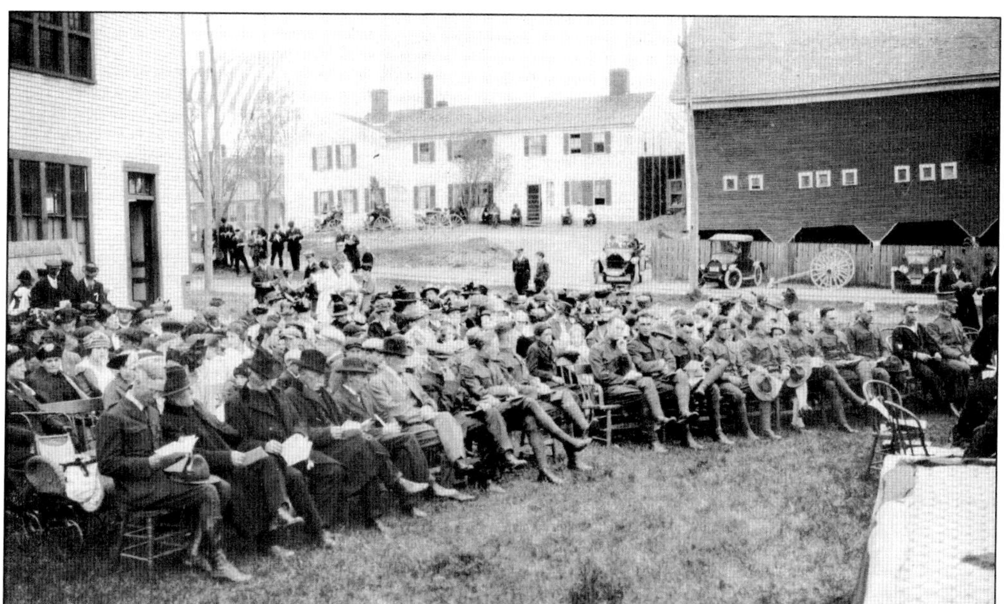

This is another view of Armistice Day of 1918, during a gathering behind the old Hill village Congregational church for an address to the military and civilian guests. (MW.)

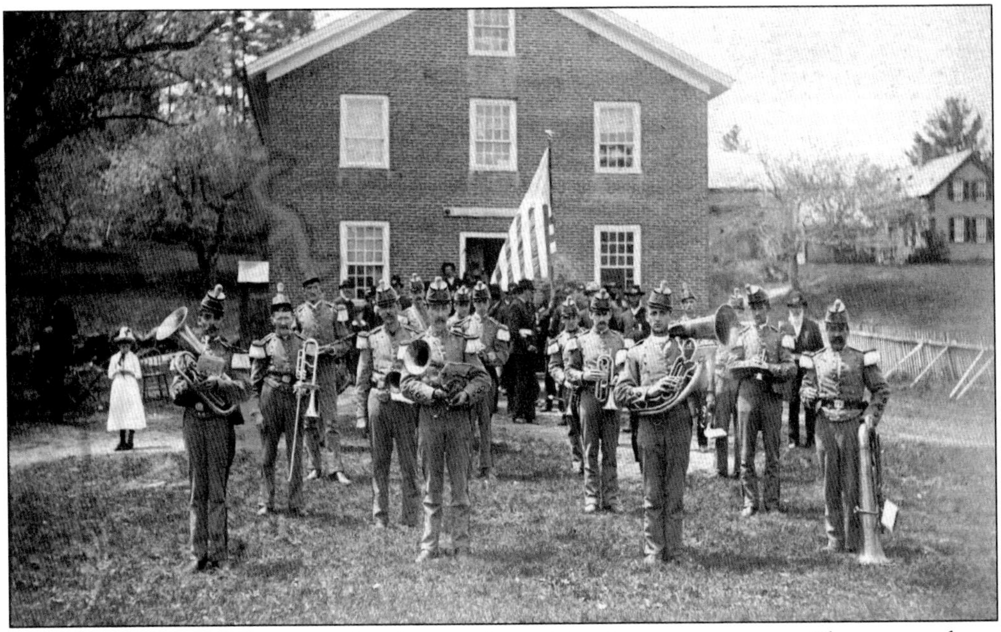

Soon after the Civil War, town bands were formed in almost every town. There was a keen interest in providing a band for memorial dedications and patriotic parades. Towns would often make appropriations for the purchase of uniforms and instruments. Bandstands were being built on the common, where the town band would give Sunday concerts during the summer months. Although some towns still have a uniformed band, few bandstands remain today. Old Hill village proudly displays its town band in this early photograph taken in front of the old Academy. (HHS.)

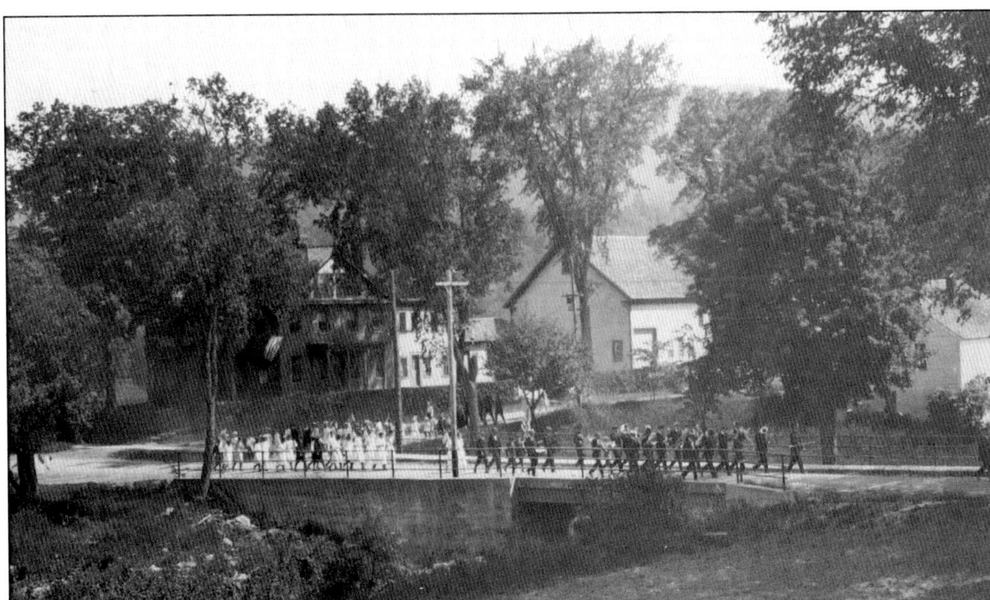

Parades have always been an important feature in a celebration. In this view, the old Hill village marching band leads the parade along tree-shaded Main Street. (HHS.)

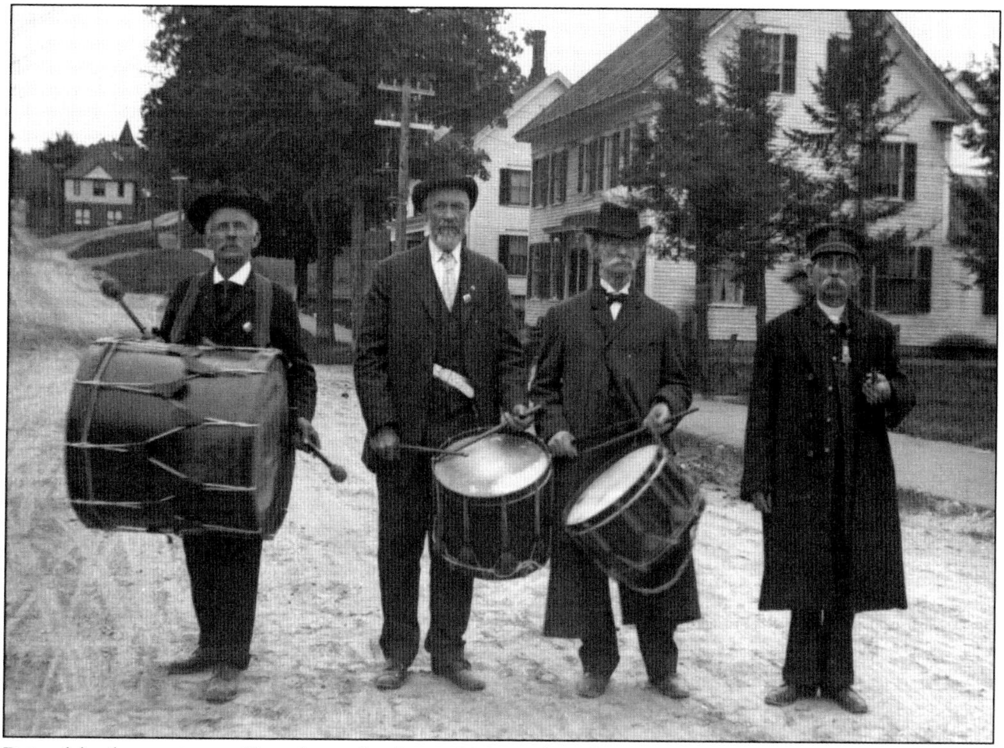

Bristol had a variety of bands in the late 1800s and early 1900s, including the Fife and Drum Corps pictured here. The houses in the background were those of Dr. Davis, a dentist, and Mr. Philpot, the proprietor of the old hotel. These houses were later torn down to make way for a filling station. The fire station is pictured in the distant left. (BHS.)

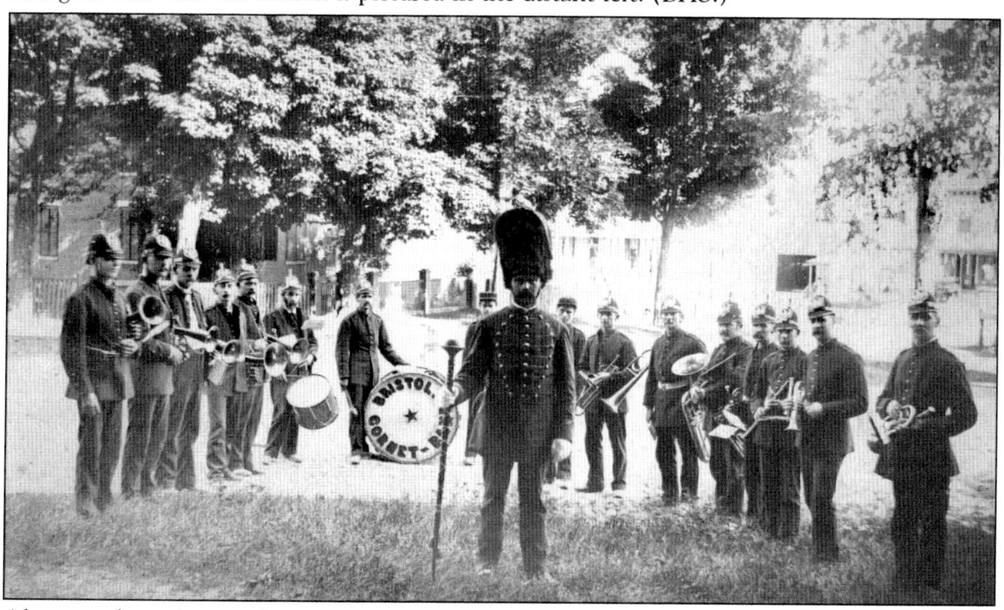

Along with a 24-member-strong fraternity band, Bristol's Cornet Band was enjoyed at many a celebration. The members are shown here in their Civil War-style uniforms. The plume-helmeted drum major creates a striking presence. (BHS.)

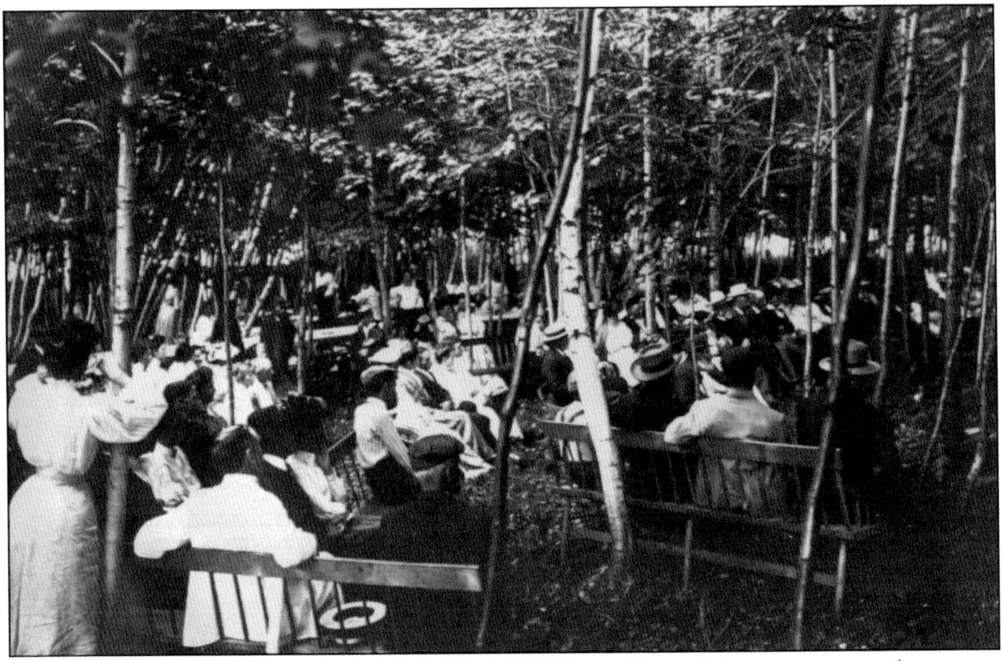

Band concerts are commonly included as part of Old Home Day celebrations, as was this one in Bridgewater *c.* 1898. Benches were taken from the old meetinghouse to the rear of the building for an evening of music and relaxation. (BWHS.)

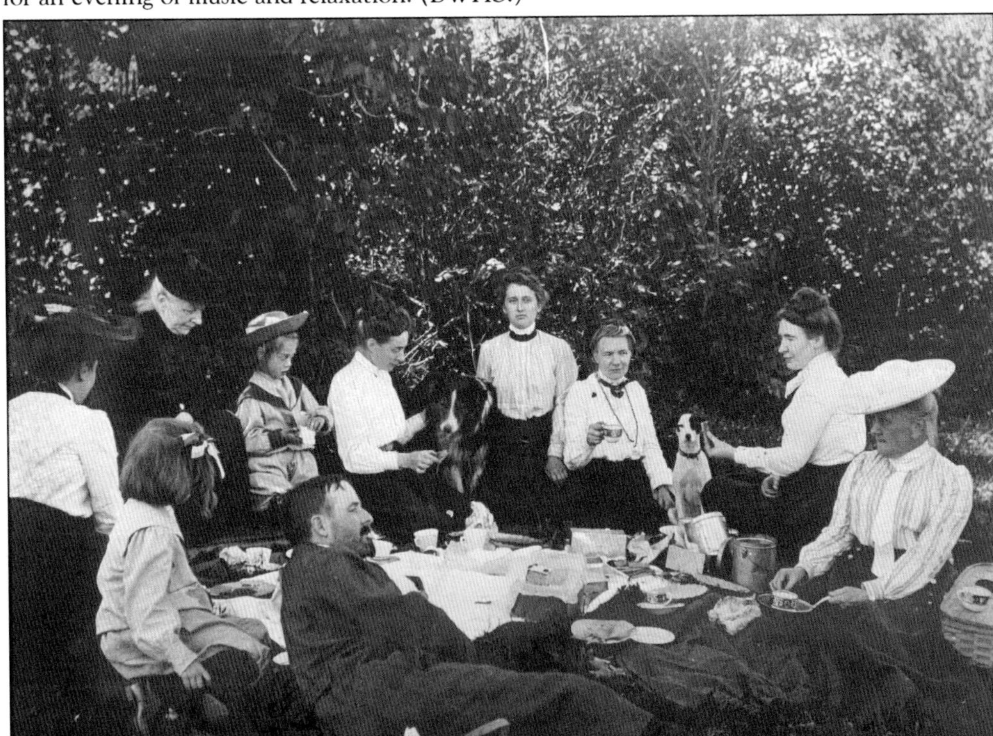

In 1903, members of the Webster family enjoy a Fourth of July picnic at their farm in Bridgewater. (WF.)

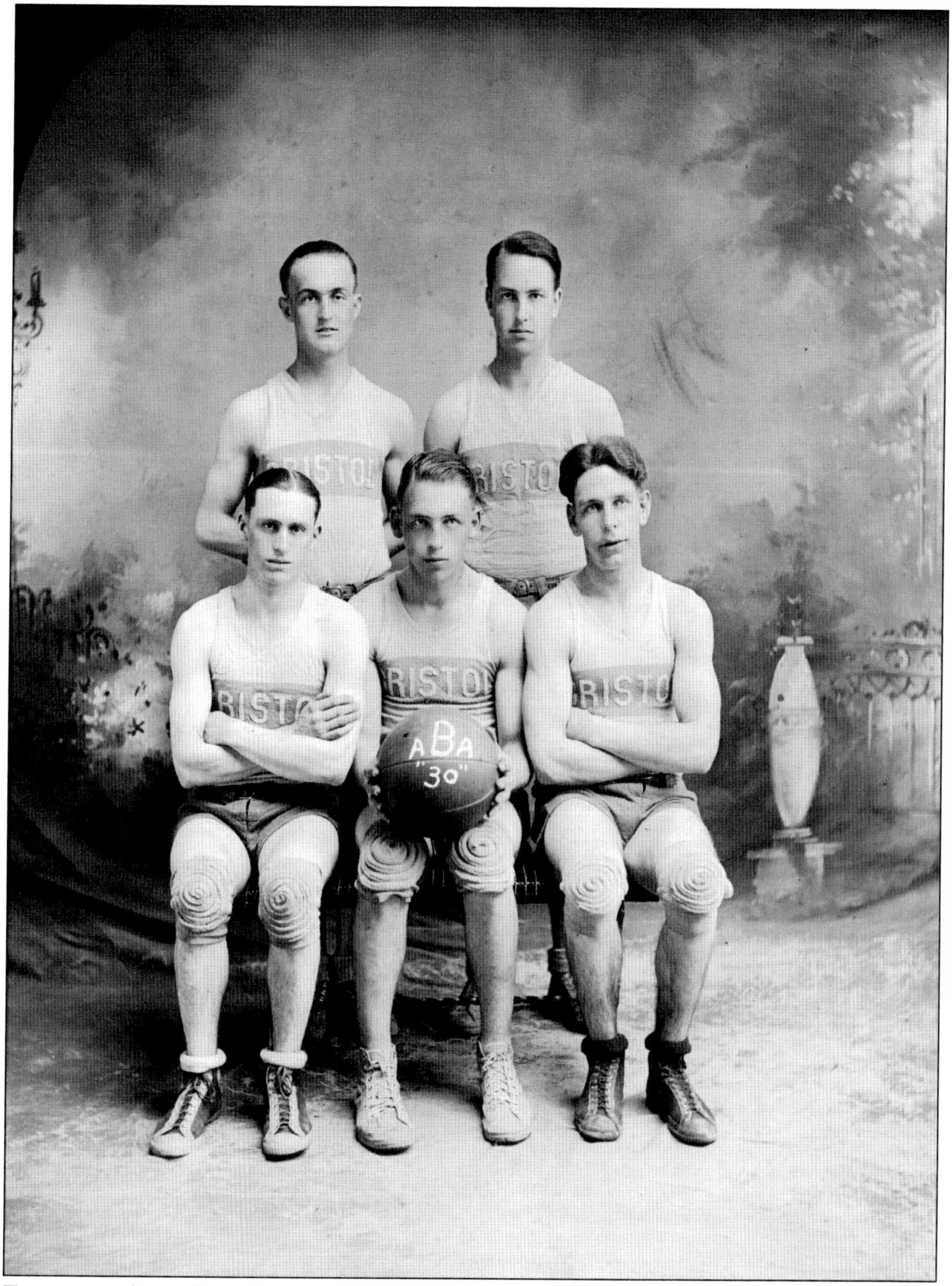

Team sports have always been an important leisure-time activity. Organized and supported by schools and by employment and town associations, many people have enjoyed the challenge and friendly rivalry of sports competitions. Pictured here is the Bristol basketball team in 1930. Members are, from left to right, as follows: (front row) Chet Wells, Bus Martin, and Clair Merrill; (back row) Fred Bliss and Howard Haskell. (BHS.)

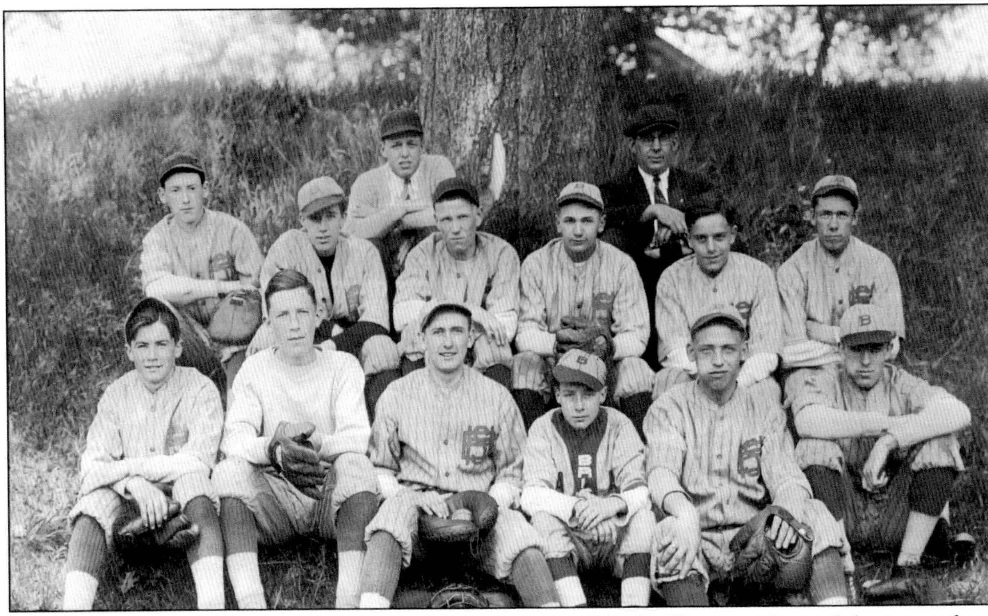

Pictured here is the Bristol High School baseball team of 1929. The members of the team, from left to right, are as follows: (front row) Willis Hatfield, Bob Tapply, Perley Wells, Dan Higgins, Bus Martin, and James Bryan; (middle row) Henry Wells, Howard Geddis, Jean MacDougall, Kenneth Platts, Fred Morgan, and Albert Webster; (back row) Rodney Brock and Ray Smith, coach. (BHS.)

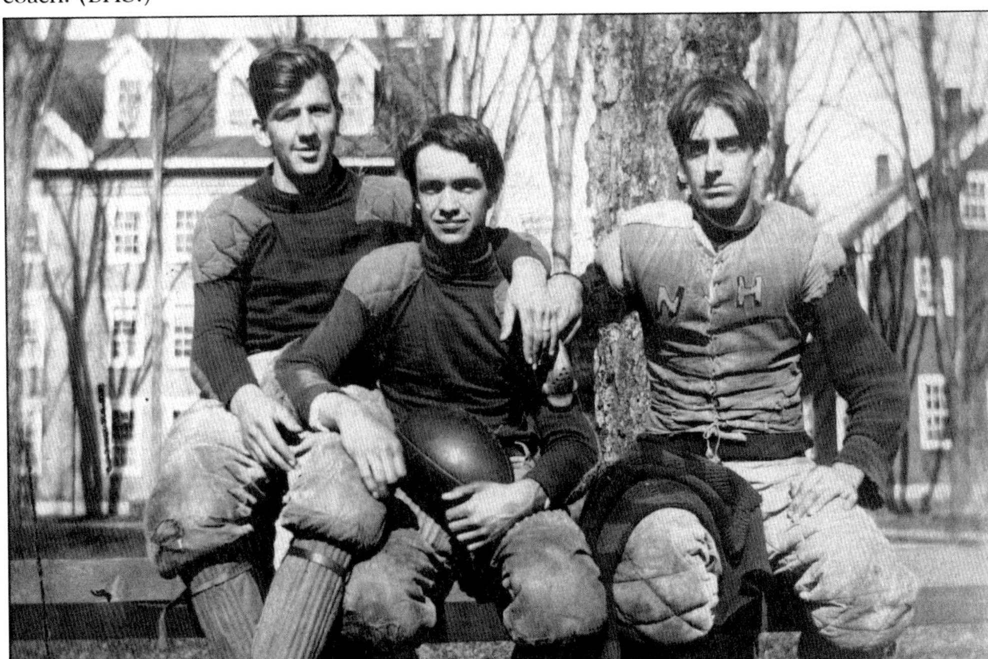

The New Hampton Literary Institution offered football, and three young players pose for this photograph in 1908. Note the nose guard in the hand of the player on the right. They were constructed of a very hard rubber and would cause one to wonder if perhaps they may have created injury rather than protection. (NHHS.)

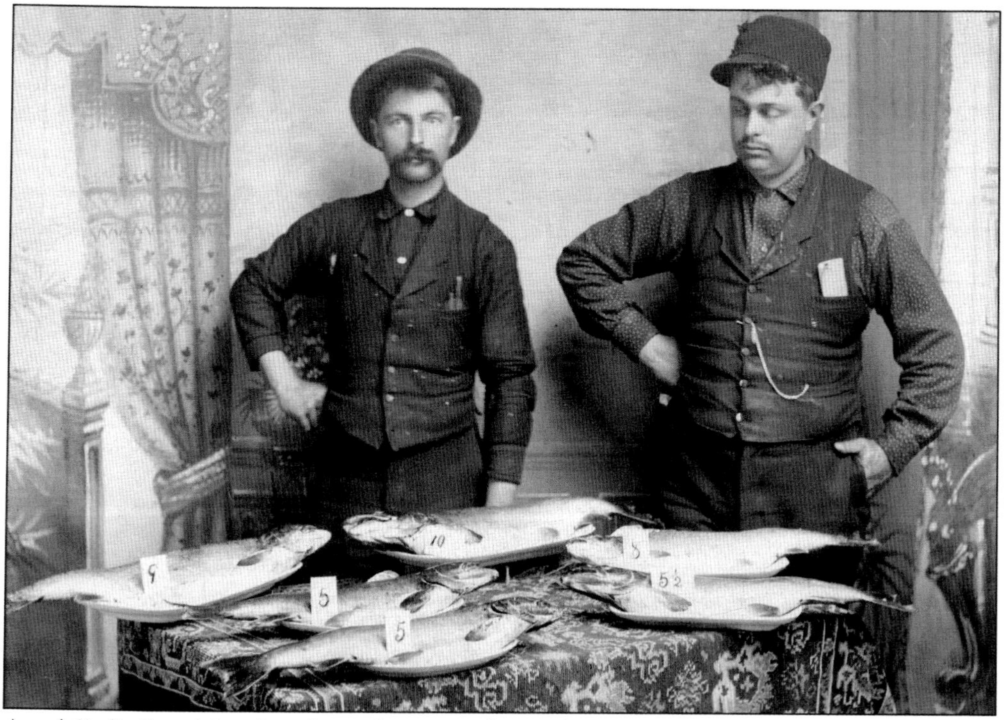

Ansel Dolloff and his friend are shown in this early-1900s photograph with an impressive catch, probably taken from Newfound Lake. The fish range in weight from five to ten pounds each. (BHS.)

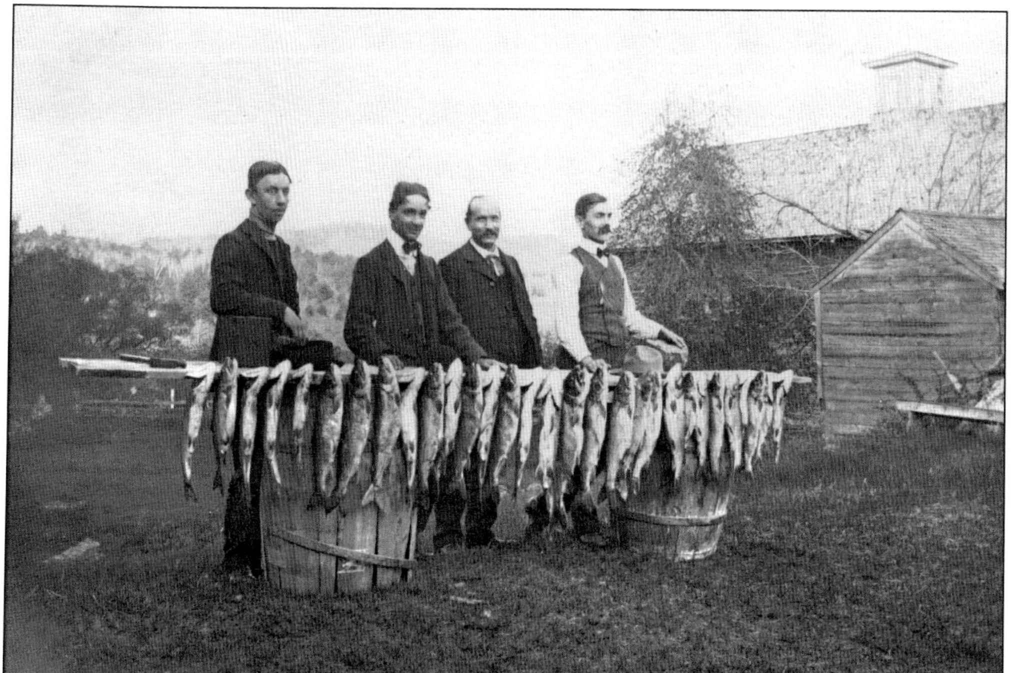

In this view, four residents of Hill display their good-luck catch in 1902. From left to right they are E.C. Smith, H. Carr, E.S. Little, and E.H. Colby. (HHS.)

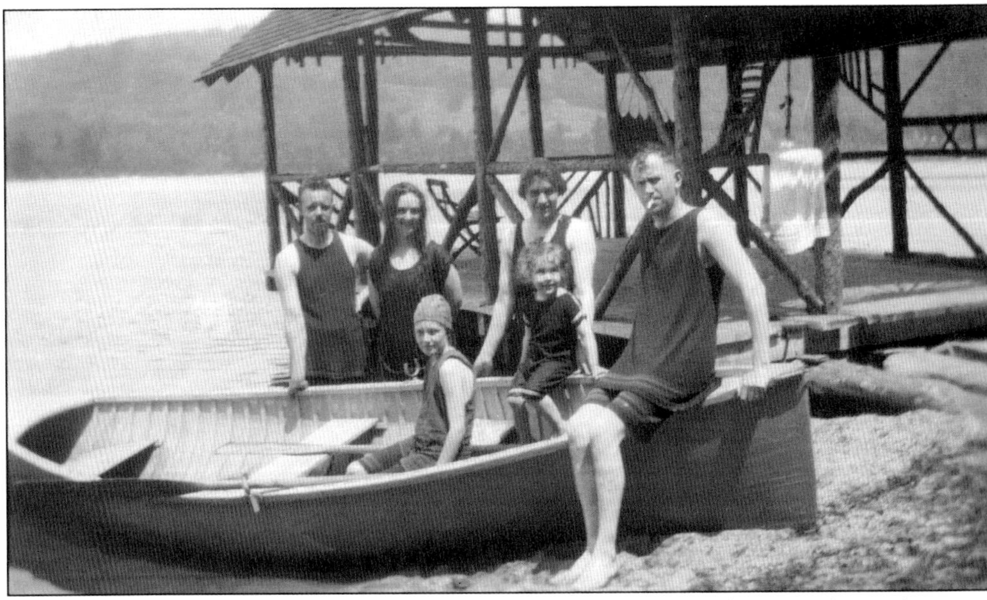

Swimming and boating on Newfound Lake has always been a favored activity for residents and summer visitors alike. Seen in this early view is a swimming and boating party, fashionably attired for the occasion. (BHS.)

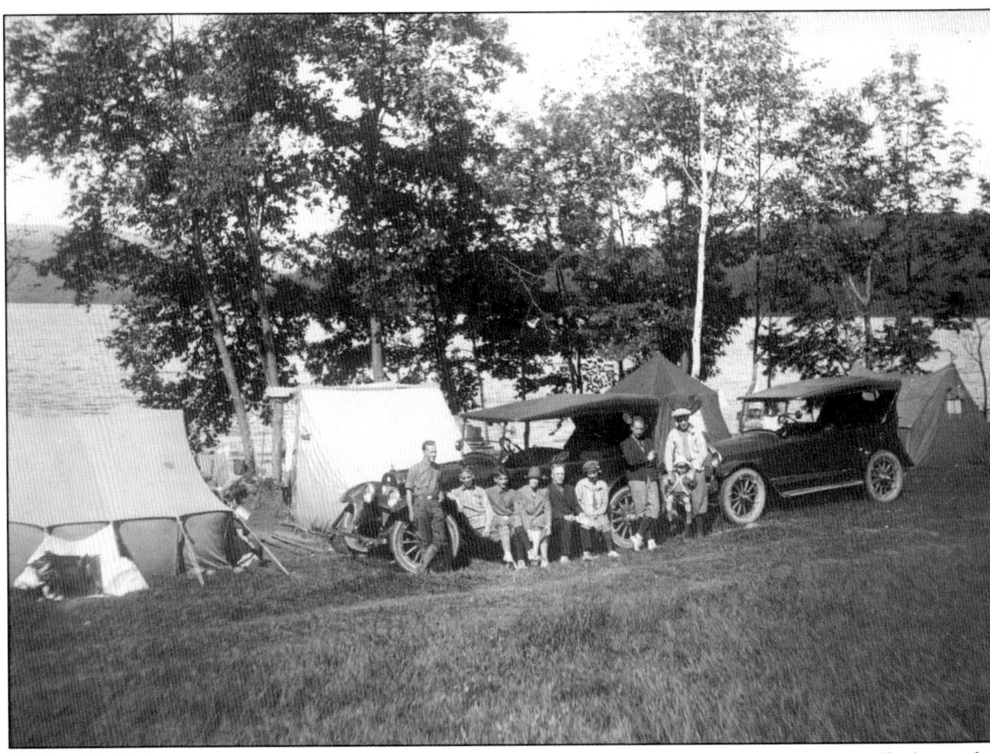

During the first half of the 20th century, it was not uncommon to see tents set up all along the shores of Newfound Lake. City dwellers came to cherish the quiet beauty of the lake and the surrounding countryside on carefree weekends and summer vacations. (HBHS.)